Contents

Preface   *page* vii
Acknowledgements   xii

1   Consent: Nuremberg, Helsinki and beyond   1
    Introduction   1
    Beginning at Nuremberg   2
    Extending scope: from research ethics to clinical ethics   4
    Raising standards: explicit and specific consent   6
    Improving justifications: the quest for autonomy   16
    Regulatory reinforcement: consent requirements   22
    Conclusion   24

2   Information and communication: the drift from agency   26
    Framing informed consent   27
    Two layers of distortion   34
    Information and the drift from agency   34
    What the conduit and container metaphors hide   38
    Conclusion   48

3   Informing and communicating: back to agency   50
    Agency   50
    Communicative actions   54
    Communicative norms   57
    Two 'models' of information and communication   64

4   How to rethink informed consent   68
    Introduction: two models of informed consent   68
    Why consent transactions matter: beyond autonomy   69
    Justifying consent transactions: consent as waiver   72
    Scope and standards   77
    Consent transactions: standards for communication   84
    Consent transactions: commitments   90
    Conclusion: consent in practice   94

5   Informational privacy and data protection   97
        Informational privacy   100
        Informational rights and obligations   101
        Informational privacy as a right over content   105
        Data protection legislation: second-order informational obligations   111
        Rethinking informational privacy   121
        Confidentiality: regulating communicative action rather than
            information content   123
        Conclusion   128

6   Genetic information and genetic exceptionalism   130
        Questions about genetic information   131
        Genetic privacy and genetic exceptionalism   133
        Is Genetic information contained within DNA?   145
        Conclusion   149

7   Trust, accountability and transparency   154
        Consent, paternalism and trust   154
        Placing and refusing trust intelligently   159
        Accountability and trustworthiness   167
        Accountability, trustworthiness and trust in biomedicine   169
        Accountability with transparency   177
        Appendix: the structure of accountability   181

    Some conclusions and proposals   183
        Informed consent and epistemic norms   184
        Informed consent and individual autonomy   185
        Informed consent as waiver   187
        Practices and policies for informed consent   189
        After rethinking: the possibility of change   198

    Bibliography   201
    Institutional sources and documents   207
    Index   211

Preface

Informed consent is now widely seen as fundamental to medical and research ethics. This has not always been the case. Informed consent first rose to prominence in biomedical practice with the Nuremberg Code of 1947, which responded to the abusive treatment of human beings by Nazi medical researchers. Consent requirements were subsequently extended from research to clinical ethics, and more recently to procedures regulating the acquisition, possession and use of personal information, including genetic and medical information. Across the last fifty years informed consent requirements have also supposedly been made more rigorous: standards for 'consent disclosures' are now more exacting; demands for more explicit and more specific consent are widely endorsed; ever more elaborate consent forms are increasingly devised and required. This huge expansion and elaboration of informed consent requirements is generally seen as indispensable if we are to respect individual autonomy. Informed consent, it is argued, ensures that patients and research subjects can decide autonomously whether to permit or refuse actions that affect them.

Yet current approaches to informed consent have led to many problems. If patients and research subjects consent without reading or understanding informed consent 'disclosures' – and it is clear that they do – is their consent inadequate? If consent 'disclosures' omit certain information – and it is clear that they do – is consent given on the basis of such disclosures inadequate? Should we forbid medical treatment and research whenever informed consent is defective? Or should we persist with current consent practices, in the full knowledge that defective consent will not ensure the autonomy of research subjects or of patients? Neither option is appealing.

In this book we consider how we might rethink the use of informed consent in biomedicine. We begin by exploring received views of informed consent, and the arguments usually given for requiring the consent of patients and research subjects to biomedical interventions. We try to identify and make explicit the underlying assumptions that shape contemporary thought, talk and debate about informed consent. We conclude that standard accounts of informed consent, standard arguments for requiring consent in clinical and research practice and standard ways of implementing consent requirements lead to intractable problems. We then propose an alternative, less ambitious, account which we hope and believe provides a more plausible account of the part that informed consent procedures can and should play in shaping ethically acceptable biomedical practice.

This approach to rethinking informed consent is not, perhaps, the obvious one; it is certainly not the preferred one. Most of the vast contemporary literature on informed consent in biomedicine looks for ways of improving informed consent procedures, typically by finding ways of making 'consent disclosures' more perspicuous or complete, and consent requirements more user-friendly for patients and research subjects. We think that these ameliorative approaches have limited potential, because they do not address the underlying difficulties of current conceptions of informed consent.

As we see matters, informed consent is sought and obtained by distinctive sorts of *communicative transactions*. We are unlikely to understand informed consent unless we consider the sorts of communicative transactions it requires and the standards they must meet. Many current accounts of informed consent represent such transactions quite passively, as a matter of *information transfer*. Information is seen as *located* or *held* in one or another place, or as *flowing* from one place to another. Information flows are seen as the *transfer* or *transmission of* information from one *source* or *container* to another, through one *conduit* or *channel* or another. These metaphors have their uses: they provide a common vocabulary for discussing the transfer of information between technological devices and between people. But they also have their dangers: they encourage us to think of information in abstraction from human activity, and specifically in abstraction from the normative framework that governs successful communicative transactions between people.

Many current discussions of informed consent are shaped by these impersonal metaphors. For example, discussions of informed consent requirements often focus narrowly on the proper 'disclosure' of information by clinicians and researchers; discussions of patient privacy often focus narrowly on requirements to 'process' medical data in prescribed ways. Yet if we rely on these impersonal metaphors we may miss matters that are basic to communicative transactions between people, including the transactions by which they request, give and refuse consent.

A more plausible and illuminating framework for thinking about informed consent would start from the fact that the communicative transactions by which it is sought, given or withheld are rationally evaluable social transactions between agents. They include or consist of speech acts. Speech acts are governed and constrained by a rich normative framework, and fail in various ways if the relevant norms are ignored or flouted. So any convincing account of informed consent transactions must begin by considering the epistemic and other norms that must be observed for successful communication. We identify many of these norms, and discuss the part they play in shaping the successful use of informed consent transactions to permit clinical or research interventions that would otherwise be unacceptable.

In successful informed consent transactions, communication is used to *waive* specific ethical, legal or other rights, obligations or prohibitions. Such transactions therefore presuppose the rights, obligations and prohibitions that are to be waived. So the obligations of medical practitioners and researchers to inform patients and research subjects, and to seek their consent to specific interventions, are always *secondary* obligations. Our rethinking of informed consent sets out the standards that communicative transactions must meet if they are to be used to waive obligations, rights and prohibitions in specific ways. Properly used, informed consent can render action permissible that would otherwise constitute (for example) assault, false imprisonment, deception, or some other breach of significant ethical requirements.

We take a parallel approach to the use of informed consent transactions in contemporary debates about specifically informational obligations, including those grouped under headings such as *information privacy* and *genetic privacy*, *data protection* and *right to know*, *accountability* and *transparency*. Many current debates about informational obligations begin with the thought that certain classes of information have intrinsic and distinctive ethical importance. On the one hand they see personal information, including personal, medical and genetic information, as information that nobody else has a right to know, which should be kept inaccessible unless there is informed consent to its disclosure. On the other hand they see institutional information, and in particular information about institutional and professional performance, as information that everybody else has a right to know, which should be disclosed in the name of transparency, accountability and freedom of information.

We argue against such views that informational obligations are not best understood by trying to identify rights over putative classes of information. Informational obligations are better articulated in terms of ordinary epistemic and ethical requirements on communicative transactions. Respect for others' privacy is best seen as a set of requirements on communicative transactions, rather than as requirements that certain types of information be kept inaccessible. Demands for accountability are best seen as requirements on communicative transactions that offer and take account of past action, rather than as requirements that certain types of information be transparently and universally 'available'. Where informational obligations are construed simply as a matter of keeping types of information hidden or making it available, there is a real danger that we adopt and require institutional policies and practices which are of little use, or even damaging to biomedical practice – and beyond. Where they are construed as a matter of epistemically and ethically acceptable communication, there is at least a possibility of establishing policies and practices that support rather than undermine good practice, and that may help secure or restore trust, in biomedicine – and beyond.

The approach that we take to informed consent is not novel or unfamiliar. It is a matter of emphasising the continuing importance of norms of intelligibility, relevance, accuracy and honesty (and other norms) in all communicative transactions, rather than of demanding ever fuller or better consent 'disclosures', or ever tighter control of certain types of data. The conclusions we reach challenge a number of current orthodoxies. We suggest that informed consent is best thought of as part of a wider ethics of communication. We argue that informed consent does not and cannot offer free-standing ethical justifications, but rather is used to waive other, more basic ethical standards (which informed consent requirements invariably presuppose). We show why informed consent cannot, *a fortiori* should not, aim to be fully specific or fully explicit. We argue that some of the informed consent requirements that have been built into contemporary legislation and codes (ranging from legislation governing Data Protection to the Declaration of Helsinki) are implausible, even incoherent. More positively, we believe that the approach we propose provides a clear and convincing account of the purposes of informed consent requirements in biomedicine and of the standards that they should meet.

Acknowledgements

This book could not have been written without the support, interest and hard work of a number of institutions and individuals. On the institutional side we would like first to thank the Wellcome Trust for generously funding our three-year research project 'Informed Consent and Genetic Data', including funding a full-time research fellowship. In the course of the project, the Trust supported a number of workshops, and provided the major financial support for a large 'discussion event' held at King's College, Cambridge, in early 2005. This event brought together some eighty helpful, interested and authoritative people, from a range of relevant disciplines (including philosophy, law, medicine and social science) to discuss the draft document that formed the basis of this book. We would also like to thank King's College, for providing a superb work environment, and for hosting both the workshops and the January 2005 'discussion event'; we are particularly grateful to the King's College Research Centre Convenor, Simon Goldhill. Thanks must also go to the Department of History and Philosophy of Science, Cambridge University, which provided administrative support, and especially to Tamara Hug for all her patience, help and advice.

Our research project only came into being thanks to the hard work of our co-investigators, Pat Bateson, Peter Lipton and Martin Richards, who put a great deal of work into the original grant proposal. We would like to thank them all for that, and for supporting the project in a variety of ways at many stages, including taking part in many workshops and in the major 'discussion event'.

The workshops held during the project focused primarily on the philosophical issues which we thought most important to rethinking informed consent in biomedical practice, including the epistemology of communication; the role of trust in communication; informed consent; and epistemic responsibility. We would particularly like to thank those from beyond Cambridge who gave talks on these occasions – Paul Faulkner, Lizzie Fricker, Angus Dawson and Tony Coady – as well as to others who took part and helped us shape our views. We owe special thanks to Peter Lipton for his clear and incisive contributions to these workshops, in which it repeatedly fell to him to summarise and integrate a complex set of themes.

Our work on these topics has constantly benefited from many people in Cambridge who share an interest in normative issues that surround medical practice, genetic technology and the uses of new genetic knowledge. We have learned a lot from talking with, arguing with and listening to, amongst others: Oonagh Corrigan, Stephen John, Cathy Gere, Kathy Liddell, John Macmillan, Bryn Williams-Jones, Bronwyn Parry, John Spencer and Marilyn Strathern. Thanks in particular to Tim Lewens for the central role he has played in bringing us together by organising and chairing the regular 'Bioethics Forum', which has provided a stimulating forum for discussion and debate.

The discussion event in 2005 provided invaluable critical discussion and commentary, and helped us to reshape and refine our key claims and arguments. We would particularly like to thank the commentators on that occasion: Tom Baldwin, Karen Sparck-Jones, Roger Brownsword, Angus Dawson, Mike Parker, Martin Richards, Ross Harrison, David Archard, Ron Zimmern and Bill Cornish; and also those who chaired discussions: Dan Wikler, Patricia Hodgson, Pat Bateson, Simon Goldhill and Alex Oliver. We are also grateful to those who gave us detailed comments and criticism, and in particular to Cyril Chantler, Peter Furness, Jane Heal, Tim Lewens, Bill Lowrance, Anneke Lucassen, Stephen John, John McMillan, Tom Murray, Peter Singleton, Tom Sorell and Suzanne Uniacke. And we are particularly grateful to Jane Lane for all the hard work she put into making the occasion a success.

Finally, we would like to thank the Public Health Genetics Unit, in association with the Cambridge Genetics Knowledge Park, and its

CHAPTER I

Consent: Nuremberg, Helsinki and beyond

INTRODUCTION

Informed consent has a long and distinguished history in liberal political theory and economic thought that goes back to the great debates of the European Enlightenment. The core of the social contract tradition is the claim that freely given consent legitimates action that would otherwise be unacceptable, and in particular the use of coercive power by governments. The basic arguments for market economics appeal to the moral legitimacy of consensual transactions, and contrast them with illegitimate economic transactions based on force, coercion or fraud, such as theft, confiscation and forced labour. These traditional claims have been reworked and reinvigorated in the last thirty years in influential revivals of liberal contractualism in political philosophy and of market thinking in economics.

These debates in politics and economics have been paralleled in biomedical ethics, where informed consent has come to play a larger and larger part, and is now the most discussed theme in Western medical ethics and research ethics.[1] Informed consent procedures

---

[1] Jeremy Sugarman et al., 'Empirical Research on Informed Consent: An Annotated Bibliography', *Hastings Centre Report*, Special Supplement, January–February 1999, 1–42. The bibliography lists and summarises 377 articles. The torrent continues. A search on the database MedLine reveals that, for example, in the year 2002–3 there were over 300 articles (in English) with 'informed consent' *in the title*, and, even more impressively, over 1,800 with 'informed consent' in the 'subject' field: six new articles *per working day* in the journals cited in MedLine (which covers clinical and medical ethics, but not social sciences, non-medical law, philosophy, political theory, and so on).

have been embedded in clinical and research practice, and in a range of legislative and regulatory regimes that govern the use of personal and medical information and human tissues. Appeals to informed consent and its role in justifying clinical and research practice are now so well entrenched that their presence, indeed their necessity, and their justification are rarely questioned.

In this book we raise a number of questions about standard views of the role of informed consent in biomedical ethics. We begin with an overview of ways in which conceptions of informed consent and its role have developed in biomedicine. In this chapter we sketch changes in received views of the *scope*, the *standards*, the *justification* and the *regulatory use* of informed consent. All four have been transformed over the last thirty years.

These changes are generally seen as improvements. We shall argue that the quest for wider scope, for higher standards, for better justifications and for regulatory reinforcement, which aimed to make consent the lynchpin of biomedical ethics, has created intractable problems. We do not conclude that informed consent is unimportant in biomedicine, or that there is a case for reverting to a paternalistic medical or research culture. Rather we argue that received views of informed consent and of its role in biomedicine need fundamental rethinking.

BEGINNING AT NUREMBERG

The Nuremberg Code of 1947 is generally seen as the first authoritative statement of consent requirements in biomedical ethics. The issues that it was designed to settle were stark and horrifying. Human beings had been callously abused and murdered in the name of medical research, both in pre-war Nazi Germany and subsequently in the concentration camps.[2] During the Nuremberg trials of the

---

[2] For discussion of the abuses of medical research both in the 1930s and in the death camps see Michael Burleigh, *Death and Deliverance: 'Euthanasia' in Germany, c.1900–1945* (Cambridge: Cambridge University Press, 1994); *Ethics and Extermination: Reflections on Nazi Genocide* (Cambridge: Cambridge University Press, 1997).

doctors charged with these crimes, the defence argued that the Nazi experiments had been no worse than medical research elsewhere. The Code was drafted to help the prosecution by setting out some of the differences. It asserts emphatically that in all research on human beings: 'The voluntary consent of the human subject is absolutely essential.'[3] It glosses the phrase 'voluntary consent' in these words:

This means that the person involved should have legal capacity to give consent; should be so situated as to be able to exercise free power of choice, without the intervention of any element of force, fraud, deceit, duress, over-reaching, or other ulterior form of constraint or coercion; and should have sufficient knowledge and comprehension of the elements of the subject matter involved as to enable him to make an understanding and enlightened decision. This latter element requires that before the acceptance of an affirmative decision by the experimental subject there should be made known to him the nature, duration, and purpose of the experiment; the method and means by which it is to be conducted; all inconveniences and hazards reasonably to be expected; and the effects upon his health or person which may possibly come from his participation in the experiment.[4]

The Nuremberg Code's reasons for requiring 'voluntary consent' echo those traditionally offered by political philosophers for grounding the obligations of citizens in consent. The basic idea of the social contract tradition can be encapsulated in the old tag *volenti non fit iniuria*: no injury is done where the subject is willing. The Nuremberg Code elaborates this thought in a quite traditional way by viewing informed consent as providing assurance and evidence that there has been no 'force, fraud, deceit, duress, over-reaching, or other ulterior form of constraint or coercion'. Codes don't usually

---

[3] The Code was initially drafted by Andrew Ivy and Leo Alexander, doctors who worked with the prosecution during the trial. On 17 April 1947, Dr Alexander submitted a memorandum to the US Counsel for War Crimes, outlining six points defining legitimate research, and responding to defence claims that there was no distinction between Nazi practice and medical research elsewhere. The verdict of the Nuremberg Tribunal reiterated these points, and extended six points into ten. Subsequently, the ten points became known as the 'Nuremberg Code'. For the text see http://www.ushmm.org/research/doctors/Nuremberg_Code.htm. The legal status of the Code remained unclear, but it is treated as a landmark document.

[4] *Ibid*, p. 181, principle 1.

offer explicit justifications, but we can find in the text of the Nuremberg Code an appeal to these widely accepted ethical standards, which would form part of virtually any ethical system or outlook. In effect, the Code forbids research that is based on overwhelming or undermining the will, or on forcing the body. Hence it forbids research on those who lack 'sufficient knowledge and comprehension of the elements of the subject matter involved . . . to make an understanding and enlightened decision', and forbids force and duress of all sorts. However, the Code says nothing more explicit about consent, and never mentions information or autonomy.

Contemporary discussions insist that informed consent should play a wider role in biomedicine than was envisaged at the time of the Nuremberg Code. Informed consent requirements have been extended from research to clinical ethics, and standards for seeking and giving informed consent have been made more explicit and more demanding. The justifications given for requiring informed consent have supposedly been strengthened by appeals to various conceptions of autonomy. Finally, informed consent requirements have been extended from medical treatment and research to the secondary use of information and tissues, by incorporating them into the regulation governing data protection, uses of human tissues and genetic technologies. Each of these four developments creates significant problems, which we discuss in the following sections of this chapter.

EXTENDING SCOPE: FROM RESEARCH ETHICS
TO CLINICAL ETHICS

Contemporary discussions of informed consent in biomedicine may have started with the Nuremberg focus on research ethics, but they are now taken to apply equally to clinical ethics. The transformation of medical ethics that began in the late 1960s, and has continued since then, seeks to protect patients by requiring their consent for all medical interventions. This was often justified by claiming that it was important not to treat patients paternalistically, on the basis of a physician's estimate of their best interests, and that informed consent requirements would ensure that the patient rather than the doctor was in control.

The extension of informed consent requirements from research ethics to clinical practice proved highly problematic from the start. The Nuremberg Code demands that research not be done without informed consent: this is a coherent requirement.[5] A parallel demand that medical treatment not be given without the patient's informed consent is clearly unacceptable. Patients who cannot give informed consent can hardly be denied treatment, and medical ethics cannot parallel research ethics by making informed consent a universal, or even a normal, requirement.

This is not a minor problem.[6] Incompetence and impaired competence to consent are more common in medical practice than elsewhere, since impaired cognitive capacities are a common effect of illness and injury. Very many patients are unconscious or too ill, cognitively impaired or mentally confused, too young or too frail to grasp the relevant information, so cannot give informed consent to their medical treatment. Few of them are likely to (re)gain competence in time to consent. Even those 'in the maturity of their faculties'[7] find it hard to grasp information about complex diagnoses or treatments, or severe outcomes. They may ignore or fail to grasp information they are given, mistakenly dismiss important information as routine or trivial, or react to routine information with misplaced or disproportionate dread or fear. Mustering the cognitive grasp and emotional strength to give or refuse informed consent to complex or threatening proposals taxes even the most competent of

---

[5] However, it is not uncontroversial. Should we forbid all medical research – even research that is minimally intrusive or risky – into conditions that undermine competence to consent, such as severe learning disabilities or dementia? Is it right to do so if these conditions cause great suffering?

[6] Vanessa Raymont *et al.*, 'Prevalence of Mental Incapacity in Medical Inpatients and Associated Risk Factors: Cross Sectional Study', *The Lancet* 364 (2004), 1421–7 argues that incapacity to consent is more common than supposed and under-recognised in the acutely ill.

[7] John Stuart Mill, *On Liberty and Other Writings*, ed. Stefan Collini (Cambridge: Cambridge University Press, 1989), p. 13.

us. These problems have become more intractable as medical interventions have become more complex, thereby adding to the cognitive demands of giving informed consent.

A vast and often repetitive literature, as noted above, has addressed
these unpromising realities by using two strategies. Some writers argue
that supposedly near alternatives to consent, such as *proxy consent* or
hypothetical consent, can justify interventions where patients lack (full)
competence to consent. In doing so they come close to disregarding or
short-changing the very standards to which proponents of consent
requirements aspire: actual consent is set aside in favour of somebody
else's consent, or of consent that might be given under different conditions, or by somebody with different capacities. Others propose ways
of making consenting easier and more user-friendly for marginally
competent patients, for example by improving procedures for providing information (e.g., better information leaflets) or by using
intermediaries (e.g., counsellors) to help those whose capacities are
challenged.[8] Unfortunately gaps between actual cognitive and
decision-making capacities and the capacities needed for informed
consent to proposed action often cannot be bridged by these methods. Attempts to make informed consent the guiding principle of
medical ethics have proved, and are bound to prove, uphill work.

RAISING STANDARDS: EXPLICIT AND SPECIFIC CONSENT

Contemporary discussions of informed consent requirements not
only extend their scope from research to medical practice, but seek
to raise standards. The Nuremberg standards were open to a range
of criticisms. Was it enough to ensure that research subjects – or

---

[8] For example, there is evidence that *video* presentations may help patients to understand informed consent disclosures: see J. Weston, M. Hannah and J. Downes,
'Evaluating the Benefits of a Patient Information Video During the Informed
Consent Process', *Patient Education and Counselling* 30 (1997), 239–5. Others
have argued that *written* 'disclosures' are less effective than face-to-face communication: see K. Cox, 'Informed Consent and Decision-making: Patients' Experiences
of the Process of Recruitment to Phases I and II Anti-cancer Drug Trial', *Patient
Education and Counselling* 46 (2002), 31–8.

for that matter patients – 'have legal capacity to give consent' and are 'so situated as to be able to exercise free power of choice'? Or were these requirements too weak, or too vague? On a natural reading, tacit or implicit consent would meet these standards, provided that those to whom it was ascribed had legal *capacity* and *could* exercise 'free power of choice'. And were the standards clear enough to ensure that those whose consent was sought understood what they were consenting to? The Code requires only that anyone whose consent is sought should have 'sufficient knowledge and comprehension of the elements of the subject matter involved as to enable him to make an understanding and enlightened decision'. It does not require that they *actually* make 'an understanding and enlightened decision'. Should adequate standards for informed consent in biomedicine be clearer about the level of information to be provided and understood, and about the quality of the consent *actually* given?

Once again discussions of standards for consent to research interventions led the way. Contemporary discussions of research ethics commonly refer not to the Nuremberg Code but to successive versions of the Declaration of Helsinki, and to a range of congruent conventions and reports.[9] The most recent version of the

---

[9] The *Declaration of Ethical Principles for Medical Research Involving Human Subjects* was first promulgated in 1964, by the World Medical Association. For the text of the 2004 revision of the Declaration see http://www.wma.net/e/policy/b3.htm. For the history of the Declaration see http://www.wma.net/e/ethicsunit/pdf/chapter_4_decl_of_helsinki.pdf; and Robert V. Carlson, Kenneth M. Boyd and David J. Webb, 'The Revision of the Declaration of Helsinki: Past, Present and Future', *British Journal of Clinical Pharmacology* 57 (2004), 695–713.

Other landmark documents include the *Belmont Report* on *Ethical Principles and Guidelines for the Protection of Human Subjects of Research*, 1979 (US Department of Health, Education, and Welfare; http://ohsr.od.nih.gov/guidelines/belmont.html) and Article 16 of the *European Convention for the Protection of Human Rights and Dignity of the Human Being with regard to the Application of Biology and Medicine: Convention on Human Rights and Biomedicine*, http://conventions.coe.int/treaty/en/Reports/Html/164.htm which prohibits research on human subjects unless 'the necessary consent as provided for under Article 5 has been given expressly, specifically and is documented'.

For secondary literature see B. Brody, *The Ethics of Biomedical Research: An International Perspective* (New York: Oxford University Press, 1998); Sue Eckstein,

Declaration of Helsinki, approved in 2004, sets out strict and strong requirements for (highly) explicit and (fairly) specific consent. Similar demands are often set out in other codes for research ethics.

The relevant articles of the Declaration of Helsinki read:

20. The subjects must be volunteers and informed participants in the research project.

22. In any research on human beings, each potential subject must be adequately informed of the aims, methods, sources of funding, and any possible conflicts of interest, institutional affiliations of the researcher, the anticipated benefits and potential risks of the study and the discomfort it may entail. The subject should be informed of the right to abstain from participation in the study or to withdraw consent to participate at any time without reprisal. After ensuring that the subject has understood the information, the physician should then obtain the subject's freely given informed consent, preferably in writing. If the consent cannot be obtained in writing, the non-written consent must be formally documented and witnessed.

Setting aside the Declaration's careless habit of conflating *physicians* with *researchers*, we can see that it promulgates more exacting standards and processes for seeking and obtaining informed consent from research subjects than those set out in the Nuremberg Code. In effect, *Helsinki* 2004 requires researchers to use *explicit* written and documented procedures in requesting and obtaining consent, and to seek *specific* consent to envisaged research projects. It repeatedly emphasises the information that researchers are to provide to research subjects. It goes beyond the Nuremberg demand that research subjects grasp in a general way what is proposed, and its likely effects and risks for them, and requires researchers to inform them about a range of scientific and institutional matters, including 'the aims, methods, sources of funding, and any possible conflicts of interest, institutional affiliations of the researcher, the anticipated benefits and potential risks of the study'. Asking research subjects to

ed., *Manual for Research Ethics Committees*, 6th edn (Cambridge: Cambridge University Press, 2003).

grasp this complex of scientific and institutional information is highly demanding, even in the 'best' case where highly competent research subjects are recruited for a prospective study. And some seek to raise the standards even higher.[10]

These standards may demand too much. Many research subjects fail to understand common features of prospective research design, such as the use of randomised trials and placebos.[11] Where they fail, their consent will not meet the Helsinki standards. Does this show that such research should not be done? In other cases, where research is not prospective, but rather based on further analysis of existing data or tissues, it is even harder – indeed often impossible – to see how Helsinki standards could be applied. Research proposals for secondary data analyses, population studies or epidemiological investigations may not be formulated until well after information was recorded or the tissues were removed. The 'research subjects' (if that is how they are best thought of) would have to be recontacted if explicit and specific prior consent were required. Doing so is often impossible. Does this show that retrospective research should not be done, because it cannot meet the Helsinki standards? If it does, and we prohibit all research that does not meet the Helsinki standards, many sorts of medical research will not pass muster and will have to be abandoned.

The quest for higher standards for informed consent has also become vigorous in clinical ethics. In the very years in which some have tried to make consenting *easier* in order to accommodate

---

[10] For example, one author suggests that 'unless subjects are informed of the researchers' personal characteristics, views, and sponsors whenever they would be likely to consider them significant, their autonomy is being overridden'. T. M. Wilkinson, 'Research, Informed Consent, and the Limits of Disclosure', *Bioethics* 15 (2001), 341–63 (p. 363).

[11] Randomised trials have been in use since the late 1940s. They are commonly required in studies aimed at establishing the relative efficacy of treatments; but there are also persistent criticisms of the method, and queries about its acceptability. On the specific issues of research subjects' consent see Angus Dawson, 'What Should We Do About It? Implications of the Empirical Evidence in Relation to Comprehension and Acceptability of Randomisation?', in S. Holm and M. Jonas, eds., *Engaging the World: The Use of Empirical Research in Bioethics and the Regulation of Biotechnology* (Netherlands: IOS Press, 2004).

patients' cognitive limitations, others have tried to make it *more exacting*. The desire to make consent and consenting rigorous is understandable, but has raised many problems. Even if past standards had been good enough – and there may be reasons to doubt that they were – the growing complexity both of the information relevant to specific clinical interventions and research protocols and of their medical and scientific settings, may now require more exacting procedures.[12] However, simultaneous attempts to make informed consent *easier for patients* and to make it *more exacting* are likely to backfire.

In effect attempts to make informed consent more rigorous argue for two distinct types of improvement. They claim that acts of consenting should be *explicit*, rather than *implied* (*tacit, presumed*), and they claim that adequate consent should be *specific* rather than *generic* (*general*). In effect, they generalise the position taken in the Declaration of Helsinki, and extend it from research into clinical practice. Demands for *explicit* and *specific* consent may have started in research ethics, but have now penetrated into clinical practice, into medical ethics and into regulatory requirements. One result has been the development of increasingly complex, lengthy and (at worst) incomprehensible consent forms – and a large literature lamenting the fact!

The distinction between *explicit* and *implied* consent contrasts ways of consenting. Explicit consenting is a two way process. Those who request consent must provide an explicit statement of the nature and purposes of a proposed course of action, its effects, risks and other features, to those whose consent is sought. Those who are asked to consent must show explicitly that they understand

---

[12] Genetic information, for example, is challenging for many patients and others, who may find the information complex, and the reproductive or clinical risks they face hard to grasp and in some cases threatening. This is particularly likely where patients have to understand the *causal* significance of genetic claims (e.g., base rate fallacy; intuitions of determinism; lack of understanding of penetrance etc.). Indeed, the problems may not lie only with patients. Physicians too may lack an up-to-date grasp of genetics, yet are supposed to inform patients about genetic matters. See J. A. Kegley, 'Genetics Decision-making: a Template for Problems with Informed Consent', *Medical Law* 21 (2002), 459–71.

this information and agree to the proposal. Explicit consenting is typically done using documents, signatures and formal statements, and in some cases witnesses who confirm and provide evidence that proper procedures for consenting have been followed. Procedures for explicit consent create enduring records of a patient's participation in the consent transaction which (it is hoped) will reduce later uncertainty about the limits of the consent given, and forestall subsequent dissatisfaction, complaint or litigation. Such records may be important not only for ethical reasons but as a way by which professionals and institutions can limit their liability in the event of mishap or failure. Where patients explicitly consent to proposed interventions they cannot later legitimately complain that an action injured or wronged them, or was unexpected, provided that it respects, or respected, their consent. Consent requirements can be used to limit complaints and litigation. By contrast, *implied consent* is inferred from a patient's action. For example, I may agree to have blood taken by extending my arm. Since no documentation of implied consent is required, sought, given or recorded, defence against subsequent allegations of injury or wrong may be more difficult in the event of later complaint or litigation.

The distinction between *specific* and *generic* consent applies not to acts of consenting, but to the propositions to which consent is given. The longer and more elaborate 'consent forms' now routinely used in the NHS, and in medical practice elsewhere, extend demands for (more) specific consent into the routine procedures of hospitals, the daily life of physicians and the daily experience of patients. These demands are seen as raising ethical standards for clinical practice by sharpening up not only processes of consenting, but the specificity of consent given.

This programme for making informed consent more exacting is problematic in many ways. The supposedly higher standards make demands that are achievable neither in theory nor in practice, and they are not well designed for achieving ethically acceptable clinical practice and medical research. In effect, demands for explicit and specific consent insist on formalistic, uniform and, strictly speaking, impossible procedures and standards, rather than looking for feasible, proportionate and normatively justified requirements.

Explicit consent cannot be necessary, because it is not always possible. Implied consent can be replaced by explicit consent in some, but not in all, cases. For example, it would be possible – if burdensome – to replace implied with explicit consent for certain interventions now done on the basis of implied consent, such as taking blood or taking a temperature. But it would not be possible to do entirely without implied consent, because any explicit consenting presupposes and relies on implicit assumptions and agreements – including assumptions about the methods and conventions for requesting, offering and refusing consent. The thought that since some consenting can be made explicit, all consenting can be made explicit commits a fallacy of composition. The aspects of consenting that are made explicit always presuppose and rely on understandings that are not made explicit. So there can be no complete programme for replacing implied with explicit consent.

Similarly, while generic consent can be problematic, a demand that consent be fully specific is unachievable. Generic consent is consent to a proposed intervention, specified or described in a reasonably general way. Although that description can always be made more detailed, so more specific, it is in principle impossible to make it fully specific: descriptions of proposed interventions are unavoidably indeterminate. There are always further clauses or qualifications that we could correctly add to *any* description of *any* proposed intervention.

Moreover, we cannot assume that consent will travel from a more general account of proposed intervention to more specific aspects that were not mentioned. Consent is a *propositional attitude*,[13] and no transfer of consent from one to another description of an intervention, for example, from (more) generic to (more) specific aspects of a proposal, is guaranteed. I may consent to some intervention under a given description, without grasping other propositions that follow logically from the one to which I consent. I may consent to research or treatment whose standard corollaries and consequences include states of affairs

---

[13] Propositional attitudes are attitudes that take propositions as their objects. They include cognitive states such as knowing, believing, hoping, desiring, imagining, dreaming and many others.

that I do not know, overlook or fail to understand, so do not consent to. Consent – like all other propositional attitudes – is *opaque*: John and Jane may both consent to intervention *x*, yet have quite divergent views of the implications, the corollaries and the consequences of *x*.[14]

Some examples drawn both from research and from clinical medicine will illustrate the point. Suppose a research subject consents to be given lysergic acid diethylamide as part of research into 'the psychological effects of a new drug'. The inferences that many of us would draw if told that the drug is called lysergic acid diethylamide may differ from those we would draw if told that the drug is LSD: yet LSD *is* lysergic acid diethylamide. The researcher who tells subjects that they will be given lysergic acid diethylamide speaks truly, but *pragmatically* this may mislead them because the chemical is *better known* as LSD, or is *likely to be known as* LSD by the research subjects.[15] The underlying point is that the research subjects 'think of' LSD in one way, but of lysergic acid diethylamide in another. The conclusions that research subjects can reach will vary with the inferences they are able to draw from the terms used, *and may differ even where the terms used refer to the same things*.[16]

---

[14] We say more about what 'opacity' means in Chapter 2. For now, an example may help. Clark Kent is Superman. Lots of statements that are true of Clark Kent are also, thereby, true of Superman. For example, 'Clark Kent is 1.9 metres tall' implies that Superman is 1.9 metres tall. But the truth of the statement 'Lois Lane thinks that Clark Kent is a wimp' does *not* imply the truth of 'Lois Lane thinks that Superman is a wimp'. In general, statements of the form 'So-and-so thinks that *x* is F' is 'opaque' in that the truth-value of such statements depends upon *more than* just what '*x*' and 'F' *actually* denote. Similar points apply to 'So-and-so *consents* to *x*'s doing F'. Lois Lane may consent to be kissed by Superman, but not by Clark Kent even though, *de facto*, being kissed by Superman *is* being kissed by Clark Kent.

[15] Could the researchers defend their action by arguing that they want to avoid the research being skewed by people's *misbeliefs* about LSD? Could they defend choosing more anodyne descriptions of genetic conditions if popular conceptions of genes and genetic conditions are likely to give rise to disproportionate anxiety? Or are such actions unacceptably paternalistic?

[16] The LSD example is noted in Ruth R. Faden and Tom L. Beauchamp, *A History and Theory of Informed Consent* (New York: Oxford University Press, 1986), p. 183. Faden and Beauchamp do not expand upon this example in the way that we have here, nor do they seek to draw conclusions about how the nature of inference puts limitations on the scope of consent.

Analogous issues arise in clinical practice. For example, James may consent to prostate surgery, but fail to grasp that one consequence of the surgery is sterility. This could happen either if he were not told of this effect, or if he were told but did not 'take in' the information. Does James then consent to an intervention that may make him sterile? Although it is true to describe the action that he agrees to as 'an action that will cause sterility', he may not consent to the action *so described*, even where he consents to the action described as prostate surgery.

Similar issues can arise where research makes use of information or human tissues originally legitimately obtained for other purposes. For example, the parents of a dead child may consent to 'tissue' originally removed for a coroner's autopsy being retained and used for research. The researchers may then retain whole organs, holding (correctly) that these consist of human tissues. But the parents may have inferential commitments that differ from those of the researchers. They may think of whole organs as something *other* than tissue, and think that organs – hearts, brains, livers, and so on – are not tissue. (This example is based on a simplified version of some of the cases at Alder Hey Hospital in the 1990s.[17])

All of these examples have in common the failure of consent to transfer from one proposition to others that are also true of the intervention for which consent is sought. In the first type of case, the LSD case, the failure derives from the fact that different terms, with differing inferential significance, may apply to the same thing. In the second type of case, the failure derives from the subject's ignorance that prostate surgery causes sterility, and from his consequent inability to draw certain inferences about the proposed action. In the third type of case, there is an intersubjective difference about the meaning of the term 'tissue'. The clinician takes 'tissue' to have a much broader reference than do the parents. In the LSD case we have two terms referring to the same thing, in the 'tissue' case we have one word used in two ways by different persons. The underlying point, which applies

---

[17] See *The Royal Liverpool Children's Inquiry Report* (The Redfern Report), http://www.rlcinquiry.org.uk/contents.htm.

to each of these types of example, is that consent is shaped by the inferences people draw, which commonly differ from those that others draw. Our inferences reflect a range of factors, including our varying understandings of certain concepts or words, and our varying beliefs. We shall say more about the role and importance of our inferential abilities – and about their limits – in Chapter 3.

The fact that consent, like other propositional attitudes, is opaque has many implications. Put very generally, it means that A's consent to *p* cannot ensure that A consents to *q*, *r*, *s*, even where *q*, *r*, *s* are entailed by *p*, or where *q*, *r*, *s* accurately specify corollaries or consequences of the states of affairs of which *p* is true. Since those who consent need not – and often do not – grasp entailment relations, corollaries or causal connections, their consent may not travel to other propositions, even if these are closely related to the one to which they consented.

These considerations show that fully specific consent cannot be ethically necessary, since it cannot even be properly defined. The act descriptions contained in any proposition for which consent is requested, given or refused are always incomplete, and could always be augmented by further and more specific detail. So if we insist that informed consent must be specific, we may reasonably be asked how *specific* it ought to be. Answering this question in any uniform or simple way is impossible, just as it is impossible to answer the pseudo-question 'How long is a piece of string?'. Demands for fully specific consent are in principle unmeetable. Indeed, demands for a *uniform* level of specificity of consent may not be definable.

Neither *full* explicitness nor *complete* specificity is possible. Yet versions of these excessive demands are constantly repeated in the standard 'literature' on informed consent. The problem runs deeper than the much-discussed worries about the level and standard of informed consent 'disclosures'. Some discussions of these worries ask whether standards of specificity should be set (for example) by what the 'reasonable doctor' would expect to disclose, or by what the 'reasonable patient' would want to know, or (more demandingly) by what the 'individual subject' would want to know. Yet even if we accept the most radical of these views, and hold that consent disclosures should be tailored to what the individual subject would want to know, we still could not determine what this required. For how are we to tell what a given patient (or research subject) would judge adequately specific in a given situation? Finding this out would be time-consuming and intrusive, indeed might require us to seek prior consent for taking up the subject's time in order to find out what she would think of as adequately specific: but then we would be off on a regress. We could avoid the regress by holding that some interactions that impose upon subjects do not require explicit and specific consent: but then we would concede the general point that explicitness and specificity cannot set general conditions on consensual social interaction.

The underlying point is that for human agents, with varying beliefs, varying inferential commitments and varying vocabularies, the best that we can hope for is a mutually agreed level of specificity in the disclosure for a particular transaction. And once we concede this point, we concede that explicitness and specificity cannot be general requirements on all consent. Full or complete specificity is unobtainable, and unnecessary for valid consent; full explicitness can be achieved in some cases – but only if we accept numerous implicit assumptions. If we try to improve, or shore up, standards for informed consent in these ways, we not only ignore the real limitations of competence of some of those asked to consent, but risk digging ourselves into deep theoretical holes.

IMPROVING JUSTIFICATIONS: THE QUEST
FOR AUTONOMY

Why, we may ask, are these unattainable standards taken so seriously? What is their point and purpose? Are medical practice and research that fail to meet these inflated informed consent requirements really unacceptable? Is explicit and specific informed consent to all interventions really morally indispensable? And is consent that does not meet these exacting standards bogus, and insufficient for justification?

The Nuremberg Code was rather clear about reasons for thinking that consent justifies. It views informed consent as assurance and evidence that a proposed action will not involve or be based on force, fraud, deceit, duress, constraint or coercion, and the like, and so will neither force the body nor overwhelm or undermine the will. Consent matters because it can be used to protect research subjects and patients against grave wrongs. However, this approach to the justification of consent requirements has been superseded in recent discussions of the justification of informed consent in medicine and research, which deploy a more sweeping justificatory strategy. They argue that informed consent is required because we must respect the autonomy of research subjects and patients.[18] Informed consent is needed in order to secure respect for autonomy, which is presumed to be fundamental to ethics. However, the general agreement that informed consent is required for the sake of autonomy, and that autonomy is a basic ethical value, is more apparent than real, since there is substantive and persistent disagreement both about conceptions of autonomy, and about their importance in biomedicine.

Three conceptions of autonomy are commonly invoked and commonly confused in writing on bioethics. One of them, the Kantian conception of *principled autonomy*, can be set aside. It is often mentioned with respect, but hardly ever discussed in writing on medical and research ethics. Those who invoke Kant's legacy and authority almost invariably overlook the fact that Kant used the term *autonomy* to refer not to a characteristic of individuals,[19] but to the formal properties of principles of action that can serve for all, and in particular to the combination of law-like form and universal scope. This understanding of autonomy lies behind and makes sense of Kant's thought that the 'Formula of Autonomy' is a version of the

---

[18] The most cited works on autonomy and informed consent in biomedical practice include Tom L. Beauchamp and James F. Childress, *Principles of Biomedical Ethics*, 4th Edn (New York: Oxford University Press, 1994); Faden and Beauchamp, *A History and Theory of Informed Consent*.

[19] See Thomas E. Hill Jnr, 'The Kantian Conception of Autonomy', in his *Dignity and Practical Reason* (Ithaca, NY: Cornell University Press 1992), pp. 76–96; Onora O'Neill, 'Self-Legislation, Autonomy and the Form of Law', in *Recht, Geschichte, Religion: Die Bedeutung Kants für die Gegenwart*, eds. Herta Nagl-Docekal and Rudolf Langthaler, *Sonderband der Deutschen Zeitschrift für Philosophie* (Berlin: Akademie Verlag, 2004), pp. 13–26.

Categorical Imperative, and of his famous claim that '*Autonomy* of the will is the sole principle of all moral laws and of duties in keeping with them'.[20] In speaking of 'autonomy of the will', Kant refers to a property of the practical principle an agent adopts or 'wills'. He, of course, thinks that agents can choose freely – but their doing so does not make their willing autonomous: heteronomous – that is non-autonomous – action is also free and imputable.

Some contemporary writers on autonomy – libertarians in particular – echo Kant in claiming that autonomy provides the entire basis for morality. But since their conceptions of autonomy are remote from Kant's views, they cannot draw any support from his arguments for linking autonomy and morality.[21] Although Kant also argued for the importance of consent in certain contexts – most obviously in his distinctive writing on the idea of the social contract – his conception of autonomy has a broader, strategic role in his philosophy, which cannot be operationalised by informed consent procedures.[22]

Contemporary work on autonomy is quite different. It views autonomy as a property of individuals, and specifically as a form of individual independence. Conceptions of *individual autonomy* have risen to prominence with the revival of liberal political and economic thought during the last forty years, and have also now become central themes in medical ethics and research ethics. It is easy to see why those who see autonomy as a matter of individual independence link it so closely to informed consent: informed

---

[20] Immanuel Kant, (1787) *Critique of Practical Reason*, in Immanuel Kant, *Practical Philosophy*, tr. Mary Gregor (Cambridge: Cambridge University Press, 1996), 5: 33. The pagination is that of the Prussian Academy and is given in the margins of this and other good editions and translations.

[21] For a more systematic account of discrepancies between Kantian and contemporary conceptions of autonomy and some of their implications for the justification of consent procedures in biomedical practice see Onora O'Neill, 'Autonomy: The Emperor's New Clothes, The Inaugural Address', *Proceedings of the Aristotelian Society*, supp. vol. 77 (2003), 1–21; and *Autonomy and Trust in Bioethics* (Cambridge: Cambridge University Press, 2002).

[22] To anticipate Chapter 4: Kantian autonomy expresses an underlying principle for a theory of basic duties; Kant's comments on informed consent propose ways of waiving those basic duties in certain cases.

consent procedures protect individual choice, and with it individual independence, hence individual autonomy. So if we can show that individual autonomy is a fundamental value – still better, *the* fundamental value – and that it can best be protected and implemented by informed consent requirements, it may prove possible to justify informed consent procedures as required if we are to respect autonomy. However, neither point is easily established.

One problem arises simply because much medical and research provision is not and cannot be chosen, so does not provide an arena for individual choice, nor therefore for individual autonomy. Public health measures aim to provide *public goods*, which if provided for any must be provided for many to the same standard. Food safety standards, air quality levels, levels of professional training, standards for pathology or genetics services and research ethics procedures cannot be varied on the basis of individual choice, informed or uninformed.[23] Nor can other public goods such as environmental measures that promote public health and safety, standards for non-clinical uses of genetic technologies, or the running of blood banks, tissue banks or genetic data banks, be matters of individual choice. Nor can externalities, such as the unintended consequences of public policies, be chosen. Consequently individual autonomy cannot be the *sole* principle of medical or research ethics, and consent requirements that protect individual autonomy cannot be the *sole* criterion of ethically acceptable action.

Other aspects of medical and research provision are *private goods*. They are thus, at least potentially, matters for individual choice or consent. Yet even in these cases it is not obvious whether consent requirements can be justified by appealing to individual autonomy. Different difficulties arise for different conceptions of autonomy. Those who seek to interpret individual autonomy minimally as *mere, sheer choice* may be able to show that informed consent operationalises autonomy conceived in this way, but will find it hard to show that this conception of autonomy is fundamental to ethics. Those

---

[23] Onora O'Neill, 'Informed Consent and Public Health', *Philosophical Transactions: Biological Sciences* 359 (2004), 1133–6.

who interpret individual autonomy more ambitiously as some form of rational or reflective choosing may be able to make a better case for thinking that it is fundamental to ethics, but will have difficulty in explaining how it can be operationalised by informed consent requirements.

If we think of autonomy as a matter of *mere* choice, arguments will be needed to show why *all* choices (however irrational, however poorly informed) should be protected. Mere independence, we might think, can lead to choices and acts that are good or bad, right or wrong, kind or callous, prudent or risky. If, on the other hand, we think of autonomy as a matter of *reasoned or reflective choice*, further arguments will be needed to show why *only* these choices should be protected, and it will be hard to show that actual consent (so often less than rational, so often unreflective) operationalises autonomy.

If individual autonomy is seen as fundamental to ethics, but merely as a matter of choice, then the only permissible restrictions on choice will be those required to protect others' individual autonomy. All choices that leave others' autonomy intact – however bizarre, however self-destructive, however offensive, however degrading – will be permissible, and restrictions on them will be unacceptable. Nothing will be prohibited or unacceptable between consenting adults. Some libertarians endorse this strong, monistic form of ethical individualism. Others would argue that further principles are usually relevant, even in the case of 'self-regarding' action, where no further issue of harm, offence or injustice to others arises. For example, they might regard consensual cannibalism, markets in human body parts or action that degrades others even with their consent (dwarf throwing, consensual sadism) as unacceptable.[24] They are likely to think that other, equally important 'other-regarding' ethical principles, such as the relief of suffering, beneficence, respect for human dignity and justice, sometimes legitimately limit individual autonomy. If it were possible to show that

---

[24] See the 'dignitarian' position discussed in Deryck Beyleveld and Roger Brownsword, *Human Dignity in Bioethics and Biolaw* (Oxford: Oxford University Press, 2001).

individual autonomy, thought of as mere sheer choice, was the fundamental ethical principle, then it could be operationalised by informed consent procedures; since it is not possible to show this, those who think of autonomy so minimally cannot show that informed choice provides an ethical panacea for medical or research practice, or for other areas of life.

Those who seek to make conceptions of *rational autonomy* fundamental to ethics face rather different problems. There are many conceptions of reason, and therefore of rational autonomy. Some see it as a matter of choosing that is well informed, or reflectively evaluated, or endorsed by second-order desires.[25] We do not want to enter these complex debates here, or to argue in favour of one rather than another conception of rational autonomy, but rather to point out why it is difficult to base justifications for informed consent requirements on conceptions of rational autonomy. One central difficulty is that rational autonomy (however conceived) is more cognitively demanding than a minimal conception of individual autonomy as mere, sheer choice. If appeals to rational autonomy are used to justify informed consent requirements, this will set a higher hurdle for cognitively adequate consent, so shrink the range of cases in medical and research practice for which informed consent could be required. A second problem is that if rational autonomy (however conceived) could be shown to be fundamental to ethics, then other ethical concerns, including the relief of suffering and beneficence, would have to be seen as subordinate, or dismissed. A third, and decisive, problem is that if we could satisfy ourselves that some conception of rational autonomy was fundamental to ethics, we would then lack reasons for thinking that it is best operationalised by informed consent procedures. Informed consent requirements protect actual choices, which are often not rational choices.

---

[25] John Christman, 'Constructing the Inner Citadel: Recent Work on the Concept of Autonomy', *Ethics* 99 (1988), 109–24; and essays in John Christman, ed., *The Inner Citadel: Essays on Individual Autonomy* (New York: Oxford University Press, 1989); O'Neill, *Autonomy and Trust in Bioethics*.

All of this suggests that appeals to individual autonomy, however conceived, are unlikely to provide convincing justifications for informed consent procedures. The question of justification has not been settled by decades of insistence that informed consent is required in order to respect individual autonomy.

REGULATORY REINFORCEMENT: CONSENT
REQUIREMENTS

Informed consent requirements became important in medical and research ethics because they were used to set standards for *invasive* treatment, which might impose risks as well as benefits, pain as well as relief from pain. Across the last fifteen years, informed consent requirements have acquired a secondary use in the regulation of potentially *intrusive* uses of information and tissues that have already been legitimately obtained, where no further invasive procedures are envisaged. In later chapters we shall look at aspects of a few regulatory regimes of these sorts.

The regulation of clinical medicine and of medical research is a vast topic, which has attracted a correspondingly large critical literature. Much of that critical literature argues that regulation is often excessively complex, bureaucratic, expensive, time-consuming, and at times dysfunctional or even damaging to medicine and research, and so to patients and to the wider public.[26] In this book we shall consider only a limited range of regulatory requirements for informed consent to certain types of non-invasive action. Even within this circumscribed area there is more complexity, more legislation and more regulation than we shall be able to discuss in any detail, and we shall focus specifically on some of the implications of informed consent requirements for *further* uses of information and tissues *already* legitimately held.

Data Protection legislation, such as the UK *Data Protection Act 1998 (DPA 98)*, requires consent from the 'data subject' to any

---

[26] See Charles Warlow, 'Over-regulation of Clinical Research: a Threat to Public Health', *Clinical medicine* 5 (2005), 33–8 for an overview of effects of UK regulation.

further use of information classified as personal or sensitive, including information pertaining to medical conditions and treatment, and information obtained in the course of biomedical research, even if it was legitimately obtained and retained.[27] Legislation on Human Tissues, such as the UK *Human Tissues Act 2004* (*HTA 04*), introduces similar provisions, requiring further consent from individuals (or their next of kin) for any further study or use of tissues already legitimately obtained and stored. Genetic Privacy legislation, such as the numerous bills laid before the US Congress in recent years,[28] generally proposes analogous consent-based regulation of further uses of genetic information already legitimately obtained and recorded. These forms of legislation and regulation seek to extend informed consent requirements beyond invasive interventions to activity that is seen as *potentially intrusive*, whether or not it is *actually intrusive*.

Each of these extensions of consent requirements is likely to encounter the difficulties already noted. There is no reason to suppose that extending the scope of informed consent requirements from invasive medical treatment and research to non-invasive activities will prove unproblematic. There is no reason to expect that demands for explicit and specific consent will prove more manageable here than elsewhere. There is no reason to suppose that appeals to autonomy will provide more convincing justifications here than elsewhere. On the contrary, there is good reason to think that placing detailed consent requirements on all further uses of legitimately held information (including genetic information) and of lawfully held tissues will raise further difficulties.

Some of these difficulties are easy to identify. If further uses of information are subject to informed consent requirements, it will be necessary to pick out the sorts of information to which these requirements apply. Yet classifying information as *medical* or *personal* or *sensitive* is fraught with problems, as we shall show in Chapter 5.

---

[27] We discuss data protection legislation, and issues about 'information privacy', in more detail in Chapter 5.

[28] See the US National Institutes of Health, *Privacy and Discrimination Federal Legislation Archive* for a list of bills – and a few Acts – bearing on genetic privacy and their current status. http://www.genome.gov/11510239.

Even if those problems could be solved, the demands that data protection requirements place on patients and research subjects may be excessive. Yet prohibiting all further uses of legitimately held information would damage patients (by restricting the information that their doctors can bring to bear on their treatment) and the public interest (by limiting medical research).

Analogous issues arise in regulating all further uses of legitimately held human tissues. Prohibiting all further uses of legitimately held tissues unless further consent is obtained for each specific subsequent use, may harm patients (physicians may not be able to study or compare their tissues with tissues lawfully obtained and retained in other similar cases), and also the public interest (since research done on 'surplus' tissues, that would otherwise be discarded as clinical waste, will be prohibited).

It may seem that these difficulties could generally be overcome by securing the requisite consent for further uses of legitimately held data and tissues. However, requirements to obtain further specific consent set high cognitive hurdles for those from whom the consent must be sought, and high administrative (and financial) hurdles for clinicians and researchers.

CONCLUSION

In this chapter we have discussed a range of problems that have arisen in the course of attempts to make informed consent central to ethically acceptable medical and research practice. We have not (as yet) offered any systematic diagnosis, or suggested any remedies to these numerous problems. However, we have covered enough ground to show that the difficulties are large and intractable. The question now is what to do.

There are choices to be made.[29] We could shut our eyes to these problems and to the very widespread failure to achieve standards of

[29] See Dawson, 'What Should We Do About It', which argues that we face a choice between (i) stopping research because the conditions for consent cannot be met; (ii) continuing with research, but keeping quiet about the fact that we know that the ethical standards have not been met; or (iii) – in our view the most promising option – reviewing and revising informed consent procedures.

consent and consenting that meet the prescribed standards. In effect we could pretend that, despite all these problems, current clinical and research practices meet the standards prescribed and should be continued. But systematic hypocrisy is hardly appealing.

A second possibility would be to try to live up to the standards prescribed by contemporary informed consent requirements. This option would require radical changes. In clinical practice we would have to classify a far larger proportion of the patient population as lacking competence, effectively conceding that they cannot give genuine consent (the alternative would be to refuse them treatment). In clinical trials we would have to ensure that nobody enrols unless their consent genuinely reaches the standards supposedly required. No clinical trial could go ahead unless it could recruit research subjects who genuinely understood the research design, including the nature and significance of randomisation or the use of placebos where these were planned, and could grasp the scientific, institutional and financial context of modern medical research. Retrospective studies could not take place unless specific further consent to newly envisaged uses of information and tissues could be obtained by 're-consenting' those whose information or tissues were studied. In effect we would treat many patients as non-competent, limit medical research and put a more or less complete stop on retrospective studies and population studies.

Neither of these two broad options is appealing. But there is a third possibility. The third option is to rethink informed consent in more fundamental ways, with the aim of identifying an approach that is both feasible and justifiable. This is what we propose to do in the following chapters. We shall begin by thinking not about consent, but about informing and information, before returning to a less exorbitant and more plausible account of consent. We shall then consider how this more modest view of consent can be justified, what implications it might have for the further use of legitimately held information and tissues and for wider issues of trust and accountability in biomedicine.

CHAPTER 2

Information and communication: the drift from agency

We have argued that current thinking about informed consent is problematic, and that we need to rethink the part that it can play in biomedical practice. But how exactly should we go about this? One approach would be to focus first on the underlying *ethical* justifications for such demanding consent requirements. We might, for example, raise questions about the coherence of putting so much weight on respect for individual autonomy in biomedical ethics.[1] Or we might, if we were of a consequentialist bent, focus on the costs and implications of current informed consent procedures and argue that in certain cases their costs outweigh their benefits.

Our preferred, rather more radical, approach is to expose ways in which current thinking about informed consent rests upon a *distorted* conception of the nature and significance of information and communication. In fact, we shall argue, there are two different kinds of distortion implicit in current thinking about informed consent. One distortion derives from reliance on autonomy-based justifications for informed consent; we postpone discussion of these issues until Chapter 4. The second, more *general* distortion derives from the metaphorical framework that we use to think and talk about information and

---

[1] The limits of appeals to autonomy are often emphasised in non-liberal (often anti-liberal) writing in bioethics, much of it communitarian, religious or conservative. See, for example, Daniel Callahan, 'Can the Moral Commons Survive Autonomy?', *Hastings Center Report* 26 (1996), 41–2; P. Wolpe, 'The Triumph of Autonomy in American Bioethics', in R. Devries and J. Subedi, eds., *Bioethics and Society: Constructing the Ethical Enterprise* (Englewood Cliffs, NJ: Prentice Hall, 1996), pp. 38–59; Leonard R. Kass, *Life, Liberty and the Defence of Dignity: The Challenge for Bioethics* (New York: Encounter Books, 2002).

communication. Contemporary thinking about information hides and downplays many important aspects of communication and information, including the fact that communicating and informing are types of *action* and *interaction*, so depend on a normative framework against which such action succeeds or fails. In Chapter 3, we aim to bring these often-hidden elements to the fore, and propose what we hope is a more adequate account of information and communication, that takes full account of the action and interaction by which they are achieved. Contrasting these two frameworks for thinking about information and communication provides us with a basis for rethinking informed consent, and for a critical discussion of a number of other contemporary normative issues to do with information and communication.

FRAMING INFORMED CONSENT

The informed consent procedures now used in biomedicine require certain agents (researchers; clinicians; genetic counsellors, etc.) to disclose information *about* certain things (proposed research; proposed medical treatments; costs; benefits; risks; alternatives) to certain others (potential research subjects; patients; those deciding whether to proceed with genetic testing). On the standard view that informed consent is required in order to respect autonomy, these 'informational' obligations are seen as justified because they protect and enhance individual decision-making. On this view, what matters ethically is that the patient or research subject *choose* or *decide which* course of action she favours, or *whether* to proceed with a certain course of action. Ethically sound biomedical practice ought to respect individual choice. If a research subject or a patient lacks adequate information about proposed courses of action that may impinge upon her, she cannot decide properly whether or not to consent to that course of action. So clinicians and researchers *ought* to disclose or make available the information that patients or research subjects need for autonomous decision-making. They should then wait for the patient or research subject to make a free decision, *based upon the disclosure of adequate, relevant information*, and should act only within the terms of that decision.

A number of distinct assumptions underlie this standard line of thought, which we shall discuss in turn. The order in which we list these assumptions does not amount to a claim that some are more fundamental or important than others.

Assumption 1: classifying information

Discussions of informed consent assume that certain *types* of information – information *about* certain things – ought to be disclosed to patients and research subjects, while other *types* of information about different matters need not be disclosed.[2] This may seem entirely reasonable. Clinicians and researchers cannot be obliged to inform their patients about *everything* about which they could inform them. That would be absurd. In the past doctors would inform their patients about proposed interventions if they thought it important, or polite, or worthwhile for some other reason. Now that informed consent procedures are incorporated into the professional codes for clinicians and researchers, other views of the types of information they ought to 'disclose' to patients or research subjects are assumed. These codes cannot specify rigid rules for disclosing types of information in every case. Professional guidelines will acknowledge that different courses of action, in different contexts, may require disclosure of more or less, or different information. If a treatment or a research intervention has a risk of severe side effects, for example, then professionals will typically be required to disclose extensive and detailed information about those effects; if the intervention is minimally invasive, less complete disclosure may be enough.[3]

However, variability in disclosure requirements does not challenge the underlying assumption that we can classify information by considering what it is about. Information may, for example, be *about*

---

[2] For example: 'Modern guidelines try to ensure that consent is informed, by giving researchers a list of information that they have a duty to disclose regardless of whether potential subjects ask for it.' T. M. Wilkinson, 'Research, Informed Consent, and the Limits of Disclosure', *Bioethics* 15 (2001), 341–63 (p. 343).

[3] We noted in the last chapter that it is not feasible to disclose *everything*: fully specific consent and consent disclosures are impossible.

risks, *about* consequences or alternatives; *about* diagnoses or prognoses; *about* this patient or that one; *about* this cohort of research subjects or that one. It is not our aim to provide a complete checklist of the *kinds* of information that should be disclosed in different situations. Our aim is to argue – in the next chapter – that the seemingly innocent assumption that we can classify information by considering what it is about hides a range of problems which create complications for current approaches to informed consent.

Assumption 2: first-order informational obligations

A second assumption implicit in current informed consent procedures is that specific agents – e.g., clinicians, researchers – ought to use the information that they have in certain ways. In particular, they should disclose that information to those others whom their action may affect, but not to others. Disclosure is not just a matter of making information 'available'. Information about, say, the effects and risks of a particular type of medical intervention is often 'available' to a subject or patient in a wide variety of ways. Such information may be available in medical textbooks, on the internet, and so on. We can imagine a world, unlike our own, where, say, self-reliance was taken to be of such fundamental importance that it was held that patients ought to take the initiative in finding out about the risks and consequences of proposed medical interventions prior to treatment. In that world the obligation to acquire information would fall upon patients, who might have to sign a document stating that they had come to know enough about a proposed intervention, and that they were willing (or unwilling) to proceed on the basis of what they knew. In such a world, researchers and clinicians would not have such stringent informational obligations. They would not need to disclose information to the individual patient or research subject, but only to ensure that the relevant information was indeed available (rather than a commercial secret, or an unpublished research result).

In practice, assigning all responsibility for finding the relevant information to research subjects would not be feasible. Researchers have to recruit research subjects with specific characteristics, who may have no prior knowledge of the research proposal for which they volunteer. Unless the research can be done without the subject's knowledge and co-operation (which would raise other ethical issues), the researcher must inform the subject about a number of things: for example, *that* certain research is proposed; *that* the researcher would like the (potential) subject to consider taking part, *what* this is likely to amount to, *what* effects it may have, and so on. Similarly, assigning all responsibility for finding the relevant information to patients would seldom be feasible. It is true that patients typically take the initiative in going to the doctor. But they often go because they do *not* know what is wrong, and want a diagnosis. Moreover, when we are ill we may lack the energy, or the ability to attend or think clearly, so may be (perhaps temporarily) unable to find and assimilate complex information.

Yet these hypothetical examples highlight an assumption that underlies current thinking about informed consent. A quite specific obligation to convey or disclose information *about* certain things, and not about others, is seen as falling on clinicians and researchers. These specific 'informational obligations' are owed *only* to (prospective) patients and research subjects. Clinicians are under no obligation to broadcast details of the risks associated with chemotherapy to all and sundry. Such informational obligations are defeasible. In cases where a person is unconscious, or is three months old, it would be absurd to disclose information about a proposed course of action that the patient cannot understand. In short, our second assumption, that some agents (but not others) have first-order obligations to disclose or convey information (of certain types) to others in specific contexts, rests on a range of enabling and defeating conditions. Informational obligations come into play *if* but *only if* certain conditions are met. Reflection on these conditions has generated a great deal of debate, in particular in the vast literature on ethically appropriate action when informed consent procedures *cannot* come into play. These remarks may seem to be obvious truisms. But they are important if we are to be clear about what is involved – and what is *not* involved – in informed consent procedures.

Assumption 3: second-order informational obligations

Contemporary informed consent procedures typically reinforce and secure first-order informational obligations with a range of *second-order* informational obligations. The distinction is readily illustrated. The obligation of clinicians to disclose information to patients is a first-order obligation. An obligation to see that this obligation is met in a specific way may be a second-order obligation: for example, an obligation to create and store a (signed, witnessed) record of the informed consent transaction. These second-order obligations are derivative: they refer to aspects of the first-order obligations, and may (for example) ensure, and allow others to know, that the first-order obligations are met in certain ways. If a researcher whispers details about proposed research into a research subject's ear she may satisfy the first-order obligation to inform the subject, but she may fail to discharge second-order obligations to do so in ways that allow others (employers, research funders, ethics committees) to *know* that it has been discharged. Such failure might be seen as unprofessional and might lead to later uncertainty both for the research subject and the professional.

Clinicians and researchers are obliged not only to inform their patients or (potential) research subjects of certain things, but to ensure that information about the consent they sought and were given is knowable by other parties. Although the distinction between first and second-order informational obligations has received little attention in discussions of informed consent (in contrast to the vast attention given to the relevant first-order informational obligations), it is an important distinction, and one to which we shall return repeatedly.

Assumption 4: purposes and justifications

Informed consent procedures are complex social and communicative transactions, yet contemporary discussions tend to privilege one account of their point and purpose. Informed consent transactions are seen as a matter of providing, or disclosing, information to the relevant parties as a basis for their autonomous decision-making. But informed consent transactions serve a variety of purposes over and above the provision of material for decision-making. Some of these other purposes are more obvious than others. For example, many have noted that one function of informed consent procedures is to ensure that doctors and researchers are protected from the threat of legal action – and here certain *second-order* obligations are particularly pertinent.

Informed consent transactions may also contribute to a range of other purposes. For example, the fact that a clinician or researcher communicates with a patient or research subject may be important in establishing trust relations.[4] But, in this context, the *content* 'disclosed' may not be the only important thing. Even if the patient does not understand what is disclosed, or understands it poorly, he may (reasonably) infer that the clinician is trustworthy simply because 'she is not trying to hide anything'. Informed consent transactions may also show patients that the clinician has *reasons* for doing certain things, and communicating those reasons may inspire confidence. By contrast, a clinician who is either unwilling or unable to explain *why* a proposed course of action is worthwhile is unlikely to inspire trust or confidence. In some cases a patient may base her decisions, not on the content of the informed consent disclosure, but on her background knowledge that certain kinds of communicative action, or reason-giving, or forms of respectful behaviour, have taken place. It is clear, then, that a single informed consent transaction can serve a number of purposes. Informed consent procedures may be important for a *variety* of reasons, and *not* simply or only because they provide informational material for decision-making.

Yet so long as we assume that informed consent is justified by considerations of 'respect for autonomy', we will tend to focus upon, or highlight, that particular purpose and to ignore the other purposes of these complex communicative transactions. We will tend to focus

---

[4] See Chapter 6.

only on the 'disclosure' or 'delivery' or 'transfer' of information from one party to another. We will tend to assume that clinicians and researchers have information about certain courses of action (and their attendant risks, costs, benefits, and so on) that patients and research subjects typically *lack*, but need to acquire or receive in order to *decide* or *choose* whether to 'authorise' a proposed course of action. The clinician or researcher is thus under an obligation to *disclose* the information that she possesses *to* the patient or research subject so that the latter can make a 'valid' decision and give her 'informed' consent.

By framing things in this way, it may seem that the shifts in informed consent, outlined in Chapter 1, are inevitable. If respect for individual autonomy is a good thing, then, surely the expansion of informed consent practices into new areas is also a good thing? If informed consent disclosures provide the necessary material for decision-making, then surely disclosing *more* information, and *more specific* information, is a good thing, and supports more and better *choice*? After all, if the patient *doesn't* receive specific, detailed, relevant information about proposed interventions, how can she decide what to do? We cannot do without informed consent, for this would entail, or risk, a return to a pre-Helsinki (or, worse, pre-Nuremberg) state of affairs, where clinicians and researchers often *withheld* information from patients and research subjects, whether for paternalistic reasons, out of idleness, or for more sinister reasons. Returning to such a world is surely not a course of action that any of us would advocate.

Perhaps the very idea of 'rethinking' informed consent is problematic, indeed unacceptable. If patients and research subjects can make decisions only if they have information, then perhaps the best that can be hoped for, given the kinds of problem noted in Chapter 1, is that better ways of disclosing or conveying information to patients and research subjects are discovered and introduced. Yet the range and difficulty of the problems discussed in Chapter 1, and their persistence despite the volume of work already done on ameliorating consent procedures, suggest that this would be a difficult task.

TWO LAYERS OF DISTORTION

We believe that it is possible and useful to 'rethink' informed consent, and that this can be done without advocating or supporting a return to paternalistic medical practice or to a pre-Nuremberg or pre-Helsinki approach to medical research.

We note first that standard thinking about informed consent involves two layers of distortion. The first layer of distortion is introduced by the assumption that informed consent is justified as a means to securing autonomy. The standard *justification* of informed consent stresses the *conveyance or transfer of information* (*from* researcher or clinician, *to* research subject or patient), sees this information as material for individual decision-making, and insists that individual decision-making (autonomous choice) *ought* to be respected. This line of thinking distorts informed consent by downplaying or hiding both the complexity of informed consent transactions and the numerous purposes they serve. Such transactions may be ethically important for a variety of reasons and in a variety of ways: they are not just devices to enable 'autonomous choice'. We will return to this in Chapter 4.

In the remainder of this chapter, and in Chapter 3, we will focus on a second layer of distortion that is implicit in current thinking about informed consent. This sort of distortion derives not from the arguments used to justify informed consent procedures, but from deeply entrenched aspects of our thinking about *information* and *communication* themselves.

INFORMATION AND THE DRIFT FROM AGENCY

Information as action and as content

The original meaning of 'inform' is *to give form to something*: to give it determinate shape, to arrange it, or modify it. A sculptress informs the clay that she shapes with her hands. In English 'inform' came to be used more narrowly, first as a synonym for 'instruct' or 'educate'. When a teacher informs her students she, in a metaphorical way, shapes them, moulds them, and in doing so impresses knowledge upon their minds. The abstract noun 'information' used to be deployed to denote the *process* or *activity* of informing – just as one use of 'formation' denotes the process of forming (e.g., compare 'She played a key part in the formation of the UN'; 'She played a key part in the information of her students'). 'Information', in its modern sense, has its roots as an abstract noun that denotes a certain species of *communicative action* (just as 'communication' does), where one speaker intentionally and successfully brings it about that another party comes to know certain things.

In contemporary English, however, 'information' is not mainly used to denote *acts* of communicating or informing. The term is now used mainly as a metalinguistic term for that which *is conveyed* in the process of informing: ideas, knowledge, the *contents* of our thoughts, or the *contents* of communication. It is instructive to note that whilst 'information' has shifted in this way, 'communication' has not so far, and is still primarily used to talk about the *action* of communicating, rather than the *content communicated*.[5]

The conduit and container metaphors

When we talk about information as the 'content' of communication, or as something that is *acquired, stored, conveyed, transmitted, received, accessed, concealed, withheld*, we draw upon a range of metaphors. There is nothing odd about the use of such metaphors. They are a firmly entrenched part of our talk about communication. But these metaphors are not random. They are thematically linked as variants upon an underlying theme or metaphor, that Michael Reddy has called the *conduit metaphor* for communication.[6] The conduit

---

[5] However, communication may be drifting in the same direction. We now refer to 'communications', meaning what is communicated, not acts of communicating.

[6] Michael Reddy, 'The Conduit Metaphor: A Case of Frame Conflict in our Language about Language', in A. Ortony, ed., *Metaphor and Thought* (Cambridge, Cambridge University Press, 1979), pp. 284–324. Reddy notes that the use of such a framework of metaphors both reflects and underscores certain commitments that we have about the nature of communication: '(1) language

metaphor views communication as the *conveyance* or *transfer* of something – of meaning; ideas; information, or most generally of content – which is 'contained' in speech, texts, emails, hard drives and CD-ROMs.[7] These metaphors highlight the *dynamic* aspects of communication, which shifts or transfers content. The metaphors are equally apt for discussing the transfer of ideas between people and the transfer of data between technological devices.

These metaphors are closely linked to a further set of thematically linked 'static' metaphors, which see information as located in one place or another, so as contained – whether in a text, a display or a human mind. These *container* metaphors allow us to represent information as something that can be *possessed* by people, that is *contained* in signals, messages, texts, CD-ROMs. The two sets of metaphors work well together. They allow us to think of information as coming in 'discrete' chunks ('packets'; 'messages'; 'signals'), and of the communication of information as a process, whereby something that exists in one container is transferred to another. For example: information in the mind of a speaker (something that is 'possessed by' the speaker) can be 'put into' words (perhaps *stored* on a hard drive, or in a library) then 'passed on', 'disclosed', 'revealed', 'conveyed to', or 'accessed by' a 'recipient'. If the recipient is suitably

---

functions like a conduit, transferring thoughts bodily from one person to another; (2) in writing and speaking, people insert their thoughts and feelings in the words; (3) words accomplish the transfer by containing the thoughts or feelings and conveying them to others; and (4) in listening or reading, people extract the thoughts and feelings once again from the words' (p. 290). See also Ronald E. Day, 'The "Conduit Metaphor" and The Nature and Politics of Information Studies', *Journal of the American Society for Information Science* 9 (2000), 805–11.

[7] We should note that *within* the broad conduit framework there are other more specific frameworks: *transport* frameworks (information is 'carried' in 'vehicles'); *postal* frameworks ('messages' are 'stored', 'sent' and 'delivered' and 'received'); *transmission* frameworks ('signals' are 'transmitted' along 'channels'); *broadcast* metaphors (information is 'posted' on the internet (the village tree), or 'broadcast' to all). Each of these retains some of the core elements of the conduit framework, especially the idea that communication involves the *movement* (posting; transference; delivery; relaying; transmission) of 'meaning' (messages; signals; information) from one party (speaker; sender; broadcaster) to another (audience; recipient; receiver). For further details see James Carey, *Communication as Culture* (New York: Routledge, 1990).

placed and meets certain conditions, she 'receives' the information and comes to 'possess' it herself. She may then 'use' this information in her deliberation and action, or she may 'store' it, or choose to 'pass it on' to another party (perhaps breaching confidentiality as she does so).

These metaphors shape the way that we tend to think and talk about informed consent. Patients do not *possess* certain information; they need to *acquire* it if they are to make valid decisions based upon such information. Clinicians who *possess* such information ought to *pass it on*, or *disclose* it to the patient (rather than, say, withholding such information). Informed consent thus requires the transmission or disclosure of something from one party to another.

The container and conduit metaphors shape the ways in which we think about communication in a direct way. But they also shape them less directly, but still significantly, because the same metaphors have been adopted in the theoretical vocabulary of the mathematical theory of communication which is – at least partly – familiar to all users of 'information technology' or 'information and communication technologies'. The mathematical theory of communication deploys a quantitative notion of information – measured in *bits* and *bytes* – and it is based upon, and framed in terms of, the same conduit and container metaphors that shape our normal everyday talk about communication. Talk of information as quantitative and measurable, as 'stored' and 'transmitted' via 'channels' is ubiquitous in contemporary life, and helps to entrench the conduit/container metaphors (and so to maintain this particular way of thinking about information and communication).

This assimilation of several ways of thinking about information has a wide range of effects. 'Information', in its everyday sense, is an epistemic notion. Information is *what is known* by someone, or *what is communicated* in certain kinds of (epistemic) speech acts such as acts of informing (bringing it about that another *knows* something). Information, in this sense, is 'semantic': it is *about* things. The mathematical theory of communication, by way of contrast, uses a *nonsemantic, nonepistemic, quantitative* notion of information. To say that a signal contains one 'bit' of information is just a measure of probability, or the reduction of 'uncertainty' that the transmission of the signal brings about. If I toss a coin, it will land one way out of two possibilities. The coin-toss 'contains' one *bit* of information. But this is not information *about* anything at all. It is a *measure* of 'reduction of uncertainty', not a way of talking about the content of knowledge and communication.

We say more about these matters in Chapter 6, when we discuss how our thinking about *genetic* information is shaped not only by the conduit and container metaphors, but also by the fact that molecular biology adopted the terminology of the mathematical theory of communication in the 1950s.

WHAT THE CONDUIT AND CONTAINER METAPHORS HIDE

These deeply entrenched metaphors may not seem to matter to an account of *normative* issues to do with informed consent. And yet they do.

Linguistic theorists who study metaphor stress – among other things – that metaphors structure our thought in an *implicit* way, and in particular that they often *highlight* certain things whilst *hiding* or *occluding* others.[8] So while the conduit and container metaphors may be ubiquitous and familiar, we may not be aware either of the fact that, or of the ways in which, they influence our thinking. Suppose we talk of *getting across* or *putting across* our ideas. This way of talking assumes that there is something – e.g., an idea or content – already there, that is then to be put across. When we *convey* or *transfer* material items, this suggests that they exist independently of the process of conveyance (we distinguish the *creation, generation* or *production of* material items, from their conveyance). The use of metaphors supports certain inferences, or metaphorical entailments. If information *about* certain things is *conveyed* in the process of

---

[8] For example, see 'Metaphorical Systematicity: Highlighting and Hiding', Chapter 3 of George Lakoff and Mark Johnson, *Metaphors We Live By* (Chicago: University of Chicago Press, 1980). Lakoff and Johnson use Reddy's *conduit* metaphor as an example to discuss how metaphors highlight certain aspects of a process and hide others (pp. 10–13).

communication – rather than generated, negotiated, constructed or produced – then it seems evident that there is some kind of stuff that is *about* other things, that is possessed, stored, transmitted, broadcast, and so on. Yet the ways in which the conduit/container metaphors support certain entailments, and thereby structure our thought, may not be obvious to speakers. Such structuring is *implicit* in the use of the metaphors, not an explicit part of our understanding of, or our talk about, communication.

In structuring our thought and talk, the conduit/container metaphors highlight certain aspects of communication, or certain aspects of certain *types* of communication. Communication is cast as the 'conveyance' of semantic content from agent to agent. But communication is not really like this. When we communicate with one another it may seem – particularly if we rely on the conduit and container metaphors – that there is some determinate, context-free, extensional 'material' that is passed from speaker to audience.[9] If we think of communication as the conveyance, disclosure, broadcast, or even *communication* of information (with the conduit metaphors in play), we radically downplay the importance of the rich set of background commitments and competencies that are essentially involved in the activity of communication.

For example: suppose Tom arrives at work and asks his colleague Sue, 'Have you seen Jane?', and Sue replies 'Oh, she went to the bank'. What information does Sue 'convey'? By itself, the *sentence* 'Oh, she went to the bank' could mean a great many things. The pronoun 'she' could pick out any woman. The tensed construction 'went' does not, by itself, inform Tom *when* Jane (if it is she) went to the bank (last week? a year ago?). Talk of 'the bank' is ambiguous: financial institution? side of a river? or some other 'bank' (a blood bank? brain bank? data bank?)? Why is Sue saying this at all? Tom's

---

[9] Extensional contexts are ones where the truth of a claim does not depend upon how the objects it is about are described or referred to. Extensional contexts are typically contrasted with referentially opaque contexts, already mentioned in Chapter 1. If we assume that all information is extensional we will ignore or downplay the essential links between information and propositional attitudes like belief and intention.

question was whether Sue had *seen* Jane. Tom *might* ask this question for all sorts of reasons: for example, he might be testing Sue's vision, or checking to see whether she is a liar.

Sue, however, can draw upon her knowledge of the context of utterance, and her assumptions about which practical and cognitive commitments are likely to motivate Tom to ask his particular question ('Tom doesn't know where Jane is'; 'Tom wants to find out where Jane is').[10] She frames her response accordingly. Tom will, likewise, make assumptions about Sue: that she is honest; that she wouldn't say where Jane had gone without evidence; that if Jane had – unusually – gone off to the *river* bank then Sue would surely mention that odd fact, and so on. Acts of informing (and communication more generally) *only* succeed within a rich practical and normative framework in which speaker and audience (a) *have* certain practical and cognitive commitments; (b) *know something of each other's* cognitive and practical commitments; (c) *adhere* to, and act in accordance with, relevant communicative, epistemic, and ethical norms; and (d) *assume that* the other party is acting in accordance with such norms. The conduit and container metaphors hide, or radically downplay, these essential aspects of communicative activity.

We have already noted how 'information' has undergone certain semantic shifts, from denoting a certain kind of *action* to denoting the content of such action. This shift, we have suggested, is hidden by our daily reliance on the conduit/container metaphors, which highlight the *content* of communication and knowledge, rather than the acts in which and by which that content is used. There is of course nothing wrong about using the term 'information' to mean 'the content of informing': but there are real risks in relying too heavily or inappropriately on metaphors that 'hide', or lead us to ignore many central features of communication.

---

[10] We say more about what we mean by 'practical commitment' and 'cognitive commitment' in the next chapter. For now, suffice to say that a practical commitment is a commitment that an agent has to *doing* or *bringing about* certain things, a cognitive commitment is a commitment to things *being* a certain way.

We do not think it would be feasible to list all the different aspects of communication that are likely to remain hidden when we rely on the conduit and container metaphors. However we will comment briefly on eight aspects of communication that tend to be obscured or ignored in using the conduit and container metaphors.

Informing is context-dependent

What is communicated in an act of informing – the information – will depend upon the context, and, more importantly, upon what participants take the context to be. There are two points here. First, there is the general point that informing, at least in its everyday sense, is done by human action, for example, by speech-acts undertaken in seeking knowledge, finding out, testing hypotheses, telling others, stating, asserting, letting know, and so on. Which information is actually conveyed, disclosed, acquired, passed on, in a communicative transaction depends both upon *what people want to do*, and upon *what they are capable of doing*. Informing also depends upon what the participants in a communicative transaction believe and expect about one another, as we saw in the example of everyday communication between Tom and Sue. Information is not a context-independent 'stuff' that flows from person to person.

Informing is norm-dependent

These remarks may make it seem that informing and communicating are something rare and difficult. How on earth do we ever communicate with one another, how do we *convey* or *acquire* information to or from one another, if communication is so complex? Communication is indeed a complex activity, but it is not unconstrained or random. When a child learns how to speak a 'natural' language (like English or Arabic) she learns to shape her behaviour in accordance with a rich set of *normative* constraints. She learns how she *ought* to make sounds, she learns which sounds (or marks) *ought* to be used if she wants to refer to this or that object, she learns the subtleties of how she ought to *structure* her speech to create complex utterances which, in turn, *achieve* a wide variety of results (e.g., she learns how to *ask* questions, and how to distinguish *asking* from *stating* something, or *ordering* someone to do something). This is not a solitary activity. Learning a language is learning to *communicate*, that is, it is learning to engage in a certain kind of norm-bound *social* activity. In learning to communicate we tacitly learn that *others* too shape their speech and communication by the same norms. Unless speakers and audiences adhere to certain mutually accepted epistemic and ethical norms, and take one another to adhere to those norms, *communication cannot succeed*. If a speaker cannot shape her communicative actions in accordance with the requisite norms, she cannot hope to communicate with others. If an audience is suspicious, or mistrusting, and assumes that a speaker has violated certain epistemic or ethical norms – e.g., is lying, or misleading, or irrelevant – they may not follow, let alone accept, what the speaker says: a speaker cannot *inform* a radically mistrusting audience. This rich normative context – we shall say more about it in later chapters – is occluded or downplayed when we think of communication merely as the transmission or flow of information from person to person.

Informing is propositional

Informing is also distinctive in being 'propositional'. What do we mean by this? One simple way of understanding what propositions are is to focus on the idea of *proposing* something. Often this is done by stating something, asserting it, claiming it, or denying it. Such propositions make claims or statements that are *about* something and may be *true* or *false*. Descriptive propositions need not be true, but they are the kind of thing that *can* be true (or false).

Other propositions make practical proposals. For example, a doctor may tell a patient that he ought to take regular exercise, or ask a research subject to answer particular questions. Practical propositions are not true or false. Their function is to guide action, for example, to *ask* or *recommend* or *require* that action of certain sorts be done, and in effect that the world be adapted to fit the proposition in certain respects.

The conduit and container metaphors hide the fact that information is propositionally *structured*.[11] Talk of *conveying* information from one party to another hides the fact that *what is conveyed* is not merely content, but specifically *propositional* content. We inform each other – we convey information – that certain things are the case, or that certain things would be good to bring about, or that certain things are possible, unlikely, impossible, hard to countenance, and so on. We stress the propositional nature of information because propositional content is central to *reasoning* and is needed for evaluation of action and of reasons for action.

Informing is a type of rational action

People act for *reasons*. When we talk of people acting for reasons we do not mean merely that their actions have causes. We might, for example, claim that a bridge collapsed for some specific reason. But talk of reasons for action implies something more than mere causality. The reasons that an agent has for acting must be *known* to her. The agent herself must see that there is something to be said for acting in *that* way, in *that* context (as she takes things to be). We say more about action and reasons in the next chapter, but for now, the point to stress is that communicating is a type of action typically *done* by agents, *for reasons*. This does not mean that communicating is always a course of action to be favoured (i.e., 'the rational thing to do'), it simply means that, as with other actions, communicating is done for *reasons*, and reasons are the kind of thing which we may formulate in propositions, can ask for, offer to one another, accept or reject.

---

[11] On the mathematical theory of communication, where information is measured in *bits* and *bytes*, information is unstructured, and not capable of being true or false. We can of course make statements *about* information (in this sense) that are capable of being true or false, but this does not imply that a coin-toss stores, states or expresses the 'bit of information' contained within it: notions like truth, responsibility, truthfulness and 'getting it right' simply do not apply to this notion of information.

Not all communication is intentional. Others may draw inferences that we do not intend or anticipate from our actions. A *manner* of speaking, for example, may allow others to conclude something about the emotional state or attitudes of the speaker. However, our concern here will be with *intentional* acts of communication, especially with communicative transactions by which some agents consciously *aim* to bring it about that others come to *know* certain things (e.g., acts of *informing*) or that others take a practical stance towards certain acts (e.g., acts of *permitting* or *committing*).

Informing is rationally evaluable

Notions of rationality and reasoning come into play in a distinctive way in acts of informing. When we state something we put it forward *as true*. When we put forward truth-claims we are responsible for ensuring that, by our lights, such claims are likely to be true and may be asked to give an account of *why* we hold such claims true. We expect others to be able to offer reasons for their claims, and are startled and thrown off course if they refuse. For example, if Tom tells Sue that the bank is closed, Sue will expect Tom to have reasons for holding it *true* that the bank is closed. If she asks 'How do you know?' and Tom says 'Oh, I have no idea, I was just *speaking*', we have a serious – and bizarre – breach of the pragmatic and epistemic norms that govern acts of informing.

The importance of the rational evaluability of informing and of information is apt to be lost if we rely on the conduit and container metaphors. It is likely to be entirely obscured when we speak of 'information' in ways derived from the mathematical theory of communication. 'Information', a proponent of this approach might insist 'is merely a reduction in uncertainty'. With this view in mind, they might claim that all of us 'broadcast' information all the time. For example, if you stand in front of an audience, they will have their 'uncertainty' reduced in all sorts of ways. When Tom stands up to give his report to the board, members of the board find that various forms of uncertainty are reduced: Tom is standing rather than not standing, speaking rather than not speaking etc. Yet Tom does not intend to communicate that he is standing, or that he is speaking, and these claims are not part of the content that he communicates.

Information, in its everyday sense, is bound up with the *claims* and *proposals* that people make. When Tom says 'Revenue is falling' he puts forward a claim, and he can be corrected, asked for evidence, asked for his reasons. His reasons will be further *propositions*, typically propositions that he takes to be true, which, as he sees it, *favour* or *support* the truth of his claim. When he recommends to the board that they cut back on expenditure, he proposes a course of action for which he will once again be taken to have reasons.

Informing is referentially opaque[12]

If we think about information in abstraction from communicative transactions, we focus on semantic content. But if semantic content is to be conveyed to others in communicative transactions, it becomes important to take account not only of the content, but also of the beliefs of the intended audiences. For example, if Tom tells Lois Lane that Clark Kent is late for work he does not inform her that Superman is late for work. Lois Lane does not know that Superman is Clark Kent. But if Tom makes the same claim to somebody who knows that Superman is Clark Kent, that person will also come to know that Superman is late for work. Lois Lane's ignorance about who Clark Kent is makes Superman's lateness *opaque* to her – even when she is fully informed about Clark Kent's lateness.

This commonplace feature of communicative transactions is often called *referential opacity*, meaning that those to whom a proposition is conveyed may understand what it means, without realising (fully) what or whom it is about. Many propositions are opaque in this sense, and this is one reason why effective communication has to take account of the range of beliefs that its audiences already hold.

---

[12] We have already introduced the notion of referential opacity in Chapter 1.

Informing is inferentially fertile

The conduit and container metaphors lead us to focus on informational content rather than on communicative transactions. This focus hides the implications both of referential opacity and of other ways in which the inferences audiences can draw will vary with their beliefs. Communication typically enables participants to make a wide variety of *inferences*, and successful communicative transactions essentially *depend* upon the proper use of inferential abilities by participants. This fact is hidden if we rely too heavily on the conduit/container metaphors in thinking about information. By contrast if we think in terms of acts of informing we will from the start be aware that communicative transactions depend upon context, upon adherence to common rules, and upon the participants' capacity to draw inferences.

When we inform someone of some matter of fact, we do not just transfer a discrete item from one agent to another (perhaps to be 'stored' in her memory). For example, suppose you tell me that Tom is a smoker when, before your saying so, I had no view on the matter. In accepting your statement as true I become entitled to make further truth-claims about Tom, claims that are not part of the semantic content of your statement. Just which inferences an agent is licensed to make on the basis of gaining knowledge of any particular proposition depends both upon what the proposition is and upon the agent's other beliefs. Suppose I know that smokers are much more likely to die before the age of 60 than are non-smokers. On coming to know that Tom is a smoker I become licensed to conclude that Tom is more likely to die before the age of 60 than the average non-smoker.[13] One of the major problems with framing

---

[13] It would be epistemically irresponsible to take it to be true that Tom is more likely to die before 60 than non-smokers if I have no idea whether or not he is a smoker. It would also be epistemically irresponsible to conclude anything about the absolute likelihood of Tom's dying before 60, unless I have some knowledge of the relevant base rate (e.g., if very few non-smokers die before 60, then the fact that Tom is much more likely to die than non-smokers is consistent with the claim that he is still very unlikely to die before 60). We note this point because informational

normative debates about information and communication in terms of the conduit and container metaphors is that the *inferential fertility* of information is hidden. Knowing that Tom is a heavy smoker allows one to draw conclusions about his likely future health (indeed, one may not be able to *avoid* drawing conclusions about his future health). We explore some of the implications of the 'inferential fertility' of information in Chapters 5 and 6.

Informing must be audience sensitive

Finally, the conduit metaphor makes it seem as if information gets into us, into audiences or 'recipients', provided only that we are awake and (as it were) pointed in the right direction. Now it is true that we sometimes acquire information without intending to, or without effort or attention. In the context of communication, however, coming to know something on the basis of another's actions (e.g., another's speaking, or passing over a written note), requires attention and engagement on the part of the audience. If we are tired, distracted, excited, bored, more interested in the odd behaviour of the person outside the window than in what others are seeking to convey, the act of communication may fail. There is a great deal of difference between reading a book with questions in mind and a familiarity with the background context that is relevant to the topic at hand, and reading the same book passively, hoping that enough of it will 'sink in' to allow one to 'regurgitate' it later in an exam, interview, or on some other important occasion. Very often audiences or 'recipients' need to *do* far more than just 'listen' and 'absorb information'. In consequence, merely making information 'available' on a website or elsewhere may fail completely as a communicative action. The intended audience may not be able to afford, or use, or have the patience to use the technology necessary to 'access' such information. Audiences too are agents, with complex sets of practical and cognitive commitments by which they shape their response to others' communications, and thereby the nature

transactions are sometimes distorted by people's *poor* inferential competences, and this seems to be especially common with statistical inferences.

and success of communicative transactions. These ubiquitous realities about the active nature of 'receiving' information are easily occluded by reliance on the conduit and container metaphors.

Our reason for making these points about information is not to suggest that the conduit metaphor *fails* or *'gets it all wrong'*. It is often useful to have a common vocabulary to cover the possession and transfer of information both by human agents and by techno- logical devices. The conduit metaphor provides a common vocabu- lary and does not have to be seen as a full account of communication.[14] Our claim is simply that over-reliance on this metaphor is risky. Once we identify information as content, rather than as action, and rely on the 'conduit' framework for thinking and talking about information, we are likely to highlight or accentuate *some* aspects of communication (either of knowledge or of practical proposals), but hide, downplay or ignore the many significant features of communication that depend on agency, and in particular the normative constraints on communicative transactions between agents.

Much current thinking about informed consent is problematic in a number of ways. In particular, it does not take enough account of the ways in which communication rests upon a rich, but largely implicit, framework of assumptions of different kinds and at different levels. In this chapter we have begun our process of rethinking informed consent by making some of these assumptions explicit. We have noted how the – orthodox and ubiquitous – 'autonomy'-based justifications for informed consent assume that *information* is to be thought of as material of decision-making, and that individual decision-making ought to be respected. If information is what we need in order to decide, and if ethically sound medical practice is all

---

[14] The conduit metaphor, however, *does* underwrite some entailments and inferences but not others, and it does provide the basis of many substantive theories of communication. See John Fiske, *Introduction to Communication Studies*, 2nd edn (London: Routledge, 1990).

about respecting individual decisions (or 'choice'), then a specific and narrow range of *informational* obligations is highlighted, but others may be overlooked. This approach distorts the reality of informed consent transactions by downplaying or hiding their rich, multifaceted character, which involves much more than the 'transfer' of information.

Contemporary thinking about informed consent thus involves *two* sorts of distortion. The constant emphasis on the *disclosure* of information and on *individual* decision-making fosters a narrow view of the justification of informed consent practices as a way of respecting individual autonomy. And the habit of seeing information merely as content to be transferred and conveyed detaches that content from the full demands of successful communicative trans-actions, and downplays the complex social and normative framework that must be in place and must be respected for effective communication.

As we see matters, much contemporary discussion of information, including discussion of informed consent, manifests a 'drift from agency'. Information is viewed as detachable from the action by which communication is achieved and from the norms that govern action. This is neither inevitable nor obligatory. To show this we now turn to a fuller and more revealing characterisation of acts of communicating and informing, and consider aspects of such action that are often hidden or ignored when we focus too narrowly on the transfer of content.

CHAPTER 3

Informing and communicating: back to agency

We have seen that the conduit and container metaphors emphasise some elements of information and communication whilst downplaying others. We suggested that this happens when we rely too much on conceptions of 'information' that are detached from action. A 'drift from agency' easily happens if we think of information as a kind of quasi-spatial semantic stuff – stuff that is *about* things – that can be *possessed, conveyed, disclosed, acquired, used,* and so on. In Chapter 2 we exposed the 'highlighting' and 'hiding' effects of these metaphors; in this chapter we aim to say something more about the key elements and aspects of communication that tend to be 'hidden' by incautious use of the conduit and container metaphors. By the end of this chapter we will have two 'models' of information and communication in play: the conduit/container model and what we shall call 'the agency model'. We hope then to be well placed to rethink informed consent, and to discuss certain other normative questions that bear on 'informational' issues.

AGENCY

There are many kinds of communicative behaviour, and we shall not discuss the full range. For example, we shall not discuss unintentional communication, important as it often is. The clothes that we wear, our posture, certain hand gestures or movements of the eyes may be viewed as 'communicating' something about our social status, our interests, our emotional states, our trustworthiness, and so on. The person wearing no-longer-fashionable shoes may not intend to communicate anything at all by wearing them. She may be unaware that her shoes have any significance at all, other than as footwear. She may be entirely unaware that others draw inferences about her character on the basis of her wearing such shoes. This is quite typical of unintentional 'communication'.

Our focus in this book is upon *intentional* communicative acts, and the normative issues that bear on them. In our discussion of informed consent we have already noted that informed consent procedures impose specific informational, or communicative, obligations on certain parties. Like other obligations, these obligations prescribe intentional actions. Suppose a paternalistic doctor aims to withhold information from his terminally ill patient. Despite his intention, the doctor may unintentionally – by his bodily posture, the configuration of his facial muscles, or other unintentional 'gestures' – reveal his dishonesty (i.e., he makes the kind of revealing bodily gesture that poker players call a 'tell'). A sensitive patient may be able to 'read' these unintentional gestures and draw a correct conclusion about the diagnosis. Our point here is not directly about the ethics of withholding information, but about the fact that the obligations upon doctors to *tell* their patients certain things concern *intentional* acts of communication.

By contrast, a great deal of everyday communication is intentional. Intentional communication is a species of action, one that is done only by agents with certain basic capacities.[1] At a bare minimum, agency involves two distinct kinds of *commitment*. Agents have *practical* commitments that stem from their desires, needs, whims, preferences, principles, and so on. Agents also have *cognitive*

---

[1] We restrict our focus to the actions of mature, language-using human beings and do not discuss how *our* type of agency differs from that of chimps, dolphins, frogs or flies. We also restrict our focus to actions that are done for reasons, where the agent herself knows her reasons for acting. We are not concerned with questions such as: is drumming one's fingers whilst bored properly an *action*, and if so, what are one's *reasons* (if any) for doing it? Nor are we concerned with cases where an agent's own conception of her reasons for action runs up against some other account, or theory, of her actions (e.g., psychoanalytic explanations, where an agent's own explanations of her actions may be contextualised as a 'rationalisation' thrown up by defensive psychological mechanisms). These exclusions leave plenty to focus on, including the kinds of action on which normative constraints bear.

commitments: they take certain things (but not others) to be the case; some things to be likely, others to be impossible, and so on. Practical commitments and cognitive commitments have different 'directions of fit' to the world. Cognitive commitments aim to fit the way the world is: they succeed if they match the way the world *is*. Practical commitments, in contrast, aim to make the world (in small part) fit our commitments.[2]

When an agent acts on her cognitive and practical commitments she intentionally does something that she believes will be a step towards satisfying her practical commitments – given the way she takes the world to be. Such actions can be described – correctly and truly – in a wide variety of ways. Suppose I switch on the kettle in order to boil water to make some tea. My switching on the kettle may be the ten-thousandth time that the switch is pressed. By switching on the kettle I bring it about that the kettle has been switched on ten thousand times. It may also be the third switching-on that day, and the fifty-third that week, and so on. In acting, certain cognitive commitments are *privileged*, in the following sense: they capture what it is that the agent intended to do, or sought to achieve. In our everyday talk about agency we tend to give special weight to people's *own* conceptions of, and accounts of, what it is that they seek to achieve. There is much philosophical debate about *why* we should privilege such accounts, and about the *limits* of such a privilege, but we shall not be concerned with such questions here.[3]

---

[2] Our focus is on practical commitments to *bring about* certain situations. A weaker notion of practical commitment might identify such commitments with a 'pro-attitude' to certain situations (e.g., world peace), or even with a mere wish, or with 'meaning well', without any corresponding commitment to adjust one's actions in any positive way towards achieving any change.

[3] We stressed in Chapter 1 that statements of consent are referentially opaque and in Chapter 2 that *informing* is intensional. Agency too is intensional, in that a correct description of an action must be attuned to the *agent's* cognitive commitments (including further beliefs that she has) that bear on her action. For example, if Lois Lane is getting on the bus to go to meet Clark Kent for lunch, the fact that in meeting Clark Kent she also meets the unique individual who is Superman, does not imply that Lois Lane is getting on the bus to go to meet Superman. She (still!) has no inkling that Clark Kent *is* Superman.

Agency involves both practical and cognitive commitments. Agents need to grasp inferential relations between their cognitive commitments and their practical commitments, including the descriptions under which they act. The action, as the agent views it, must be something worth doing in the light of those cognitive and practical commitments. This type of inferential reasoning about action is a ubiquitous part of our everyday life. The fact that actions rely on our grasp of inferential relations to our various practical and cognitive commitments does not, of course, mean that we must 'go through' a chain of reasoning prior to acting. If you go to the kitchen to put on the kettle, you know where the kitchen is, and you know why you are going there. Typically this knowledge – of where the kitchen is – does not involve any occurrent mental event, or accompanying process of 'inner speech' in which the agent explicitly thinks through the rational steps that underlie and justify his actions (we tend to engage in such explicit thinking only in cases where we are undecided, or are finding it hard to settle which cognitive and practical commitments we ought to undertake). This point takes on considerable importance once we take account of the ubiquitous role of inference in effective communication.

One striking feature of our inferential capacities, as we noted in the last chapter, is that they are extremely fertile. Normal human adults have a vast stock of background knowledge, which allows them to make an indefinitely large number of reasonable inferences from any particular factual proposition. Consider, for example, the proposition 'Tom is a man'. One can infer (assuming ordinary 'background' knowledge) that he is a human, that he has blood, that he has a Y-chromosome, that he lives on Earth, that he breathes oxygen, that he is larger than 10 cm but smaller than 10 m tall, and so on and on. Such inferential fertility may seem pretty pointless. What purpose could be served by making all these inferences? Yet the very simplicity of the example is telling. In real life we make inferences all the time. Inferences are indispensable both for communicating successfully with one another and for acquiring new knowledge without having to *do* anything new by way of discovery (other than drawing upon the stock of knowledge that we already have). Our background knowledge licenses countless inferences, which we need not make, and need not make explicit.[4] We realise how important these daily inferences are when (to our surprise) somebody fails to infer something that we take to be obvious.

This sketch of some of the key features of agency is not, we hope, contentious. It simply draws attention to the fact that agency involves commitments with different 'directions of fit', the ability to grasp rational relations between propositions, and the ability to put one's commitments to act *into action*. Discussions of agency need to acknowledge that actions are a manifestation of the agent's point of view, and to take into account both how *the agent* conceives of things and the rich rational and inferential context of agency. But the inferential relations that are essential to rational action are rarely, at least in everyday life, explicit in the stream of consciousness. So there are key features of agency that are 'hidden', in that they are neither 'up front' nor obvious. When we think about action we may fail to note, or to give due weight to, some of these implicit, but essential features. The conduit and container metaphors that are so often deployed in talking about information and communication downplay or 'hide' the complex set of rationally evaluable practical and cognitive commitments, and the inferential relations between them. This can have damaging implications since these commitments underpin agency.

COMMUNICATIVE ACTIONS

We have now said a little about agency, and about the practical and cognitive commitments that underlie action. *Communication* – of the intentional kind that we are focusing on here – essentially involves the practical and cognitive commitments of agents in two broad

---

[4] This is not to say that we are capable of making *all* the inferences that our beliefs entail. I know that there are 60 seconds in an hour, 24 hours in a day, 7 days in a week, and 31 days in January – now this *entails* that there are 312,480 seconds in January, but it takes some *effort* to get that result. For our purposes what matters is that our cognitive commitments are inferentially fertile; the fact that there are limits to our (unaided) inferential fertility does not count against this.

ways. First, given that communication is a species of action, communicative acts presuppose the practical and cognitive commitments both of those who seek to communicate, and of those with whom they seek to communicate. For example, in asking a question a speaker intentionally does something with the aim of finding out *where* something is, or *what* something is, or *when* something will happen, and so on. Precisely *what* the speaker asks depends upon her specific practical and cognitive commitments. But communication also involves practical and cognitive commitments in another way. Communicative actions have to take account of the cognitive and practical commitments of others, and may aim to alter their practical and cognitive commitments.

Consider a simple example. Tom has a practical commitment – not just an idle wish – to have a party. Having a party (let us assume) requires guests. Let's assume that Tom has some cognitive commitments that make it easy for him to say whom he would like to come to his party – Sue and Bob, but *not* Jane. These, in turn, generate more specific practical commitments: Tom has to *do* something to try to bring it about that (just) these people come to his party. By modifying the material environment in certain systematic ways (e.g., by speaking, making marks on paper, tapping on the keys of a computer hooked up to the internet etc.), Tom can bring it about that certain other people – in this case his intended guests – come to acquire certain *cognitive* commitments that are related to Tom's *practical and cognitive* commitments (e.g., they come to know that Tom *wants* them to come to his party; they believe that the party will take place when Tom says that it will). Sue and Bob may then acquire, or undertake, new practical commitments: to go to Tom's, at the time stated, to buy some fashionable shoes, and so on.

Tom, of course, does not have to *say* all of this. Tom may just send a note saying 'Party, my place, this Saturday, 8.oopm. Tom'. Nevertheless, most of the commitments mentioned above are implicit. When one invites others to a party, those invited will assume that on the stated occasion there will be festive arrangements: food, drink, music perhaps. *Inviting* someone to a party involves a number of elements: the speaker must have certain cognitive and practical commitments; he must then aim to bring about very specific cognitive (and practical) commitments in others. The audience, in turn, must have a rich set of cognitive commitments, and, in understanding the import of a communicative act, must achieve some grasp of the speaker's practical and cognitive commitments.

If Tom, Sue and Bob had to start 'from scratch' this would be impossible. Tom's act of *inviting* (and Sue and Bob's *being invited*) is made feasible thanks to the fact that each of them has a rich stock of cognitive commitments, and that each of them *knows* that the others do too.

Here, then, are some of the essential features of intentional communication to be found in our simple example. First, speaker and audience must *share a language*. Tom and his audience share a language in the sense that Tom knows *how* to modify the world in certain ways that will engage with the others' existing cognitive and practical commitments and alter those commitments in specific ways. Similarly, his audience starts with cognitive and practical commitments that enables it to grasp *what* Tom means when he modifies the world in certain ways.

Second, speaker and audience must share a great deal of *background knowledge* about the world, and about the social conventions that govern their behaviour. They will know something about parties, about ways of inviting, accepting or declining an invitation, and so on. They will know what sorts of things are *feasible*. There is no point in Tom inviting people to a party on a mountain top thousands of miles away in one hour's time.

Third, speaker and audience must be able to *draw* upon that knowledge in making the right kinds of inferences: both must exercise inferential competence. Simply sharing a broad stock of background knowledge is not sufficient. Finally, speaker and audience must have some knowledge of *each other's* commitments and competences. For example, Tom must have some grasp of the limitations and competences of his audience. If he tries to invite people by posting a note on the tree outside his house, he is unlikely to inform friends in another city successfully. If he writes to them in a vague and ambiguous way, or leaves out crucial information, communication will fail.

Now, inviting is an action that we can do, and can only do, by communicating with others. Such action, as we have seen, involves an intentional attempt to engage with and to adjust others' cognitive and practical commitments. But inviting is only one of countless types of speech act. We can, for example, give orders, ask for directions, show our sympathy, encourage another to join our club. Agents with the appropriate socially sanctioned authority may use speech acts to *do* complex acts of many sorts: they may marry a couple; condemn someone to death; pardon a traitor; agree to a legally binding contract, and so on.

What all of these speech acts have in common is that they take place against a background of a shared acceptance of complex sets of cognitive and practical commitments, entitlements, expectations and social roles, and shared understanding of ways in which others' commitments can be modified. Communicative actions play a role in allowing agents to *do* things that affect their own and others' cognitive and practical commitments on the basis of existing practical and cognitive commitments on the part of audiences and speakers alike.

COMMUNICATIVE NORMS

Communication is a blanket term that covers a heterogeneous range of actions (and also, as we noted, some sorts of non-intentional events and processes). Since communicative action is normatively structured in many different ways, communication can fail, go wrong, be misdirected or misunderstood in correspondingly many ways. There are many kinds of normative consideration in play here. For example, if I say the words 'I promise to be there' without having any practical commitment to being there, then, I either fail to promise or promise falsely. That is, I fail to fulfil some of the conditions for my speech act being a promise. The performance of such an act might also fail in different ways. For example, there are lots of contexts where one can *say* 'I promise to be there' without making any corresponding practical commitment: such as reciting lines in a play; teaching someone how to pronounce English; testing a microphone, and so on. But many of our speech acts are produced in full knowledge that they will engage with the intended audience's commitments, and may alter those commitments. If I say 'I promise to be there' others may assume that I have a practical commitment, and they in turn may undertake certain commitments on the basis of what I say. Speaking *as if* one promises (i.e., saying the words without the corresponding and expected commitments) can, in certain contexts, constitute false promising and is generally seen as being ethically wrong.

But, even when we *do* undertake the requisite commitments to engage in certain kinds of speech act, that is not enough for successful communication. Most communication (other than simple actions such as indicating by shrieking *help!!*) is *syntactically* structured. Errors of syntax are typically readily identifiable, and typically readily corrigible. Lexical errors are also often readily identifiable and can be taken into account, as when a person uses an obviously mistaken word.

However, communication can fail where speaker and audience differ in their understanding of a particular word in the context of utterance. A surgeon may mean one thing by 'human tissue', a person with no medical training may mean something else (the former may take 'human tissue' to denote a wide range of bodily material including whole organs; the latter may assume that tissue is bodily material *other than* or *less than* whole organs). But here, the failure differs from the sort which arises from false or idle promises. The surgeon does not intend anything unusual in speaking of human tissue, nor does she intend to deceive by her use of words. She is using words in the way that surgeons do, and there is no *intention* to deceive. But the *effect* of such differences may, nonetheless, lead to failures of communication. So we need to distinguish different ways in which speech acts can go *wrong*. In particular we need to note that communication often fails without any specifically *ethical* failure.[5]

---

[5] A classical account of non-ethical failure in speech acts can be found in Austin's explorations of ways in which they can be mistaken, or botched, or more generally *infelicitous*. J. L. Austin, *How to Do things With Words* (Oxford: Clarendon Press, 1962); see also his 'A Plea for Excuses' and 'Performative Utterances', both in J. L. Austin, *Collected Philosophical Papers* (Oxford: Clarendon Press, 1962).

Communicative actions are evaluable against *multiple* kinds of norm, including, but not restricted to, ethical norms.

Acts of informing are typically, but not always, achieved by the type of speech act known as 'representatives', a class that includes acts of *asserting, telling, stating*.[6] Such acts are of central importance to cognitive and practical activity and so to communicative trans-actions. However, audiences cannot tell conclusively whether a speaker who issues a syntactically well-formed declarative utterance, even one that is intelligible to them, is actually making an assertion or truth-claim.[7] In daily communicative practice we draw on a rich knowledge of social and communicative context to identify when people are making assertions (e.g., we don't run out of the theatre when an actor in the play shouts 'The building is on fire Aunt Matilda, everybody leave!!'). Speakers have a responsibility to their audiences *not* to engage in certain forms of communicative act if their audiences are apt to be misled by those acts. One way of misleading people is to make what seems to be an assertion of fact when one is really doing something else – reciting poetry; giving examples of English grammar; testing a microphone. The same point is true for other speech acts, such as giving orders, warning, and so on.

If an agent makes an assertion of fact, with the intention that others come to believe what she says, certain obligations come into play that are absent from speech acts that are used to express suppositions, hypotheses, poetry, and so on. There is good reason why this is so. Representative communication that makes truth-claims may be true or false, and may lead others to form reliable or unreliable beliefs. Communication that leads others to form mistaken or misguided cognitive commitments is likely to affect their ability to satisfy their practical commitments reliably. If we

---

[6] Following the terminology of John Searle in his *Speech Acts: An Essay in Philosophy of Language* (Cambridge: Cambridge University Press, 1969). J. L. Austin called such speech acts 'constatives'.

[7] Worse still, there is nothing in the form of the utterance to show that the speaker is actually *stating* this, putting it forward as true, rather than just engaging in supposition, or poetic expression. See P. Geach, 'Assertion', *Philosophical Review* 74 (1965), 449–65.

are to communicate successfully with others, then our communication ought to aim to take account of the way the world actually is and to communicate the way it is to others. Successful agency, and with it successful communication, requires a certain kind of responsibility, often called *epistemic* responsibility.[8]

Epistemic responsibility includes various normative standards. It includes what we might call *individual* epistemic responsibility. For example, we ought not to be gullible; we ought not to rely on idiotic ways of reaching conclusions. However, individual epistemic responsibility is not enough. A great deal of our individual knowledge is acquired as a result of the communicative acts of other 'informants'.[9] We are epistemically dependent upon innumerable others.[10] So individual epistemic responsibility must be augmented by and linked to forms of other-directed epistemic responsibility that provide standards for judging informants: what steps must we take if we are to judge whether others make trustworthy knowledge claims? What sorts of epistemic responsibility do we have towards others?

Suppose there were a society where it was simply a matter of chance whether or not people were truthful.[11] It might seem that the consequence would be that each of us would have to rely upon our own intelligence and reason to get through the day. That is, each individual would aim only to ensure that she was individually

---

[8] Epistemologists have spent a great deal of energy discussing whether and how *knowledge* differs from other 'mere' cognitive commitments. A speaker's claim that someone *knows* that *p* entails a commitment, on the part of the speaker, to its being the case that *p*. In contrast, one can claim that Tom *believes* that *p*, without oneself being committed to its being the case that *p*. For our purposes issues about the nature of knowledge, and about the distinction between knowledge and belief, are not of central importance. What is important is that successful agency requires us to exercise a certain kind of responsibility to ensure that our cognitive commitments are in good shape and properly related to one another.

[9] C. A. J. Coady, *Testimony: A Philosophical Study* (Oxford: Clarendon Press, 1992); Michael Welbourne, *Knowledge* (Chesham: Acumen, 2001).

[10] John Hardwig, 'Epistemic Dependence', *Journal of Philosophy* 82 (1985), 335–49.

[11] Note that this is *not* a society where everybody lies all the time, for in that society one can rely on others (if they say that snow is black, I know that they think it is not).

epistemically responsible. But individual epistemic responsibility in isolation is unlikely to achieve or secure very much. Without reliance upon truthful communication by others – who are on the whole epistemically responsible – our stock of knowledge would be minimal (remember, in this hypothetical world, it is a matter of chance whether a parent responds to her child's question 'Is that ice safe to walk on?' with a 'Yes' or a 'No'). Given that we cannot check every fact that is communicated to us, we have to *rely* upon, and *trust* other parties as sources of knowledge.[12] Unless a sufficiently large proportion of a social group adhere reasonably closely to norms of truthfulness, the result will be a radical shrinking of knowledge and a dissolution of the kind of social existence that we take for granted.

These are serious reasons why speakers *ought* to be truthful. Being truthful does not ensure that what one says is correct. Suppose someone is always truthful, yet individually epistemically *irresponsible*. They themselves are willing to believe whatever pops into their head. If they then *state* what they themselves take to be the case they will be truthful, yet still fail to act as they ought. Their audiences will assume that ordinary standards of epistemic responsibility have been met, so will often be misled. It is epistemically irresponsible to *others* to state as true that which one has little grounds for taking to be true (the children's story of the boy who cries 'wolf' illustrates this type of irresponsibility).

How on earth do speakers and audiences manage to negotiate this complex situation? One very common way is by ensuring that communication is 'two-way'. Suppose Tom tells Sue that scientists have found a UFO buried in the Antarctic. This is a surprising claim. Sue does not know whether to accept the truth of this claim or not. But Sue can improve her position by asking Tom to tell her something about the provenance or source of his commitment. Tom may say 'I have just seen it on TV, all the channels are showing it!'. Tom and Sue's two-way communication allows Sue to act in an epistemically responsible way, by investigating the basis of Tom's startling

[12] John Hardwig, 'The Role of Trust in Knowledge', *Journal of Philosophy* 88 (1991), 693–708.

claim. Of course, Tom *may* be lying on both counts. Responsible action may not be successful action, and epistemically responsible action may not secure the truth.

It is arguable that Tom also has a responsibility to say more about the *source* or *justification* for his claim, if asked. Tom's aim is to bring it about that Sue – another epistemically responsible agent – adopts a particular cognitive commitment on the basis of his action. If Tom refuses to give further reasons for her to take on this cognitive commitment, or refuses to expand on his epistemic sources (e.g., he says he has an 'anonymous source', or that the only source is dead) there are a number of likely consequences (as Tom will know). He seems to leave Sue with a dilemma. Either Tom *does* have further grounds, but is not telling them, or he does not. If he does not have further grounds, then the claim is not, as it stands, worthy of acceptance. If he does have further grounds, but is refusing to say what they are, then Sue is likely to feel slighted or undermined: Tom's refusal to assist her in meeting her epistemic responsibilities in taking on cognitive commitments is unhelpful, rude and demeaning to Sue.[13] If Tom wants to have effective communication with Sue, and if he wants his claims to be taken seriously, he ought to (a) ensure that he *has* reasons for his claim and (b) ensure that he *shares* those reasons, should he be asked for them.

This picture of epistemically responsible communication is very distant from the picture we adopt when relying on the simple conduit/container model of information transfer. Rather than viewing Tom as 'disclosing' the information that scientists have found a UFO, information which Sue then 'picks up', we have to view the communicative transaction as a rich and complex, two-way exchange through which Sue may come to adjust her cognitive commitments in line with Tom's – or alternatively may refuse to believe what he says. This complexity is *not* captured by relying on the picture of some kind of quasi-material stuff or content being *conveyed* from one mind to another.

---

[13] These issues are a recurrent focus of controversy whenever political and journalistic truth-claims are backed only by unattributable sources.

Suppose a speaker is competent, capable of 'speaking a language', truthful, has reasons for taking what she claims to be true and is willing to share these reasons with others. This will still not ensure good epistemic and communicative practice. Good communicative practice must also be *relevant* to the intended audience. For example, suppose I know that your house is on fire, and that you do not know it, and I also know that it is likely that you have considerable interest in coming to know of this fact. In this case I not merely know that some proposition is true, but that its truth matters to you. If in this context I say to you 'grass is green', I say something that you understand, I am being truthful, and I can cite evidence that grass is, in fact, green: but my communication will be (at least!) a pragmatic failure. You *already* know what colour grass is, and the point of my communication is obscure, indeed irresponsible – despite the cognitive standards it meets. Equally, suppose that as your house continues to burn I tell you something else that you do not know, namely that nickel melts at 1,455 degrees. In this case you may understand what I say, it may be true, and what I say may be 'informative'. Yet my saying so in this context is pragmatically odd and might be grounds for serious criticism. In this context, *given* that your house is on fire, I should be telling you *that*. Good communicative practice involves sensitivity to specific audiences. Speakers who bombard their audiences with random truths treat them as mere 'epistemic sponges' who need to be doused in information. Communicative transactions ought to be sensitive to others' practical commitments, including their practical commitments to acquire relevant knowledge. Good communication takes account of what others already know, and of what they want and need to know at that time, in that context. Epistemically adequate communication is *relevant* communication, and has to be limited to what is appropriate to the actual context. Good communicative practice therefore always involves *withholding* information – comprehensible, true, grounded information – that could have been conveyed.

We do not think that it is possible to set out a complete list of the cognitive norms that are constitutive of good communicative practice. Norms are abstract entities, and it is always possible to refine any classification of norms. However, we now set out some of the more significant kinds of norms that govern communication, whose violation or neglect is likely to lead to various kinds of communicative failure. They include:

1. Norms needed for speech acts to be accessible and relevant to intended audiences (e.g., *intelligibility, relevance*);
2. Norms needed for speech acts, and especially those that make truth-claims, to be adequately accurate and assessable by intended audiences (e.g., *not lying, deceiving or manipulating; aiming for accuracy; not misleading in other ways; providing relevant qualifications and caveats*).

These norms should not be viewed merely as ethical norms, which it would be right and proper to observe, but which it is feasible (if wrong) to flout or neglect. They are *constitutive* norms of communication and set standards in the light of which communication can succeed or fail, go right or wrong. Even the amoralist has to take these norms seriously. Both failure to adhere to these norms and the assumption that others are not living up to them may undermine communicative transactions. If these norms are flouted or disregarded, either *no information will be conveyed or what is conveyed will be irrelevant or unreliable.* Yet on the conduit and container model of communication, these constitutive normative requirements are downplayed, and often remain entirely hidden. These are not the only norms that are relevant for communication, and in subsequent chapters we will say more about certain specifically *ethical* norms that matter for communication.[14]

TWO 'MODELS' OF INFORMATION AND COMMUNICATION

We have now distinguished two different ways of thinking about information and communication: a *conduit/container model* and an *agency* or *agent-based model*. We do not lay too much store by these labels. They merely allow us to differentiate between two different

---

[14] Such as: norms needed for speech acts not to injure others (e.g., *not insulting, defaming, threatening* or *backing speech with force or coercion*); and norms needed for some but not all speech acts (e.g., *not promising falsely; maintaining confidentiality*).

ways of thinking about information and communication. Nor should too much be read into the use of the term 'model'. We are not offering a philosophical theory of communication, or a linguistic 'model' of communication. Our claim is *not* that the conduit/container model – and the metaphors in which it is often revealed (or perhaps obscured!) – is entirely mistaken. Nor are we claiming that it is, somehow, *wrong* to talk of people conveying information from one to another. The model has some correspondence with aspects of the communicative process – e.g., it is true that an agent who believes that *p* can act in such a way as to bring it about that another agent believes that *p*, thereby 'conveying' information. Our main reason for being cautious about the conduit/container model is not that it is wholly inaccurate, but that it *hides too much*.

The alternative 'agency' model can be viewed as simply making explicit, or highlighting, aspects of communication and information that are ignored or hidden on the conduit/container model. We draw attention to – or remind ourselves of – the fact that (a great deal of) communication is *done* by and between agents. Communication is a normative affair that presupposes a rich framework of *shared* norms, and shared background commitments (practical and cognitive), as well as the requisite *inferential* competences. Communicative actions play a wide range of roles in adjusting, maintaining, indicating, correcting and revising the practical and cognitive commitments of participants in communicative exchanges. There is a wide variety of norms, ethical and epistemic, that are important for successful communicative actions. In this chapter we have offered reasons for taking a range of epistemic norms seriously; in the next we shall offer reasons for taking a range of ethical norms seriously.

Information used to be a term for one type of communicative action (informing). Nowadays it is used as a term for the content that is (or could be) communicated or that is (or could be) conveyed in certain kinds of communicative action. Information is the 'content' of communication – some kind of 'stuff' that is 'out there' (perhaps located in the heads of others, or in their words or texts). By contrast, the agent-based model of communicating and informing that we have discussed in this chapter does not identify 'information' as any kind of stuff or content that can be thought of as 'out there' independent of communicative actions in specific contexts, or of the practical and cognitive commitments of participants in communicative transactions.

Once we take due account of the importance of agents in communicative transactions, we see that 'information' is a term that is parasitic upon, and derived from, our talk about certain kinds of epistemic and communicative action, such as *acts* of informing, or *acts* of which informing is one component. Acts of informing are typically inferentially *fertile*: telling someone one thing typically licenses them to make many inferences. This aspect of information is too readily lost, or ignored, if we think of information as something that comes in discrete 'packets' that are passed or transferred from speaker to audience.[15]

On an agent-based model, information is only the content of communicative transactions, and such acts succeed only where participants are sensitive to one another as agents with their own cognitive and practical commitments, and assume one another's adherence to a range of communicative, epistemic and ethical norms. The fact that communication is a normatively rich affair may provide us with answers to at least some of the ethical and regulatory questions about uses of information. For example, being truthful, relevant and responsive to the intended audience's interests, may in some contexts be sufficient for ethically sound informed consent practices.

Once we make explicit the normative and rational context of communication and information, we establish a range of *feasibility constraints* on informational obligations. Once we accept that all communication is context-based, and dependent upon a rich *implicit* knowledge of the shared interests, competences and commitments of

---

[15] Acts of informing are, as noted earlier, *intensional*. In the abstract, we might hold that information about Clark Kent just *is* information about Superman, given that they are the same being. But from the point of view of individual agents with their specific cognitive commitments, this classification cannot cut things finely enough: someone who does not know that Clark Kent is Superman may *feel* and *act* very differently on being informed (when marooned atop a burning building) that 'Clark Kent will come to your rescue' rather than 'Superman will come to your rescue' (the latter claim may inspire hope, the former despair).

participants, we have reason to be suspicious of any claim that, say, informed consent procedures require a 'full' or 'fully explicit' statement about proposed actions. Once we grasp that *all* communication is partial, is rooted in background knowledge and inferential competences, we see that the ideal of 'fully explicit' consent is nonsense. We examine this line of argument further in the next chapter, together with related claims that consent disclosures should be fully *specific*. The formal property of *full specificity* is ill-defined; and excess specificity may be destructive rather than essential for ethically adequate communication. It is not always necessary – and it may even be wrong – to inflict full details about a medical intervention upon a patient. Relevant communication *always* involves the withholding of *some* details that one could 'disclose'.

If we are to rethink informed consent in ways that escape the criticisms set out in Chapter 1, we must do so on the basis of a coherent and rigorous account of certain informational obligations, which we can only do if we are clear about what information and communication involve. Our contention is that it is all too easy to think about information and communication in a way that fails to give due weight to the rich, but implicit, social, rational, inferential and normative framework that is essential for communication – including acts of informing, and thus *information* – to take place. In this chapter we have contrasted a fuller, agency-based account of informing and communicating with the selective, partial and we think misleading ways in which information, and with it informed consent, are often discussed. There are further points that could be made, and many further interesting historical, linguistic and philosophical questions about which we have said nothing. We hope that the limited considerations we have set out show why we think that there is some value in approaching issues to do with the ethics and regulation of information in an abstract, philosophical way. In the following chapters we shall constantly refer back to the conduit/container model and to the agency, or agent-based, model. In the next chapter we turn from discussion of some of the epistemic norms that are constitutive of communication, to some of the ethical norms that matter most in rethinking informed consent.

CHAPTER 4

How to rethink informed consent

In Chapter 1 we argued that current thinking about informed consent, its justification, scope and standards, is problematic in a number of ways. We suggested that it would be profitable to 'rethink' informed consent. In Chapters 2 and 3 we explored two distinct models of information and communication. These models, in turn, support distinct approaches to informed consent. We shall argue in this chapter that although each model supports an account of the justification, the scope and the standards for informed consent, the conceptions of informed consent that emerge from these models differ in important ways. These differences have powerful implications for biomedical practice. By making explicit two different conceptions of informed consent, we pave the way for 'rethinking' informed consent in this chapter. In the chapters to follow we then shift from general and abstract theorising about communication and consent to a number of specific and concrete issues where informed consent is of key ethical importance.

The 'standard' way of thinking and talking about information and communication is, we suggested, the conduit/container model. When information is discussed in terms of the conduit/container model, it is thought of in abstraction from agents and from the speech acts by which they communicate. When we rely on this model, we think of information as 'flowing' or being 'transferred' between agents, who are thought of quite abstractly as 'originating' or 'receiving' messages. The message or content is highlighted, but the act of communicating is hidden.

By contrast, when we view informing or communicating in terms of the agency model, we focus not only on content, but also on the speech acts by which agents communicate proposals, understand others' proposals and respond to them. The agency model takes account both of what is said (the speech content) and of what is done (the speech act). It provides a framework for recognising the *transactional* or *interactive* character of successful communication.

These two models of communication support different conceptions of informed consent. As we saw in previous chapters, the conduit/ container model of information fits well with a view of informed consent that focuses on *disclosure for decision-making*. A *disclosure-based account of informed consent* requires those who seek consent to ensure that the relevant information flows to – *is disclosed to* – those who have to decide or choose whether to consent. This selective emphasis on disclosure for decision-making highlights some aspects of consent requirements, but also hides much that is essential to giving and refusing consent. By contrast, an agency model of communication locates informed consent in *communicative transactions between agents*. It provides a framework for a *transactional model of informed consent*, which emphasises what is said and what is done *both* by those who request consent, *and* by those who respond by giving or refusing their consent.

A *transactional account* of informed consent, we shall argue, has a number of advantages. It provides a basis for deeper and more plausible justifications of informed consent than the autonomy-based justifications typically used to support accounts of informed consent that centre on disclosure-for-decision-making. A transactional account of informed consent also provides the basis for a convincing account of the scope of informed consent requirements, and for a plausible and differentiated account of the standards they must meet. In the following sections we shall first rethink the justification for consent requirements, and then reconsider their scope, and finally rethink the standards that they must meet.

WHY CONSENT TRANSACTIONS MATTER: BEYOND
AUTONOMY

We begin our rethinking of informed consent requirements by returning to questions of justification. It has become conventional to justify informed consent as a way of ensuring that information is disclosed to those who have to make decisions, thereby (it is hoped) allowing them to exercise their individual autonomy. However, as we argued in Chapter 1 under 'Improving Justifications: The Quest for Autonomy', autonomy-based justifications of consent requirements are problematic. Which conception of autonomy is to be protected and secured? How must consent requirements be structured if they are to ensure respect for individual autonomy (variously conceived)? Why should respect for the individual autonomy of patients and research subjects trump other ethical considerations?

These questions are particularly acute for minimalist conceptions of individual autonomy that identify it with mere, sheer choice. Why should all choices – even those not based on an adequate grasp of others' proposals – be protected at all costs? Is it of no importance that choices may be good or bad, right or wrong, kind or callous, prudent or risky, informed or ignorant? Or that choices may be based on misleading views of others' proposals, or of the realities, risks and benefits of consenting to – or refusing – those proposals? Does it not matter that individuals may accept proposals for action that are likely to injure them, may 'go along' with manipulative proposals, or may succumb to 'offers they can't refuse'? Respect for *mere* choice has been widely, and in our view plausibly, viewed as a shaky and questionable justification for invasive treatment.

The favoured alternative to justifying informed consent as securing such *minimal autonomy* seeks to justify it as securing (some conception of) *rational autonomy*, such as *informed*, or *reasonable*, or *reflective* (rather than *mere*) choice. Informed consent is seen as justifying invasive interventions by ensuring that patients or research subjects not merely choose or decide whether to accept such interventions, but make *informed, reasonable* or *reflective* choices to do so: only then can their choices be seen as reflecting their rational autonomy. This line of thought risks justifying both too much and too little.

Appeals to conceptions of rational autonomy may justify too much where individuals choose dire alternatives in the appropriate way: would consensual cannibalism, consensual torture or consensual killing be acceptable, provided victims choose them in the appropriate way? Even if the victim's consent cannot justify these sorts of illegal action, can it justify interventions that are within the law but more risky than available alternatives, provided they are chosen in the appropriate way? Or will such cases not arise because clinicians and researchers (not to mention research ethics committees) will not propose or sanction unnecessarily risky treatment? But if that is the situation, then can we still claim that rational autonomy, operationalised by informed consent procedures, is a fundamental principle of medical and research ethics? Or would this move concede that other standards, in which consent plays no part, are of equal importance?

In other cases appeals to rational autonomy may justify too little: they have nothing to say about the treatment of non-competent patients, or about interventions whose complexity overwhelms the cognitive capacities of (otherwise) competent patients and research participants. Yet if we require patients and research subjects to exercise demanding conceptions of rational autonomy, failure of competence will more often be overtaxed, and the number of cases in which consent cannot be given will rise.

These realities are often obscured in discussions of medical and research ethics by a range of tacit assumptions. It is assumed that clinicians and researchers will not intend to injure their patients, and that they will not propose interventions that they think useless, unprofessional, too risky or illegal. Rather, they will propose only interventions that they take to be lawful and professionally acceptable, reasonably likely to benefit (the patient or others with the same condition) and unlikely to injure. These assumptions tacitly limit the choices patients and research subjects are offered to 'approved' options. Reliance on these assumptions is in great tension with the thought that informed consent procedures are fundamental to clinical and research ethics because they ensure respect for individual autonomy. If individual autonomy presupposes a large number of normative constraints that are *not* open to choice, those other normative standards will do a lot of the ethical work, and respect for individual autonomy will *not* be the sole, nor perhaps the main, basis for justifying medical and research practice. More provocatively, one might say, the standard model of informed consent is based on disclosures that inform individual decision-making, and paradoxically sees patient autonomy and the autonomy of research subjects as merely responsive. Patients are typically asked to choose – or refuse – from a very limited menu (often a menu of one item); research subjects to choose – or refuse – to participate in a single project. Do appeals to autonomy in biomedical practice perhaps presuppose and rely on a residual paternalism that frames and protects the supposed exercise of individual autonomy?

JUSTIFYING CONSENT TRANSACTIONS: CONSENT AS WAIVER

If, on the other hand, we think of informed consent as embedded in communicative transactions, we can take a broader and (we believe) more convincing view of its justification. In this section we set out an alternative approach to the justification of informed consent, on the assumption that it is a distinctive type of communicative transaction. Informed consent transactions are typically used to *waive* important ethical, legal and other requirements in limited ways in particular contexts. Where informed consent is important or required, it has to meet a range of standards, which we discuss in the later sections of this chapter. We shall deal with questions of justification first, because arguments for the scope of consent transactions, and for the standards they must meet, cannot easily be set out without a clear understanding of the justification of informed consent.

The use of consent transactions to waive ethical or legal requirements is well understood in everyday life. In consenting we *waive* certain requirements on others not to treat us in certain ways (sometimes this will include waiving rights), or we *set aside* certain expectations, or *license* action that would *otherwise* be ethically or legally unacceptable. Informed consent has a role *only* where activity is already subject to ethical, legal or other requirements. We do not have to seek others' consent to action that we have every right to do, or to meet others' legitimate expectations. I do not have to request others' consent to cross the road, or to arrive at work on time. (The absurdity of such requirements is even more evident if we ask *whose* consent would be required.) Consent is relevant only where there are *already* legal, ethical or other requirements and the question of setting them aside arises. For example, I may have to request consent if I want to picnic in somebody else's field, or to take the morning off work.

Using consent to waive prohibitions on action that would otherwise wrong us, or frustrate our legitimate expectations, is an everyday matter. Where an act would *otherwise* wrong an individual or disrupt their legitimate expectations, that individual's consent can waive their right, or modify their expectations in particular cases, and so justify an act that would *otherwise* be unacceptable. If Jane takes her family for a picnic in Roger's garden she will be trespassing – unless he has waived his right to exclude them. His consent to their picnic justifies action that would *otherwise* be trespass. If Tony picks Sue's plum trees bare, he will be stealing – unless she has waived her right to exclude him from doing so. Her consent to his fruit-picking justifies action that would *otherwise* be stealing. If Ann goes to the head of a queue, she will be disrupting legitimate expectations – unless those in the queue have agreed to let her go ahead of them. Their consent justifies what would *otherwise* be queue-jumping. Waiving prohibitions on wrongful action and waiving legitimate expectations is a daily practice by which we permit certain others to act in ways that would *otherwise* be unacceptable, and thereby justify their action.[1]

Any justification of informed consent has therefore to start from a recognition of the underlying legal and ethical claims and legitimate expectations that are selectively waived by consent transactions, and of the reasons individuals may have for waiving them in particular cases. We do not propose in this book to argue for a definitive list of

---

[1] Cf. 'When individuals consent to undergo medical operations, to engage in sexual intercourse, to open their homes to police searches, or to testify against themselves in court, they convert what otherwise would be an invasion of their person or their rights into a harmless or justified activity.' George P. Fletcher, *Basic Concepts of Legal Thought* (Oxford: Oxford University Press, 1996), p. 109.

legal and ethical requirements or norms (let alone of legitimate expectations, which will of course vary with cases). We propose, rather, to rely on the fact that certain ethical norms or standards are very widely accepted and endorsed by an overlapping consensus among those with an extremely wide range of ethical, social and religious outlooks. Still less do we propose to offer a list of significant legal requirements. Instead we will rely on the fact that certain types of action will be prohibited in most jurisdictions. We assume, for example, that nearly all ethical outlooks, and nearly all legal systems, will converge in prohibiting action such as injury, torture, poisoning or killing. Further, nearly all legal systems will prohibit the use of force, fraud, duress and coercion, deception and manipulation, and nearly all ethical outlooks will condemn such action as wrong. The convergence is likely to be very extensive, although lists, definitions and drafting will vary.

Yet what, we might ask, can justify waiving such significant and deeply entrenched and important ethical or legal requirements? If these requirements are important, they should surely be respected in all circumstances, and there can be no case for waiving them. However, in specific circumstances refusal to waive an important ethical or legal requirement for a specific purpose may itself lead to pain, injury, damage, distress and even to death.[2] Nowhere is this more evident than in biomedicine. Patients and research subjects can have sufficient, indeed urgent, reason to consent to interventions that would *otherwise* wrong them in significant ways and violate legitimate expectations. They may consent to treatment or to participate

---

[2] The *locus classicus* for this argument is Immanuel Kant's *Metaphysic of Morals*, 6:230–31; see Immanuel Kant, *Practical Philosophy*, tr. Mary Gregor (Cambridge University Press, 1996). Kant is an aberrant social contract theorist, in that he grounds the legitimacy of government not on the consent of the governed but on the argument that while coercion is generally wrong, it is rational to waive rights not to be coerced in favour of the exercise of state power when this is needed to prevent more extensive coercion. For details see Onora O'Neill, 'Kant and the Social Contract Tradition', in François Duchesneau, Guy Lafrance and Claude Piché, eds., *Kant Actuel: Hommage à Pierre Laberge* (Montréal: Bellarmin, 2000), pp. 185–200.

in research, thereby sanctioning action which, if inflicted without consent, would be ethically and legally unacceptable. Here too consent is *not* ethically fundamental: rather it is a way of justifying action that would *otherwise* violate important norms, standards or expectations.[3]

Consent is important in clinical and research practice because physicians and researchers often cannot help patients, or develop better treatments, without invading bodily integrity in ways that may hurt or harm, and at the limit damage, health, life and limb. Invasive and potentially damaging action is generally prohibited: it may cause pain, injure, poison and even kill. However, in medical and research practice there may be good reasons for consenting to specific invasive interventions. They may benefit individual patients, or establish how to benefit patients with a certain disease. Even when potentially beneficial invasive interventions go well, they may cause discomfort, pain, anxiety and harmful 'side' effects; and where things go badly, they may lead to complications, serious injury, even death. If invasive and risky action were undertaken without consent, it would normally violate very significant ethical and legal norms. Medical treatment, let alone surgery, done without consent might constitute assault or injury. Administering powerful drugs without consent might amount to poisoning. Conducting clinical trials without consent might treat others as guinea pigs. Informed consent requirements provide effective ways of waiving requirements and expectations in limited and defined ways in some cases, while insisting that these requirements and expectations nevertheless be respected whenever they are not specifically waived. Although the centrality of consent in discussions of clinical and research ethics has

---

[3] Cf. Roger Brownsword 'it is a mistake to view consent as a free-standing or detached principle (on the same level as privacy, confidentiality and non-discrimination); rather, consent is implicated in the right to privacy, the right to confidentiality, and the right against discrimination – in each instance, the right-holder may consent to waive the benefit of the right in question'. 'The Cult of Consent: Fixation and Fallacy', *King's College Law Journal*, Vol. 15 (2004), 223–51 (p. 225). We would add that consent can be used to waive a far wider range of basic norms.

grown massively in recent decades, these realities have been recognised for far longer.[4]

Anybody who inflicts medical treatment without consent, or conducts research on others without their consent, is likely to violate important ethical norms and legal requirements. Those who intervene *against* the will of a patient or research subject are likely to breach ethical norms and laws that prohibit the use of force, duress or coercion. Those who do not intervene *against* the will of a patient or research subject, but nevertheless *act without consent*, are likely to breach ethical norms (and possibly laws) that prohibit deception, manipulation or fraud. In some cases, action without consent breaches norms of both types. Invasive investigations, treatment and experiments undertaken without informed consent *normally* violate significant ethical norms and legal requirements, and are likely to violate fundamental rights of the person, as well as to flout or neglect a range of legitimate expectations.

Consent requirements offer a routine way of obtaining a limited waiver of requirements that are *generally* inviolable. They confer a special right – a permission – on certain medical practitioners or researchers to act in ways that would otherwise be prohibited. Consent may not be sufficient to waive such norms in all cases[5] – but it functions reliably as an everyday way of permitting action that would *otherwise* violate important norms and standards. So, far from providing the *fundamental* ethical standard for biomedical practice, informed consent justifies action *only* against the background of other important ethical and legal norms, and is used to give limited

---

[4] See P. Dalla-Vorgia, J. Lascaratos, P. Skiadia, and T. Garanis-Papadotos, 'Is Consent in Medicine a Concept Only of Modern Times?', *Journal of Medical Ethics* 27 (2001), 59–61.

[5] For example, consensual cannibalism and consensual torture may be prohibited in some jurisdictions. But this is not invariably the case. For examples of legal uncertainty consider the 2004 trial of the German cannibal, Armin Meiwes, who claimed in his defence that his victim consented, where the court reached a verdict of manslaughter, and the appeal court a verdict of murder; or consider *R.* v. *Brown* [1993] 2 All ER 75 (HL), in which the lower court finding that certain sado-masochistic practices were lawful if consensual was overruled on appeal to the House of Lords.

permission to act and intervene in ways that would *otherwise* do wrong to others, or *otherwise* fail to meet legitimate expectations.[6] It provides a way by which individuals who would *otherwise* be wronged, or whose legitimate expectations would *otherwise* be denied, can waive those requirements on others in limited ways in a particular context, or agree to adjust legitimate expectations in limited ways in a particular situation.

SCOPE AND STANDARDS

We do not doubt that the consent of patients and research subjects to invasive procedures can be of high importance. There have been notorious cases in which medical treatment or research undertaken without consent inflicted injury, even serious or fatal injury. The atrocities perpetrated in the name of medical research under the Nazi regime provide incontrovertible evidence of the importance of consent.[7] So do some of the most widely discussed examples of medical malpractice elsewhere.[8] Had consent requirements been honoured in these cases, consent would have been refused, and grave injuries would not have been inflicted.

Nor do we doubt that lesser asymmetries of power and information, which are commonplace in clinical and research practice, can expose patients and research subjects to serious mistreatment if they make it easier to breach consent requirements. However, the

---

[6] In developing this account of the justification of informed consent we have learned a great deal from Roger Brownsword's far reaching criticisms of tendencies to drift towards treating consent as a free-standing ethic. See Brownsword 'The Cult of Consent'.

[7] G. Annas and M. Grodin, *The Nazi Doctors and the Nuremberg Code* (Oxford: Oxford University Press, 1992), and the works by Michael Burleigh cited in Chapter 1 note 2.

[8] For examples see James H. Jones, *Bad Blood: The Tuskegee Experiment* (New York: Free Press, 1993); Jonathan D. Moreno, *Undue Risk: Secret State Experiments on Humans* (London: Routledge, 2000). For further discussion of a range of examples see Rosamond Rhodes, Margaret P. Batting and Anita Silvers, eds., *Medicine and Social Justice: Essays on the Distribution of Health Care* (New York: Oxford University Press, 2002).

importance of consent in many circumstances does not show that where consent is needed it must be sought and given in a uniform way or to a uniform standard.

In this section we move on from rethinking the justification of informed consent to rethinking its scope and the standards it must meet. When does consent matter in medical and research practice? Where it matters, what standards should consenting meet? As we have seen, consent requirements far from being ethically fundamental, presuppose other more basic ethical and legal standards. In this section we shall argue that procedures for consenting and the specificity of consent sought and obtained must both take account of the underlying norms that are to be waived in particular cases. Consequently differing clinical and research interventions are likely to require varying rather than uniform standards for consent. We shall then move on to explore the issues that are relevant in setting standards for consent in a given type of case in the following two sections of this chapter.

Consent transactions, we suggested in the first two sections of this chapter, can be used to justify action that would *otherwise* wrong others, by failing to meet adequate ethical or legal standards, or by disregarding legitimate expectations. This suggests immediately that consent is *not* required for all 'other-regarding'[9] action, whether in biomedicine or elsewhere. Action that is already permissible, and so does not violate ethical or legal norms, needs no consent. Where no ethically or legally important norm need be waived, action will not require consent unless legitimate expectations will be breached.[10] Clinicians need not seek consent from patients to chat with them about non-medical matters, to ask them how they are feeling, to

---

[9] John Stuart Mill (*On Liberty*) introduced a useful distinction between *other-regarding* action, which may affect others, and merely *self-regarding* action which does not. It is basic to his well-known arguments for individual liberty.

[10] Permissible action that disappoints legitimate expectations may require consent, or at least agreement, even if it will wrong nobody. If Tom has come to rely on Sue's being in the office across the lunch hour, so does not lock up when he goes out, she would have reason to seek his agreement or consent if she plans to change her use of her lunch hour.

sympathise with them or to close an office window. Researchers need not seek consent from research subjects to talk about the work they are trying to do, or about its interest or importance. These and countless other permissible aspects of clinical and research practice violate no norms, and require no consent.

Informed consent is important in medical or research practice *only* when a proposed intervention would violate important norms if done without consent, or disrupt a legitimate expectation. Consequently, the *scope* of informed consent requirements is set not by the demands of autonomy (however conceived) but by a wide range of ethical and legal norms which must be waived or set aside if invasive medical or research interventions are to be acceptable.

In setting out the reasons why we think that this is the way to understand the proper scope of informed consent requirements we begin by reconsidering the Nuremberg and Helsinki approaches to consent. Although the two documents take very different views of the *standards* to be met by informed consent requirements, they take a common stand on their *scope*. Both documents are drafted on the assumption that there can be a single set of standards for all invasive research on human subjects. We believe that it is hard to make a case that any common set of requirements should hold for all medical research, let alone for all medical treatment.

The Nuremberg Code views *implied* or *tacit* consent as setting an adequate standard for all medical research. It demands that the research subject:[11]

... should have legal capacity to give consent; should be so situated as to be able to exercise free power of choice, without the intervention of any element of force, fraud, deceit, duress, over-reaching, or other ulterior form of constraint or coercion; and should have sufficient knowledge and comprehension of the elements of the subject matter involved as to enable him to make an understanding and enlightened decision.

This emphasis on capacities rather than on action may seem to demand too little. It perhaps sets plausible standards for routine

---

[11] See Chapter 1 for our discussion of the Nuremberg Code, available at: http://www.ushmm.org/research/doctors/Nuremberg_Code.htm.

aspects of research, where other safeguards are in place. Here, we may think, merely going along with proposals is treated as sufficient evidence of consent, although research that is done in the face of refusal is rightly prohibited. However, the Nuremberg Code's emphasis on 'capacity to consent' and on possession of 'sufficient knowledge and understanding' may seem to set too low a standard for more complex or risky interventions. Will assurance that an individual has the 'legal capacity to consent' (or refuse), is 'so situated' as to exercise this capacity, and 'has sufficient knowledge and comprehension to make an understanding and enlightened decision' show whether important norms or expectations have been waived or breached?

Yet, as we saw in Chapter 1, the more exacting standards proposed in the Declaration of Helsinki are also problematic. Fully explicit and specific acts of consent are never possible; even highly explicit and very specific consent is seldom feasible. Moreover, since highly explicit and very specific consent are particularly demanding for patients, the Helsinki standards, and similar standards, cannot plausibly be extended from research to medical practice. The scope of 'Helsinki-style' requirements is inevitably very narrow, precisely because the standards are set at an (unrealistically) high level. Indeed, they may be so exacting that very little falls within their scope.

These difficulties suggest that it is pointless to look for uniform standards for all informed consent transactions, for all consent procedures, or for all consent forms. If there are no uniform standards, then trying to fix the scope of informed consent requirements in the abstract may have little point – and little chance of success. Adequate consent requirements may legitimately differ for different sorts of intervention, depending on the norms that would otherwise be breached. So the thought that a single standard can be set for all research, or for all clinical interventions – let alone for both – may be illusory. Although it may be useful to devise standardised consent procedures or forms for certain routine and recurrent types of research, such as randomised clinical trials, there is little reason to think that research of all sorts can be brought within the scope of any uniform set of standards, or uniform consent procedures. (We return to this point in Chapters 5 and 6 in discussing retrospective research of the type commonly undertaken in epidemiology or secondary data analyses.[12])

Similarly, in clinical practice there are sharp contrasts between routine procedures and complex interventions. At the routine end of the spectrum consider the case of a nurse who takes blood on the basis of a patient rolling up his sleeve and extending his arm, but without offering any explicit explanation and without documenting the consent given. Although the consent is implied rather than explicit, the nurse (we may think) does no wrong. She neither forces nor uses duress, and she does not deceive or manipulate the patient, or breach other fundamental ethical or legal norms. If, on the other hand, the patient had objected, she could not have proceeded without violating important norms. If, on meeting objections, she had tied the patient down or administered a paralysing drug in order to take his blood, there would have been no implied consent, and the taking of blood would have wronged him, indeed violated legal rights not to be coerced or forced, which had evidently not been waived. Similarly, a doctor who offers a diagnosis and proposal for treatment in simplified language that omits much detail does not seek, and will not receive, highly specific consent to the proposed treatment: but this may be acceptable provided that the treatment does not deceive or manipulate the patient, and the subsequent treatment does not force or coerce.

More demanding standards may be relevant where interventions are less well understood, where going ahead without consent would violate important norms, and where risks are high. Complex medical interventions and research done without (relatively) explicit consent

---

[12] In these chapters we shall argue that the Helsinki standards are particularly implausible where research is not invasive, but merely intrusive or potentially intrusive, in that it uses (anonymised) information that has been legitimately obtained. Non-invasive retrospective research does not put patients at risk, since nothing is done to them. Retrospective research cannot use force, duress or coercion. If consent is relevant in this case, it must be in order to waive (supposed) rights to privacy.

may violate significant norms, and risk serious or long-term harm or injury. A doctor who proposes severe forms of chemotherapy with considerable 'side-effects' may need to make the nature of those effects very clear if she is not later to stand accused of having deceived the patient by prescribing a drug with effects that the patient neither understood nor would have found acceptable. Equally, a researcher who enrols subjects in a randomised trial may later stand accused of misleading them if he does not ensure that they understand that the efficacy of the drug they may receive is still unknown, and that they may receive a placebo rather than the drug. Those who consent to be research subjects need to know *what* will be done to them, *what* risks they are thought to run and *what* benefits they and others might gain. In complex, risky, unfamiliar cases there may be good reasons to seek *relatively* explicit and *relatively* specific consent.

However, a blanket approach to consent requirements that seeks to standardise procedures for consent for all treatment or all research shows a lack of understanding of the reasons why consent matters. Consent is a way of ensuring that those subjected to invasive interventions are not abused, manipulated or undermined, or wronged in comparably serious ways. It seeks to ensure that such action is done only when specific norms are waived, and is not undertaken if it would breach important ethical or legal requirements. This aim cannot be secured by making consent disclosures more and more 'complete', or by tailoring them to some uniform standard: what matters will vary depending on the case at hand; and more is not always better. Where research is non-invasive, as in the case of secondary research using anonymised data that have already been legitimately obtained and stored, nothing is done to the 'research subjects' to whom these data pertain and it may be hard to establish any case for requiring consent.[13]

We can perhaps imagine unusual cases in which respect for important norms might require researchers to meet the full Helsinki standards by informing prospective research subjects

---

[13] See Chapter 6 for further discussion of this case.

about the 'aims, methods, sources of funding, and any possible conflicts of interest, institutional affiliations of the researcher and the anticipated benefits and potential risks of the study'. But in other cases subjects for medical research, very reasonably, want to base their consent to participate on rather less. They are likely to want to know how participating in the proposed research might affect them, and what its anticipated benefits and potential risks for them and for others with the same condition are thought to be. If these matters are not communicated to them intelligibly and accurately, they may reasonably think that requests for their consent have not met adequate standards, and that their ostensible consent was based on deception or manipulation, so did not justify the intervention. In such cases they might also reasonably argue that they had not given genuine informed consent, and perhaps (depending on the circumstances) that they had been forced or duped, deceived or coerced.

It is, we conclude, pointless to hunt for a uniform view of informed consent requirements for all invasive procedures, let alone for all clinical treatment or all research participation. Cases vary hugely, and while standardised consent procedures and forms may be useful for certain ranges of cases, there is no reason to think that standardised procedures and forms, let alone the same procedures and forms, will be adequate in all cases. So there is no simple way of fixing the scope of consent requirements, beyond noting that consent will always be irrelevant where no important norms would be breached. Equally there is no simple way of fixing the standards for consent procedures: consent procedures must be robust enough to ensure that action that would otherwise breach norms is not performed unless those norms have been waived – and this may demand different standards in different cases. A procedure for gaining consent for routine interventions from competent patients with robust cognitive capacities may be inadequate for other cases.

Rather than looking for a simple way of determining the scope of consent requirements ('all medical interventions'; 'all research on human subjects'), or searching for a uniform standard for all consent procedures, we need first to consider which norms are to be waived by consenting, and will be breached if there is no consent in a particular situation. Consent matters most where the underlying norms that would be breached if they were not waived set important ethical, social or legal standards. The norms breached by going to the head of a queue without the consent of others in the queue are relatively trivial. The norms breached by administering drugs, performing surgery or detaining others for psychiatric treatment without consent are far more important. The most significant ethical and legal norms may be so important that they cannot be waived by the consent of those affected. For example, consensual killing, consensual torture and consensual cannibalism are widely seen as unacceptable, notwithstanding the consent obtained. Informed consent is indeed secondary, and lacks a context unless other norms and standards are seen as important. However, this does not show or suggest that informed consent is a trivial matter: rather the contrary.

CONSENT TRANSACTIONS: STANDARDS FOR COMMUNICATION

Where consent is used to waive other ethical or legal norms, it must be requested and given in ways that meet adequate standards. Although we do not think that it is possible to set uniform standards for all consent requirements, we hope to set out a range of considerations that are relevant if the communicative transactions by which consent is sought, given or refused are to succeed. We argued in Chapter 3 that speech acts can be used to express, convey and adjust agents' practical and cognitive commitments. Successful informed consent transactions communicate and adjust these commitments in a number of ways. In this section we shall explore some epistemic standards that successful communication, including successful informed consent transactions, must meet. In the next section we shall explore some other standards, including ethical standards, that successful consent transactions must meet.

We also saw in Chapter 3 that communication can succeed or fail in many ways. Many aspects of epistemic success in communication can be specified in terms of respect for certain norms, and communicative failure is likely where those norms are ignored or flouted. Since informed consent transactions are communicative transactions (of a specific sort), they too must respect the norms that are required or important for successful communication.

Successful communication must in the first place use a language that its audiences can follow, and make what is said *intelligible* to them.[14] It must also be *relevant* to its audiences, rather than overwhelming them with a flood of irrelevant or distracting – even if intelligible – information. Would-be communication that flouts or disregards these norms fails because it is not adequately adjusted to its audiences. Audiences may find such communication obscure, diffuse, irrelevant and (at worst) wholly unintelligible.

If those who request consent and those who respond to their requests are to communicate in ways that are intelligible and relevant to one another they must have some grasp of one another's background knowledge. There is little point in communicating things that the other party already knows, or has no need to know in a particular context. Even where others grasp aspects of communicative acts that fail in these ways, they may be unable to follow them successfully, or may read in unintended content.

Intelligibility and relevance are not always enough for successful communication. For example, speech acts that make or incorporate truth-claims aim to inform or *tell* their audiences about something. They succeed (where they do) only if they respect specific epistemic norms, and in particular norms of truth and truthfulness.[15] They are performed and received on the assumption that what is said is true, and what is done in saying it is truthful.

Of course, there are many complexities here, since what is said in some truth-claims may be untrue (or at least partially inaccurate), and what is done in saying it may be dishonest (or at least partially evasive). Some truth-claims are true, but not truthful; others are

---

[14] In other contexts it might be useful to distinguish various types of norms that are essential to intelligibility, such as syntactic, semantic and pragmatic norms, and even norms of etiquette.

[15] The speech acts which we, following Searle, *Speech Acts*, have referred to as 'representatives'.

truthful but not true; some are neither true nor truthful. Where truth-claims are true but not truthful, audiences may accept what was said as true, but fail to realise that it was said dishonestly; alternatively they may realise that a claim was dishonestly made and (mistakenly) refuse to accept what was in fact truly claimed. Where truth-claims are truthful but not true, audiences may rely on speakers' truthfulness and thereby acquire false beliefs; alternatively they may (wrongly) assume that speakers are untruthful, reject their claims, and thereby avoid false beliefs (by an unreliable method). Where truth-claims are neither true nor truthful, audiences may be misled in multiple ways. Norms of truth and truthfulness are perhaps best thought of as *regulative* rather than *constitutive* norms for making and responding to truth-claims, in that their violation does not invariably undermine, but rather disrupts and damages both communication of truth-claims and responses to others' truth-claims.

For these reasons, audiences are often cautious about others' truth-claims. They may be concerned about the accuracy of particular claims, or the honesty of particular communicators; they may suspect that certain speech acts are both inaccurate and dishonest. Yet even in cases of (suspected) inaccuracy or dishonesty, truth-claims have to be formulated and interpreted in the light of norms and practices of truth and truthfulness. Successful deception of others must simulate respect for truth and truthfulness; successful interpretation of others' truth-claims must start from, even if it later discards, a working assumption that what is said is true and truthfully said. Audiences who assume that others are not even aiming at truth, or that they are systematically dishonest, or both, no longer view their communication as making truth-claims. They may understand *what* is said by others, but not whether it was said to communicate fact or fantasy, report or rumour, illusions or truth-claims.

These difficulties extend far beyond the canonical cases of deceptive communication that is wholly false, or entirely based on carefully crafted lies, fraud, evasion and dishonesty. Deliberate deception fades into exaggeration, omission of important qualifications and mere confusion. For these reasons we often focus most intently on the negative core of norms of truth and truthfulness. We take it that communication of intelligible truth-claims is normatively adequate provided it is at least *adequately accurate for the purposes at hand* and *not dishonest*.

Even these stripped-down norms are demanding, not only for those who seek to communicate truth-claims, but for those who seek to understand and respond to them. Listeners and readers may reach a mistaken view of truth-claims, even where they find their content is fully intelligible, for many reasons. Despite adequate understanding, they may fail to realise *that* a truth-claim is at stake, and may think that what is said is intended (for example) as fiction or fantasy. In other cases they may accept truth-claims with unreasonable credulity or excessive deference to authority, or reject them with unreasonable suspicion. Or they may place and refuse belief erratically, in response to the whim of the moment. Equally, they may be excessively confident or unreasonably suspicious about others' honesty, or vacillate about the level of trust they place in others.

Informed consent transactions are communicative transactions that include truth-claims. They will therefore succeed only if the various parties to such transactions are epistemically responsible. Consent transactions require agents to respect the epistemic norms that are required for successful communication, including not only norms of intelligibility and relevance, but also norms for making, understanding and responding to truth-claims. Any request for consent will include some account of a proposed action or inter-vention, and of the effects – including risks and benefits – that are thought likely. For example, a surgeon may explain what an oper-ation involves, how it might benefit a patient and what its risks are thought to be; a researcher recruiting for clinical trials may explain the effects that the drug being trialled is likely to have and the regimen of treatment to be followed by those recruited for the trial. Informed consent transactions incorporate truth-claims, so succeed only if they respect the norms for making successful truth-claims.

These normative requirements are largely obscured if we rely on the conduit/container model of information transfer. If we think of consent transactions as based on disclosure of information (by professionals) followed by decisions (by patients and research subjects) we will gloss over many of the norms that must be met by successful consent transactions. The point is not that disclosure is unnecessary for successful informed consent transactions. On the contrary, disclosure of information is *necessary* for consent: how else could anyone know to *which* proposal consent is sought, given or refused? But disclosure alone is not *sufficient* for successful communicative transactions, so in particular not enough for successful informed consent transactions. By emphasising content while neglecting agency, the conduit/container model downplays, even hides, some of the distinctive norms that must be met by effective communicative transactions, and in particular those that are essential for understanding and responding to the truth-claims contained within informed consent transactions.

So communicating in ways that are intelligible and relevant is not sufficient for epistemically responsible and successful communication. The truth-claims contained in proposals for action and responses to those proposals must also be *adequately accurate*. We noted in Chapter 3 that the agency model of communication sees communication as an activity that draws on each party's background knowledge and inferential competencies. It follows that speech acts and, in particular, requests for consent and responses to requests for consent, cannot be fully explicit or fully specific. So we should not expect requests for consent to incorporate 'the whole truth' about proposed interventions, or expect those who respond to offer 'fully specific' consent. But we can expect requests for consent to be intelligible and relevant to those whose consent is sought, and we can expect the truth-claims they incorporate to be adequately accurate. Equally, we can expect those who respond to requests for consent to communicate their consent or refusal in ways that are intelligible and relevant to those seeking consent, and we can expect the truth-claims contained in their responses to be adequately accurate. Both requests for consent and responses to these requests fail if they do not meet these epistemic norms. Communicative transactions that are *unintelligible* or *irrelevant* to respondents, or that incorporate more or less inaccurate (at worst, *wholly inaccurate*!)

truth-claims do not provide a basis for informed consent or informed refusal. In effect, the notion of *informed consent* is a pleonasm: *uninformed consent* is not really a type of consent. If a patient or research subject remains uninformed or under-informed about what others (researchers, clinicians) propose or request, then however eagerly or fully he appears to agree to their proposals, those indications of agreement do not count as giving consent, and do not license others to act as they propose.

Mere disclosure may fail to meet these normative standards for communication in many ways. If we think of clinicians and researchers merely as disclosing information, we may think of demands for intelligibility, relevance and adequate accuracy as *additional*, perhaps ethical, requirements, rather than seeing them as indispensable epistemic norms for the success of the communicative transactions by which consent is sought, given or refused. If we assume that the sole justification for *informing* patients and research subjects is to provide them with material for decision-making, we may lose sight of the fact that consent is a *transaction*, which fails unless patients and research subjects – often thought of merely as *recipients* of informed consent disclosures – respect norms for successful communication by responding in ways that are intelligible, adequately accurate, and relevant to those who request consent. Such oversights have heavy costs. If patients or research subjects do not achieve adequate understanding of the proposals to which their consent is sought, or if they respond in ways that are not accessible to those who request consent, or if the truth-claims made by either party are not adequately accurate, 'consent' based on them will be defective, and will fail to legitimate the proposed intervention.

No doubt, those who think that disclosure is what matters for informed consent generally *assume* that what is disclosed will be intelligible and relevant to the audience, and adequately accurate. However, by focusing on disclosure at the expense of a fuller account of requirements for communicative transactions, they short-change the epistemic norms that are basic to adequate communication with others. In particular, they ignore the importance of reciprocal communication and the opportunities that it provides to check and challenge, to correct and defend truth-claims. A 'blunderbuss' approach of disclosing 'everything' – the illusory ideal to which demands for (fully) specific informed consent disclosures gesture – may or may not meet the epistemic norms required of truth-claims. *Adequate accuracy* is more important that *illusory completeness* for communicating the truth-claims that are integral to the successive stages of successful informed consent transactions. Disclosure by itself does not ensure that the epistemic norms for successful communication are met. Nor, as we shall see in the next section, does the 'disclosure-for-decision-making' model of consent offer a clear view of other norms that are relevant to consent transactions.

CONSENT TRANSACTIONS: COMMITMENTS

In Chapter 3 we noted that speech acts are often used to make, to adjust and to convey practical and cognitive commitments. Consent transactions are not merely exchanges of semantic content. They consist of speech acts by which each party both communicates with the other, and reveals and makes commitments. Requests for consent are made in speech acts that communicate *what* is proposed and *that* the proposers commit themselves to act in accordance with any consent given, and not otherwise. Those who consent to others' proposals do so in speech acts that convey that they understand *what* is proposed, and *that* they commit themselves to view subsequent action that accords with those proposals as acceptable. Those who refuse to consent convey that they understand *what* is proposed and warn *that* they are not committed to viewing subsequent action that accords with those proposals as acceptable.

More specifically, those who seek others' consent *communicate* proposals that include truth-claims about proposed action, and commit themselves to act in accordance with their proposal if, but only if, consent is given. For example, a surgeon may explain what a certain operation involves (*thereby making various truth-claims*) and commit himself to carrying out that operation (*and not some other procedure*) if, but only if, consent is given (*thereby making a conditional commitment to perform that operation if, but only if, the patient consents*). The speech acts by which consent is sought have a dual function: to communicate the content of a proposal and to make a conditional commitment.

Correspondingly, those who consent to others' requests communicate that they understand *what* is proposed (*thereby making truth-claims*) and commit themselves *not* to view action that satisfies the proposal as injury or grounds for objection (*thereby making conditional commitments*). And those who refuse requests for consent communicate their understanding of *what* is proposed (*thereby making truth-claims*) and warn that they do not commit themselves to viewing action that satisfies the proposal they have refused as other than harm or injury, and so as grounds for objection, complaint or even litigation (*thereby refusing to make conditional commitments*). The speech acts by which consent and refusal are given thus have three functions: they communicate the patient or research subject's grasp of what was proposed; they make, or refuse to make, a conditional commitment; and they communicate that commitment or lack of commitment.

Speech acts that request, give or refuse informed consent fail unless they meet not only the standards needed for effective communication of the content conveyed, but also those standards necessary for making the relevant (conditional) commitments. These standards, as we have seen, include a range of substantive and demanding epistemic norms, which set clearer and more differentiated standards for requesting informed consent than are set by appeals to respect individual autonomy, or by unrealisable aspirations to make consenting wholly explicit and specific. Communication that complies with these norms supports genuine consent or genuine refusal, without placing too much weight either on the cognitive capacities of patients and research subjects or on their capacities for voluntary action and choice.[16] Such communication, as we have stressed, need not – indeed *cannot* – be fully explicit, or fully specific.

---

[16] Cf. Bernard Williams' comment that 'morality is under too much pressure on the subject of the voluntary': *Ethics and the Limits of Philosophy* (London: Fontana, 1985), p. 194.

Successful communicative transactions must also meet a wider range of epistemic and ethical standards. In some contexts it may in fact be hard to say whether a given norm should be thought of as epistemic or ethical, but fortunately it is not generally necessary to decide the point. We note simply that some sorts of failure are more readily thought of as epistemic and others as ethical. For example, even when a proposal is intelligible and relevant to those whose consent is sought, is accurate and omits nothing substantive, the conditional commitments ostensibly made by proposers and by respondents may prove *bogus* or *unreliable*. A proposal that ostensibly meets standards for successful communication may fail if covert steps are taken to ensure that it is not *really* accessible to those whose consent is sought. More significantly, if a proposal is backed by coercion, duress, force or constraint, then any 'consent' it receives will be bogus, and any conditional commitment ostensibly made by those who 'consented' will be void. Genuine requests to waive important norms in particular cases will fail dismally if the requests themselves, or the commitments they ostensibly make, violate important epistemic and ethical norms, for example, by relying on elements of force, duress, constraint and coercion, or on forms of fraud and deceit.

Unfortunately, seeming requests for consent can easily be coupled with – and vitiated by – more or less overt uses of force, duress, constraint and coercion. Such bogus requests constitute 'offers you can't refuse', and by the same token offers that nobody can genuinely accept.[17] Genuine, legitimating consent can only be achieved where proposals communicate effectively, and where commitments reliably match proposals. Consent can be given, but cannot be extracted.

Respondents too can undermine the adequacy of informed consent by disregarding relevant ethical and epistemic norms. They may do so even when proposals are intelligible, relevant and accurate and omit nothing substantive, and when the requester's commitments are reliable and not grounded in force, duress, constraint or coercion.

---

[17] Onora O'Neill, 'Which are the Offers You can't Refuse', in *The Bounds of Justice* (Cambridge: Cambridge University Press, 2000), pp. 81–96.

Respondents do not offer genuine consent or refusal when, despite the fact that proposers meet relevant standards, they misunderstand those proposals, base consent or refusal on their misunderstandings, convey their consent in ways that are unintelligible to requesters, respond unintelligibly or with poorly articulated or targeted consent, or object to subsequent action that meets the terms of their consent. Sometimes such defects arise from a general failure in a respondent's cognitive competence or ethical standards; sometimes they have more specific sources. None of these failures is trivial; only in their absence can consent and refusal succeed.

These considerations are also relevant to cases in which we commonly think implicit consent sufficient, as in stretching the arm to give blood or shaking the head to indicate refusal. Gestures too are communicative transactions that must meet certain norms of intelligibility, relevance and accuracy. It is not enough to pretend not to grasp information that is plainly there (Nelson putting his telescope to his blind eye), or to 'consent' or 'refuse' in ways that are designed to be unintelligible (nodding or shaking one's head in the dark). It is improper, indeed wrong, to indicate consent dishonestly, for example, with a 'mental reservation' not to refrain from objecting to action that meets the terms of the consent. Consenting fails unless respondents grasp *what* was requested, and *that* it was a request (not, e.g., an order or a threat), hence something that they do not have to accept, then convey their consent or refusal with adequate intelligibility, relevance and accuracy, and accept a commitment not to see action that fits the proposal to which they consent as wronging them.

Once consent is given or refused, requesters in their turn must respond appropriately to respondents: they too have to understand *what* has been consented to or refused, and *that* it was consent or refusal. If they received consent, they may proceed with the consented-to action; if they were refused consent, they must act on their previous commitment by refraining from that action. Informed consent is achieved only when both parties respect both the epistemic norms that are relevant to communicative transactions, and the ethical norms that are relevant to making commitments.

Of course, even when requests and responses are epistemically impeccable, failure may subsequently arise if the commitments to action made by either party turn out to be unreliable. Requesters may fail to live up to the terms of the consent they received, or to respect a refusal that was clearly communicated. Such failures may be large or small, failures to observe some or many conditions, a trivial matter or a total failure of reliability, and at worst a matter of duress, force, constraint or coercion. Respondents too may fail to live up to the terms of the consent they offered, and may retrospectively claim that reliable action by requesters, which fully respected the consent they had given, was inadequate, or even an injury.

CONCLUSION: CONSENT IN PRACTICE

The conduit/container model of information and communication, coupled with the autonomy-based justification of informed consent disclosures, is apt to mislead, and to distort our thinking about informed consent. They promote a narrow focus on disclosure of information by one party, and 'autonomous' decision-making by the other. If we think of consent in this narrow way, we may forget that consent is sought, given or refused in communicative transactions that make truth-claims and commitments, and that this requires attention to a number of significant epistemic and ethical norms.

Such oversight is hardly surprising. If we think of consent merely as an exercise in individual autonomy, variously conceived, we need not take cognizance of the underlying norms that are waived in consent transactions, and can sideline the epistemic and ethical norms required for successful consent transactions. We may then come to think of requests for consent as achievable by self-regarding speech acts such as *disclosing* or *disseminating information*, and may overlook the norms that are basic to, and essential for, adequate communication. We may think of responding to requests to consent merely as a matter of autonomous decision-making, overlook the importance of communicating consent and refusal, and downplay the significance of the commitments made in consenting and refusing. We may ignore the background requirements, duties and rights, expectations and legislation against which informed consent operates, and some or many of the epistemic and the ethical norms that are constitutive of adequate communication.[18] We may think that 'autonomous decision-making' can only be respected if full, explicit, information is disclosed. If we rely on the conduit/container model, we may think of full and explicit disclosure as an *ideal* to which informed consent practice should aspire, even if we know that neither is possible in practice.

By contrast, an approach to informed consent that takes norms for adequate communication seriously has a number of advantages. A brief list might include the following. First, the justification of medical and research practice need not place sole or excessive weight on appeals to individual autonomy, variously conceived. Second, a consideration of the normative underpinnings of consent shows why medical and research practice that provides public goods cannot be subject to informed consent requirements. Third, by thinking of informed consent as waiving important norms, it becomes clear that it can never provide a complete justification of any medical treatment or research proposal, since it presupposes other ethical, legal or professional standards, norms and rules. Fourth, if informed consent transactions are seen as waiving those standards, norms and rules in limited ways, a robust distinction can be drawn between genuine and bogus ways of requesting and giving consent. Fifth, it affords a relatively clear view – although not a uniform or simple view – of the standards that those who give and refuse consent must meet. Sixth, these standards avoid reliance on excessive and questionable conceptions of explicit or specific consent.

---

[18] A nice example of a strategy that pretends to respect but in fact undermines the epistemic norms that are constitutive of good communication is the use of small print to disclaim responsibility, in, as it were, an aside. This approach, by which information is communicated, yet not *really* communicated, is in common use in activities ranging from marketing drugs to selling insurance to labelling products. Curiously, small print is deemed legally sufficient to transfer liability, even when it fails to communicate: disclosures count as disclaimers. Its ethical acceptability is another matter. See Michael Power, *The Risk Management of Everything: Rethinking the Politics of Uncertainty* (London: Demos, 2004), http://www.demos.co.uk/catalogue/riskmanagementofeverythingcatalogue/.

This understanding of informed consent transactions affirms the *importance* of informed consent, but traces its importance to the way in which informed consent transactions can provide protection against serious wrongs, evidence that such breaches have not occurred, and assurance that systematic ways of preventing them are in place. Successful consent transactions can *protect* against serious wrongs, by placing control of invasive interventions that might otherwise wrong and harm in the hands of those who would be wronged or harmed. Only those whose consent is requested can waive important ethical norms. Second, when they waive such norms, those who consent provide *evidence* that can later be cited to show that no serious wrong has been done, and used by those who perform invasive interventions to justify their action. Thirdly, the systematic use of informed consent procedures in medical and research practice can provide *assurance* to third parties that action that would otherwise be seriously wrong is routinely prevented. By contrast, where invasive treatment and research are practised without requirements of informed consent, individuals may not be protected against force or fraud, deceit or duress, constraint or coercion. In such a context, those who undertake the interventions may have no evidence to show that they did no wrong; and third parties may have no assurance that such wrongs are not routinely done.

CHAPTER 5

Informational privacy and data protection

We began rethinking informed consent by arguing that it is best viewed as a distinctive kind of communicative transaction, which agents may use to waive ethical and legal requirements in specific ways. For example, consent procedures can be used to waive norms that prohibit invasive action, thereby permitting medical treatment and research participation. Without ways of setting aside general prohibitions on invasive action, both medical treatment and research would be severely restricted. Patients would go without care; medical research would generally be impossible.

In this chapter we turn to the ways in which informed consent can be used to waive prohibitions on action that would otherwise be *intrusive* rather than *invasive*. Where *invasive action* violates either others' bodily integrity (it may force or restrain, injure or harm, even mutilate, poison or kill), or their liberty or property (it may threaten, enter, steal, damage or destroy property), *intrusive action*, by contrast, infringes a specific range of liberty rights, often referred to as privacy rights. There are many conceptions of privacy, and of privacy rights. For example, in the US discussions of privacy rights are often viewed very broadly as encompassing the liberty rights that protect individuals against invasive action, and have classically been seen as elements of a 'right to be let alone'.[1] In public debate in the UK privacy is typically understood in a more restricted way, as a right against action that is intrusive, but may not be invasive

---

[1] Samuel D. Warren and Louis D. Brandeis, 'The Right to Privacy', *Harvard Law Review*, IV (5) (1890). Warren and Brandeis cite Justice Cooley as the originator of the phrase 'right to be let alone'.

(consequently many of the actions characterised as *invasions of privacy* in US debates are seen in Millian terms as *violations of liberty* rather than of privacy in the UK). *Intrusive action* violates others' privacy in distinctive ways by seeking, revealing or publishing certain sorts of information about them without their consent. This divergence of terminology makes it useful to speak specifically about *informational privacy*, about *obligations not to misuse others' private information* and about *rights to informational privacy*.

There are very many different conceptions of informational privacy,[2] and a number of different arguments have been advanced to show that there is a right to informational privacy variously conceived.[3] We shall not offer or seek to justify a specific account of informational privacy rights, or rely on any of the justifications commonly advanced. Our focus will be on the way in which conceptions of information shape conceptions of informational privacy, and thereby obligations to respect and rights to enjoy such privacy.

Privacy rights – and their correlative obligations – have their basis in the protection of privacy *interests*. It seems uncontentious enough that each of us may have reason to keep certain information

---

[2] For example, Alan Westin defines the *right* of informational privacy as: 'the claim of individuals, groups, or institutions to determine for themselves, when, how, and to what extent information about them is communicated to others.' Alan Westin, *Privacy and Freedom* (New York: Atheneum, 1967) p. 7; Graeme Laurie defines the *state* of *informational* privacy as 'a state in which personal information about an individual is in a state of non-access from others'. Graeme T. Laurie, *Genetic Privacy: A Challenge to Medico-Legal Norms* (Cambridge: Cambridge University Press, 2002), p. 6. Parent suggests that: 'Privacy is the condition of not having undocumented personal knowledge about one possessed by others.' W. A. Parent, 'Privacy, Morality and the Law', *Philosophy and Public Affairs* 12, 4 (1983), 269–88 (p. 270); Weinreb identifies informational privacy as 'a person's control over others' acquisition and distribution of information about himself'. Lloyd L. Weinreb, 'The Right to Privacy', in Ellen Frankel Paul, Fred D. Miller Jnr and Jeffrey Paul, eds., *The Right to Privacy* (Cambridge: Cambridge University Press, 2000) pp. 24–44 (p. 34).
[3] For example, see Laurie, *Genetic Privacy*, Chapters 1 and 2 for a summary of arguments in favour of informational privacy. Standard arguments include: informational privacy is necessary for intimacy; for mental well-being; for the exercise of autonomy; for avoiding feelings of violation; for the protection of 'family life', and so on.

from becoming known by others, or by certain others, without our consent. Discussions of privacy often focus on specific types of information, such as information about a person's medical history, religious commitments, sexual orientation or intimate and personal relationships; but we may also have an interest in keeping other sorts of information private. In the first half of this chapter we shall look at some conceptions of 'informational privacy', and at the rights and obligations that would support such privacy, and at the ways in which they are shaped by differing conceptions of information and communication.

In the second part of the chapter we shall discuss a range of second-order obligations to enforce and assure informational privacy. We have already noted the importance of certain second-order obligations in discussing informed consent to clinical and research interventions. The same is true for informational privacy. Here too, second-order obligations to ensure that first-order obligations are fulfilled may be important, and may be given legal backing. For example, in the UK informational privacy is assured by the *Data Protection Act 1998 (DPA 98)*, and similar legislation has been enacted in other jurisdictions. In the second part of this chapter we shall once again emphasise ways in which specific conceptions of information and communication shape second-order obligations to assure informational privacy.

We shall argue that contemporary thinking about informational privacy, and about its second-order enforcement and assurance – like contemporary thinking about informed consent in medical and research practice – is often distorted by reliance on the conduit/ container model of information and communication. And we shall show that here too a focus on agency and communicative transactions provides a remedy for these distortions. An agency model of informing and communicating provides a framework for a clearer account of the point and the limits of informational privacy, and of the relevant rights and obligations. It also offers advantages in thinking about second-order obligations to assure respect for informational privacy, and suggests that a focus on norms of *confidentiality* may have a number of advantages over appeals to *data protection* requirements.

INFORMATIONAL PRIVACY

Informational privacy is commonly construed in terms of (supposed) privacy rights against others performing certain types of *epistemic* or *communicative* actions. Privacy rights are often seen as rights against others *coming-to-know* something about another individual, or rights against their *stating* or *communicating* or *publishing* something about another individual. So we begin by asking why coming-to-know something about another individual, or informing a third party about another individual should be thought ethically problematic where the action is not invasive, and so does not violate non-informational liberty rights.

The background is uncontroversial. It is an evident fact of human psychology that we often find it distressing and disquieting to be an *object* of others' attention. When we are performing bodily functions, or engaged in intimate acts, it can be distressing to be *seen* or *heard* or *noticed*, even if the viewing party is located in 'public' space. An action may be intrusive even if the agent does not invade another person's bodily integrity, or physically enter their property or space, or breach any non-informational liberty rights. For example, if Tom knows that his neighbour has recently bought a range of efficient 'amateur spy' equipment, he may feel that he is a victim of intrusive behaviour, because he cannot tell whether or when he is an object of his neighbour's attention.

The harmful consequences of some violations of privacy are also uncontroversial. In some states people may have reasons to fear persecution if they answer questions about religious or political commitments, or trade union membership, or questions that are posed in court or by agents of the state. These interests can be protected by informational privacy rights of 'non-disclosure'. Equally we may have strong interests in not disclosing information to individuals who might use it to violate other non-informational obligations: disclosing credit card details might provide a basis for theft or fraud; disclosing information about criminal or sexual activity might provide a basis for blackmail.

However, the aspects of informational privacy that matter in medical and research contexts are not merely rights of non-disclosure.

They are more than rights to *refuse to answer* certain sorts of questions asked by others. The aspects of informational privacy that matter in biomedicine are typically seen as rights that others not come to know 'personal' or 'sensitive' facts about patients or research subjects.

INFORMATIONAL RIGHTS AND OBLIGATIONS

We shall argue that it is important to distinguish between actions by which agents come to know certain facts from action by which they bring it about that *others* come to know those facts. Although both kinds of action are epistemic actions, and both (if successful) will bring it about that somebody comes to know something, they differ in important ways. Yet informational privacy rights are often construed very broadly to cover both the *acquisition* – or even the *possession* – of knowledge, and its *communication* to others. As we shall show, the distinction is important.

There are two broad ways in which others' *having* – as opposed to *acquiring* – knowledge about us can matter. First, what others know about us may alter how they act towards us. Others who know certain facts about us may treat us unfairly or prejudicially. Knowledge of a person's sexual orientation, religious commitments or criminal record may be taken as a reason for persecution, discrimination or other harmful treatment, even if the knowledge was acquired without intrusion. Second, we are all subject to various social emotions, like embarrassment and shame, which may be triggered by awareness that others know specific facts about us, even if they act no differently on the basis of that knowledge. So an adequate account of informational privacy needs to take account of these realities. We begin by looking more closely into the contrasts between invasive and intrusive action.

Sometimes informational privacy is violated by acts that also breach fundamental obligations not to perform invasive actions, such as obligations not to intrude, coerce, harm or act prejudicially towards others *unless* there is some overriding justification for doing so. Certain intrusive epistemic actions – such as specific ways of coming-to-know about others, and certain communicative transactions about others – may be doubly wrong because they are *also* invasive. Where others acquire knowledge about a person by invasive methods, or use that knowledge to harm, injure or act prejudicially, a range of obligations and rights will be violated.

However, breaches of informational privacy can arise without any breach of obligations to respect other liberty rights. For example, if Tom accidentally glimpses something about Sue's intimate life written in her diary, which she has left open in a public place, he does not *intend* to acquire this knowledge, he does not intrude or coerce, and his action is not invasive. Yet if he then sells the information he obtains to a tabloid newspaper, so that the details of Sue's intimate life become known to all, he breaches her informational privacy without breaching any rights other than a right to informational privacy. We shall concentrate on this type of case, in which informational privacy is ostensibly violated but other rights are not. In isolating this case we bracket – but do not dispute the importance of – obligations to refrain from invasive action and to respect the corresponding liberty rights.

Obligations to respect others' informational privacy are first-order obligations not to act in certain ways. They include obligations to refrain from attempting to find out certain things; obligations not to disclose certain things; obligations not to communicate certain things to some, or to any, others. In current discussions, these obligations are often construed as (supposed) rights over certain *types of information*. Informational privacy rights are then seen as primary, and informational obligations as derivative. This way of thinking can seem entirely natural and obvious if we rely on the conduit/container model of information, and view information about persons as a distinctive kind of stuff – in many ways analogous to personal property – that ought to be handled in a distinctive way. But if this way of looking at matters is to be sustained, we need to find some independent way of determining *which* types or items of information are to be treated as private to a given individual, just as an account of property rights has to provide a way of determining which objects are the property of a given individual. Informational privacy rights do not (on any account of the matter) pertain to *all* information, but only (it is said) to certain types of information *about* identifiable individuals. Typically rights to informational privacy are described as rights to control the use (acquisition, disclosure or communication to others) of *personal* information.

But what makes information personal? It is clear that not all of the information that is true of a given individual can count as personal information. A great deal of information about each of us can be readily known by others merely by observing us in any public place. This sort of information is freely available, and cannot count as personal information over which each individual has privacy rights. If we act in ways that others cannot help but come to know, we cannot then claim privacy rights that prohibit their knowing or coming to know about those actions. Personal information, in the sense that may be relevant to an account of informational privacy, cannot include *publicly available knowledge about individuals*.

However, this exclusion is not enough to specify the sort of information that is to count as personal. Countless propositions are true of particular individuals, are not a matter of public knowledge, yet can hardly be thought of as private. For example, Tony Blair is largely made of water; he never lived in the fourteenth century. Until our examples demanded it, nobody (we expect) has ever said or thought these things of Tony Blair. And although these propositions are true of Tony Blair, they are also true of every person alive today. So it seems that these propositions can hardly be thought of as personal information, over which Tony Blair has privacy rights.

Perhaps, then, personal information is information that pertains *uniquely* to identifiable individuals. But it cannot be the case that we have privacy interests only in propositions that are *uniquely* true of us. For example, lots of people have cancer, but each of them might well hold that this fact about their health ought to remain private.

So private information is *at most* a subset of the information that is true of a person and not already public knowledge. However, it is not easy to work out which information falls within that subset. One way of specifying the class of personal information that should be protected by privacy rights might be to appeal to a more specific account of 'privacy interests'. For example, the legal theorist Raymond Wacks suggests that:[4]

Personal information consists of those facts, communications, or opinions relating to an individual that it would be reasonable to expect him to regard as intimate or sensitive and therefore to want to withhold or at least to restrict their collection, use, or circulation.

This conception of personal information might include things like information about health, sexual activity, religious belief, political allegiance, and so on. But this definition – and others of the same type – would simply shift the classificatory burden onto a specification of what it is *reasonable* to regard as intimate or sensitive (it cannot simply be whatever people *in fact* regard as intimate or sensitive). It would be strenuous, not to mention tedious, to examine the whole range of theoretical accounts of personal information or of informational privacy rights that have been proposed in the voluminous literature. Instead we propose to take a critical look at two quite general problems that will arise if informational privacy rights are seen as rights over specific types of information.

The first general problem is that the information used in thought, communication and action does not fall into discrete types. Information, as we have already stressed, is *inferentially fertile*. Knowing that your neighbour smokes heavily – which may be public knowledge and readily accessible – allows you to make quite robust inferences about her probable future health. Sometimes we can infer what is taken to be personal information on the basis of information that is taken to be non-personal, indeed public.

The second general problem arises when we consider the *obligations* that correspond to (supposed) informational privacy rights. When we frame informational obligations by focusing on (supposed) types of information – personal information, medical information, genetic information and so on – we downplay or even ignore the fact that many different *kinds of actions* use, deploy or convey information about identifiable individuals. Because the conduit/container metaphor

---

[4] Raymond Wacks, *Personal Information: Privacy and the Law* (Oxford: Clarendon Press, 1993), p. 26.

highlights information content, but downplays the actions by which information is acquired, used and communicated, it may lead us to assume that *all* types of action that use information about persons must be classified in the same way. This, we shall argue, may lead us to misclassify morally permissible actions as breaches of putative informational privacy rights. In order to clarify and defend this claim, we will now consider in more detail some ways in which a focus on speech content rather than speech acts shapes how the acquisition, possession, use and disclosure of personal information are viewed.

INFORMATIONAL PRIVACY AS A RIGHT OVER CONTENT

A focus on content downplays the importance of intention and agency

A privacy right cannot be a wholly general right against others *knowing* or *coming to know* things about us. Knowledge can be reached – or information 'acquired' – in many different ways. Rights of any kind must have coherent corresponding obligations, and obligations are always obligations to *do* or *refrain* in specific ways. A right to privacy has to be a right that others *do* or *refrain* from certain types of action. It might be a claim right against others doing, or trying to do, certain types of *epistemic action*, such as acquiring or conveying or concealing knowledge, and so on. It might be a claim right against others doing or trying to do certain types of non-epistemic action that use information or knowledge for certain purposes. However, neither of these would amount to a right that others do not acquire knowledge about us. Since we often find things out inadvertently, there cannot, strictly speaking, be rights against others' *knowing* certain things about us.

A focus on content hides the importance of inferential fertility and obscures the variety of routes by which information may be acquired

The conduit/container view of information suggests that acquiring and communicating knowledge is a matter of acquiring, possessing or conveying *discrete* items: pieces of information, ideas, messages, images etc. But this is misleading. Recall the example of coming to know something about your neighbour's health on the basis of knowing her smoking habits. The inferential fertility of information means that we cannot prohibit others from coming to know information of specific types – including health or medical information. Inferential fertility raises problems for the very idea of rights against others' *acquisition* of specific types of information, such as 'personal' information.

Some views of informational privacy claim that there are rights to *control* 'personal' information about oneself. Such views too are problematic, given the range of different communicative acts in which information can be used. It may be plausible to argue that individuals have a right not to disclose information that is personal to them: this is a right to refrain from a specific type of action. But this is not equivalent to, and does not entail, a right that others not come to know 'personal' information by acceptable methods. We *can't* control what people think, or the conclusions they may draw from public evidence. For example, Stefan's address may count as 'personal' information: but if Maria comes to know it by consulting the electoral register, which is a public document, she has not violated Stefan's privacy. So it is highly problematic to think of informational privacy as including a *general* right against others acquiring specific types of information, as opposed to a narrower right against them acquiring it by unacceptable action. The acquisition of 'personal' information is often an unavoidable or highly likely consequence of morally permissible action. However, in some cases the *routes* or *means* by which such knowledge is acquired may be intrusive and impermissible. If we think of informational privacy rights in terms of information content, rather than in terms of the actions by which information may be acquired or communicated, we may overlook the variety of entirely permissible sorts of action and communication that may lead to the acquisition and possession of 'personal' information.

A focus on content encourages misleading analogies between information and physical objects

A focus on informational content, rather than on communicative and epistemic action, may lead us to think of informational privacy in implausible, even incoherent, terms. The container/conduit model encourages us to think of information as a kind of quasi-physical stuff, and of bits of information as analogous to physical objects that can be kept hidden or contained, or alternatively transferred and moved around. But information and knowledge are in fact very unlike physical stuff.

Suppose Peter leaves his diary open, and you unwittingly notice that he has been diagnosed as having a terminal illness. You have unwittingly *acquired* personal information. Now, had you acquired the diary itself, you could rid yourself of it: you could put it back, throw it away, or burn it: the diary is a material object. But it can be hard, even impossible, to rid oneself of knowledge once possessed. The fact that we speak of *possessing* or *acquiring* information is no reason for ignoring the profound differences between communicative and epistemic action and action that alters physical elements of the material world.

Similarly, if we rely on the conduit metaphor, it is easy to cast knowledge as the *possession* of something, perhaps most naturally as the *possession of information*. But this risks downplaying two things. First, we risk downplaying the fact that we know something only if we have *sets* of rationally evaluable commitments and if we also have the rational competencies that are required to grasp how propositions stand as evidence for, or in favour of the truth of, other propositions. Knowledge is never acquired or possessed in an isolated, atomistic, way. Second, we risk downplaying the fact that the *significance* that knowledge has for an agent (e.g., the difference it makes to how she acts) depends upon that agent's cognitive and practical commitments.

The underlying point that we want to stress here is that *information acquires ethical and normative significance not because it is about certain special aspects of the world, but because it can or may be used in certain inferences and actions.* These inferences and actions always depend on background knowledge, and on competencies, commitments and interests *other* than the mere *possession* of specific information. What is informative and significant for one person is often meaningless or irrelevant to another.

This point is easily missed because discussions of privacy, and of other normative issues bearing on information, often focus on cases that presuppose a rich and distinctive, but quite untypical, set of background knowledge, interests and inferential abilities. We may find ourselves concentrating on cases where insurers want access to medical information in order to increase premiums for those with higher health risks, or where direct marketers want information about purchasing habits so that they can target their products. Once we see possession of 'personal' information against these sorts of backgrounds or contexts, we may be led to think that the information itself has intrinsic ethical significance. We may ascribe specific motives, interests and knowledge to others, and then see their acquisition of a limited amount of 'personal' information as the decisive element in making certain sorts of action feasible or desirable for them. Yet we do not really think of the *information as such* as requiring protection or special handling, or as being subject to informational obligations. Rather we think of certain *uses of information* as raising special issues, and as subject to informational obligations. This suggests that informational obligations bear on epistemic and communicative actions and transactions, rather than on information content and information transfer. Informational privacy is better framed by an agency-based model of communicating and informing than by the content-based approach of the conduit/container model.

A focus on content obscures ways in which personal information may be used for impersonal ends

While the literature on informational privacy concentrates excessively on examples where one party has a prior *interest* in knowing or making known certain facts *about an individual*, and in using that information for distinctive, perhaps unacceptable, purposes, this is not the only or even the typical case.

In many communicative transactions nobody has the slightest interest in making facts about any individual known. For example, a great deal of medical (not to mention other) research *uses* information about identifiable individuals for entirely *impersonal* ends. Such research does not aim to find out anything about individuals, but rather to draw conclusions about populations, groups, diseases, treatments, and so on. Studies of *heredity*, for example, are based on information about *individuals*, but aim to explain the variation of traits within *populations*. Such studies may make automated computations on extant databases. The stored data are indeed about individuals, but are used to reach conclusions about populations. At no point in the process does anyone engage in any thought or judgement about the genetic, health or other 'personal' characteristics of particular individuals. Yet if we think that individuals have a right against others possessing and using their 'personal' information, such studies will be seen as breaching that right, and may seem to require consent from each individual whose data are held or processed.[5]

A focus on content hides the importance of audiences' knowledge and interests

These difficulties arise not only in possessing and acquiring information, but also in action that discloses or communicates information. Information can be 'conveyed' or 'disclosed' to others without the person who does so being in a position to understand it, to appreciate its significance, or to be concerned about it. We may disclose information that we do not *understand*, or do not see as *relevant*. Such unwitting disclosures may gain significance *only* for an audience that knows certain further facts. Jack may show Jane a holiday photograph of Bob on the beach and Jane's medical training may allow her to infer certain things about Bob's dire state of health

---

[5] See, for example, Department of Health, *Confidentiality: NHS Code of Practice* (2003), para. 38.

that Jack cannot infer. In this case, Jack discloses 'personal' information about Bob's health without knowing that he is doing so, and certainly without *intending* to do so.

A focus on content supports an over-ambitious and distorted view of informational obligations

If we rely upon the conduit/container model of information transfer we risk framing discussions of informational privacy in ways that create recurrent and unsolvable difficulties. The model hides or downplays key aspects of the speech acts by which we communicate and acquire knowledge, and assumes that we can identify certain types of information that *intrinsically* require special handling such as 'personal', medical or genetic information. It is then a short step to claims that such information should be protected by informational privacy rights, and that it is wrong to use such information unless those rights are waived by the consent of the person to whom the information pertains.

By contrast, the agency model of information and communication offers a framework that allows – indeed requires – us to distinguish different types of communicative action, so provides a basis for a more differentiated view of the ways in which personal information can be acquired, used or shared. This approach allows us to give due attention to the variety of reasons why certain types of action by which we acquire, hold, use, disclose or communicate information may be impermissible, and others entirely permissible. Rather than starting by trying to establish a putative 'right to informational privacy' over certain sorts of content, this approach provides an appropriate framework for picking out specific ways of using information that would be wrong, in order to argue for a specific configuration of informational privacy rights. The agency model of information and communication allows us to distinguish *morally permissible* acts that acquire, possess, use or disclose information about others from morally unacceptable acts that do so. Just as morally permissible acts of other sorts do not require informed consent – as we saw in Chapter 4 – so permissible epistemic and communication action does not require informed consent.

These concerns and criticisms may seem abstract and remote from practical affairs. But they are not. The way in which we frame discussions of informational privacy is of direct practical relevance to clinical medicine and medical research. Medical data about individuals can be used for many purposes: for training; for medical audit; for diagnosis; for public health and epidemiological studies; for clinical treatment of other patients; for drug development; for research into the aetiology and treatment of disease, and so on. The informational obligations of those who undertake these varied activities are likely to be complex, demanding and highly differentiated. An intelligent approach to informational privacy and its regulation needs to distinguish and argue for the informational obligations that fall on those who acquire, possess, use or disclose medical data for each of these and for other purposes, as well as distinguishing and arguing for the variety of second-order obligations that can help assure that these first-order obligations are properly met. Only if we can set out the demands of these informational obligations will we have a basis for arbitrating disagreements about the proper configuration of rights to informational privacy. Here, as elsewhere, treating rights as independent of, or prior to, obligations may lead only to uncertainty and indeterminacy.[6]

DATA PROTECTION LEGISLATION: SECOND-ORDER
INFORMATIONAL OBLIGATIONS

Accounts of informational privacy set out certain first-order obligations that bear on the use of information, including the use of information about persons. Both content-based and agency-based approaches to informational obligations often reinforce these first-order informational obligations by instituting or imposing second-order obligations to observe, report on and enforce aspects of

---

[6] See Onora O'Neill, 'The Dark Side of Human Rights', *International Affairs*, 81, 2 (2005), 427–39.

informational privacy. Regulation of personal information has been a focus of complex legislation in many jurisdictions in recent years. There are many reasons for this intense legislative and regulative activity. Typically new measures have been introduced to counter possibly adverse effects of new information technologies, by regulating their use and by enforcing that regulation.[7]

Our focus in this section will be very specifically on the second-order control of information enacted in the UK *Data Protection Act 1998* (*DPA 98*), which aims to regulate uses of specific types of information.[8] This legislation assumes and builds on a view of informational privacy as a matter of rights over 'personal' information: its starting point is a content-based rather than an agency-based account of privacy and personal information.

The Act assigns *individual consent* a large, indeed pivotal, role in controlling the lawful acquisition, possession and use of 'personal' information.[9] Individual consent is seen as a way of waiving others' obligations, thereby rendering lawful what would *otherwise* be impermissible 'data processing'. The Act assigns a wide variety of complex first- and second-order obligations to those who acquire, obtain, hold or use information of the relevant types.[10] Supposedly these obligations

---

[7] For example, see Colin J. Bennett, *Regulating Privacy: Data Protection and Public Policy in Europe and the United States* (Ithaca, NY: Cornell University Press, 1992).

[8] The text of the Act can be found at http://www.hmso.gov.uk/acts/acts1998/19980029.htm.

[9] Schedules 2, 3 and 4 to *DPA 98* specify certain conditions, at *least one* of which must be met for the legitimate processing of personal data and sensitive personal data. In each Schedule the subject's consent is listed first, followed by a number of other conditions that can exceptionally make processing of personal data lawful without consent. The Act also grants the Secretary of State certain powers to exempt specific uses of personal and sensitive information from data protection provisions.

[10] By 'informational obligation' in this context we mean both (a) obligations that pertain to the acquisition, storage and use of information; and (b) obligations to engage in, or to ensure that one is in a position to engage in, certain kinds of communicative (or informative) acts. We shall also refer to the European Data Protection Directive (Directive 95/46/EC of the European Parliament and of the Council of 24 October 1995. *On the protection of individuals with regard to the processing of personal data and on the free movement of such data*).

are correlative to each data subject's rights over 'personal' information or data held about her.[11] In the Act *personal* data are defined as:[12]

... data which relate to a living individual who can be identified (a) from those data, or (b) from those data and other information which is in the possession of, or is likely to come into the possession of, the data controller.

What are we to make of the idea of data *relating* to a living individual? Wearing a strictly-minded philosopher's hat (though we recognise that this is not the right attire for legal interpretation), we might point out that unless we are told *what* the relation in question is, we are at a loss. After all, *any* bit of data relates to *any arbitrary individual* in *some way or other* (all it takes is a little patience and ingenuity – and a lack of a decent social life – to come up with examples). But data

---

[11] (1) The right of subject access. *DPA 98* allows individuals to find out what information is held about themselves on computer and some paper records. This is known as the right of subject access.

(2) The right of rectification, blocking, erasure and destruction. *DPA 98* allows individuals to apply to the court to order a data controller to rectify, block, erase or destroy personal details if they are inaccurate or contain expressions of opinion which are based on inaccurate data.

(3) The right to prevent processing. A data subject can ask a data controller to stop or request that they do not begin processing relating to him or her where it is causing, or is likely to cause, substantial unwarranted damage or substantial distress to themselves or anyone else. However, this right is not available in all cases and data controllers do not always have to comply with the request.

(4) The right to prevent processing for direct marketing. A data subject can ask a data controller to stop or not to begin processing data relating to him or her for direct marketing purposes. This is an absolute right.

(5) The right to compensation. A data subject can claim compensation from a data controller for damage or damage and distress caused by any breach of *DPA 98*. Compensation for distress alone can only be claimed in limited circumstances.

(6) Rights in relation to automated decision-taking. An individual can ask a data controller to ensure that no decision which significantly affects them is based solely on processing his or her personal data by automatic means. There are, however, some exemptions to this.

[12] *DPA 98*, Part I, section 1. This formulation of personal data is closely based upon that found in Directive 95/46/EC where '"personal data" shall mean any information relating to an identified or identifiable natural person ("data subject")' (Chapter 1, Article 2 (a)).

protection is not meant to apply indiscriminately to everything that is true of some individual. So what is meant by speaking of data as 'personal' must be more specific. But this too is problematic. There are, as noted above (in our Blair examples), countless propositions that are true of, or state something *about*, some living individual, but which do not count as personal data in any interesting sense, or in the sense intended by the Act. Sue's name has three letters in it. Bob lives on the third planet from the sun. Rita has red blood cells. Sue has more DNA in her muscle cells than an aphid has in its whole body. Bob's name is 'Bob'. A conception of 'personal' data that covered examples of these sorts would be excessively broad, would cover many sorts of data that are in the public domain and would be exceedingly trivial.

Worse still, even if 'personal' data could be defined (and we doubt that this is possible), the Act would still be highly problematic. *DPA 98* applies to *all* uses of 'personal' data, regardless of the *purposes for which they are used*. 'Processing' as defined in *DPA 98* includes such things as acquiring, organising, altering, retrieving, consulting or using data.[13] Indeed, in the *Legal Guidance* it is noted that 'The definition [of 'processing'] in the Act is a compendious definition and *it is difficult to envisage any action involving data which does not amount to processing within this definition*' (emphasis added).[14]

In short, then, *DPA 98* exhibits exactly the kind of thinking that we have identified as problematic, in that it seeks to focus on decontextualised informational content, rather than on informational action and transactions. A significant class of information is identified, although only in a broad, unclear and uncertain way. Then obligations that pertain to (virtually) any type of action that 'processes' such information are set out. In consequence, the legislation applies to a fantastically diverse range of actions.

This way of thinking is extremely problematic. We have noted already that medical researchers often use *sets* of data about identifiable individuals for *impersonal* ends. This is common in studies of

---

[13] *Data Protection Act 1998: Legal Guidance*, p. 15. Available at: http://www.ico.gov. uk/upload/documents/library/data_protection/detailed_specialist_guides/data_ protection_act_legal_guidance.pdf.

[14] *Ibid.*, p. 15.

heredity, in epidemiology and in public health research. Such a researcher has no specific interest in any particular person, or in finding out whom the data apply to, but will need to ensure that the data that she uses are indexed to identifiers, in order to link different bits of information about the same individual. Without linked data, many lines of research, including virtually all forms of epidemiological work and secondary data analyses, will be impossible. Similar problems arise in clinical practice, where a physician may wish to revisit data about the treatment of a past patient, A, in order to inform his treatment of a current patient, B. This use of A's personal information is not done in order to treat A, so apparently breaches data protection requirements if done without A's consent.

DPA 98 prohibits all such 'informational' actions unless each individual data subject has given informed consent to the proposed use of the legitimately held information about them, subject to quite limited exceptions.[15] This requirement is highly problematic. Consent to subsequent research can seldom be sought when

---

[15] Additional legislation on the use of patient information was enacted in section 60 of the *Health and Social Care Act* 2001, under which a *Patient Information Advisory Group* (*PIAG*) was established to deal with cases where informed consent is not feasible. The legislation has led to confusion, mainly about the type of anonymisation required to ensure that information is not 'patient identifiable'. A recent consultation document on revising section 60 of the 2001 Act makes it clear that obtaining informed consent for any further use of information remains the default position: 'The Government has made it clear that informed consent is the fundamental principle governing the use of patient identifiable information by any part of the NHS or research community' ('Consultation' 2.1). Section 60, as it currently stands, gives the Secretary of State powers to authorise the use of 'patient identifiable' information without informed consent for a limited range of purposes such as: 'work to anonymise records'; 'work to identify and contact patients to gain their consent'; 'analysis of geographical data'; 'communicable disease surveillance'; 'clinical audit and monitoring of healthcare provision'; and others ('Consultation' 3.3). The first two are 'in-house' uses of data; the others are uses that do not require linkable data. But much research needs linkable data, and is impossible if anonymisation destroys links. On the account we offer here, there need be nothing ethically impermissible about uses of information that is *in principle* linkable to individuals, provided that it is *effectively* (although reversibly) anonymised. *PIAG*'s guidance can be found at http://www.advisorybodies.doh.gov.uk/piag/HealthRecords.pdf; the consultation document is available at http://www.dh.gov.uk/assetRoot/04/07/14/32/04071432.pdf.

information about a data subject is initially obtained, if only because future research cannot be foreseen at that point. Yet recontacting data subjects at a later date may be impossible, impractical or prohibitively expensive. Recontacting is also likely to lead to many problems: 'data subjects' may find it hard to understand why they are being recontacted, or what is 'being done' with their information; if some sorts of people are more likely to refuse to give consent than others, the data made available for research by recontacting may not be representative.

DPA 98 identifies a broad class of actions as impermissible simply because they 'process' 'personal' data. It might seem that the obvious solution is to insist upon *anonymisation* of personal data, so as to ensure that it does not fall under *DPA 98*. However, weaker forms of anonymisation do not satisfy the requirements of the Act, and stronger forms do not meet the needs of research. One weaker form of anonymisation, that has traditionally and routinely been used in medical and research practice, is *potentially reversible ano-nymisation*, where work is done on data that have no 'identifying' labels (such as patient names, NHS numbers) although others (e.g., the hospital or those who have gathered the data, or the custodians of a database) retain information that *could* be used to link those data to the data subject, for example, by looking up a name or an NHS number. In this case the anonymisation is reversible: the data are not actually de-linked, they are merely reversibly anonymised or 'pseu-donymised'. It remains possible, in principle, to de-anonymise such data and to link them to individual data subjects. Traditionally this sort of anonymisation was held to provide adequate informational privacy for patients. However *DPA 98* applies to all use of data in which the data subjects remain 'identifiable' even by indirect means.[16] Under *DPA 98* research may be done without consent *only* if 'personal' data are subjected to a second, stronger form of

---

[16] For definitions of *identifiable data* and of *reasonably identifiable data* see Department of Health, *Confidentiality: NHS Code of Practice*, 2003, p. 9, http://www.dh.gov.uk/assetRoot/04/06/92/54/04069254.pdf; the Code has been endorsed by the Data Protection Commissioner.

anonymisation, which removes links that *could be* used to identify data subjects. In that case the data are *de-linked* or *irreversibly anonymised*, nobody can reverse the anonymisation and the data subject will be unidentifiable not only by the researcher but by others. Irreversible anonymisation is a highly problematic requirement on the use of 'personal' data in research. Many kinds of research, including much epidemiology and all secondary data analysis, require linked data (these data can, of course, be anonymised in the weaker sense). For example, researchers may need to find out whether there is a correlation between those who were treated with radiotherapy and those who later developed skin cancer. *DPA 98* counts all data that are *linkable* to any identifying information as 'personal' data:[17]

... data which relate to a living individual who can be identified (a) from those data, or (b) from those data *and other information which is in the possession of, or is likely to come into the possession of, the data controller* (emphasis added).

This is a *dispositional* claim. Even if a researcher has no interest in acting in any way that directly affects the original data subject (such as contacting her, or informing others about her medical history), and even if she has no practical way of doing so, *DPA 98* makes such research impermissible without consent from all data subjects, because data could *in principle* be re-linked to identifying information by using other information available to the data controller. Moreover, in some cases even de-linked information can be linked *inferentially* to particular data subjects by well-informed persons – and researchers are often well informed. Where researchers are working with data about rare medical conditions, they may find it easy to identify the source subject if the data held includes a few linked details such as date of birth, age at onset of condition, number

---

[17] *DPA 98*, Part I, section 1. This definition of personal data is closely based on that found in Directive 95/46/EC where '"personal data" shall mean any information relating to an identified or identifiable natural person ("data subject")' (Chapter 1, Article 2 (a)). Since data count as personal whenever a *data controller* could identify the data subject, it will not be enough for a data controller to supply (reversibly) anonymised data to researchers.

of affected siblings/children/family members, and so on. For example, there may be only one 53-year-old female without siblings in the whole country with a specific condition, and those working on the condition who need access to such data may well know who she is.[18]

Worse still, DNA samples, *even if ostensibly irreversibly anony-mised* – that is de-linked from other identifying information – might still, it seems, count as containing 'personal' data. A data controller who holds DNA samples can distinguish each individual subject from other data subjects. Even monozygotic twins will differ in their genomic data (at the level of single nucleotide polymorphisms (SNPs)). So by possessing genetic material we possess information that *de facto* distinguishes each source subject from all other source subjects, which might in principle be linkable to other information about the source subject. It follows that possession of human tissues, which always include DNA, will seemingly put researchers in possession of identifiable 'personal' information.[19] These problems arise because *DPA 98* takes a particularly exacting, indeed excessive, view of anonymisation. The legality of anonymised research using DNA samples will depend on whether or not the researchers or data controllers *could*, given the data in their possession – or that they have access to, or that they are likely to have access to – pick out the individual who is the source of the sample. If genomic sequencing becomes cheaper and more widely used, it may be possible to form a genomic 'profile' of the traits of the source person.[20] If that becomes

---

[18] Information of this sort is classified as 'identifiable patient information' in *Confidentiality: NHS Code of Practice*, 2003; see note 19.

[19] A point that was curiously but perhaps mercifully overlooked by the drafters of the *Human Tissues Act 2004 (HTA 04)*, which established a consent-based regime for all uses of human tissues, but did not attend to the specific implications of *DPA 98* for the use of tissues. For reasons discussed in earlier chapters, consent to the use of a tissue sample in research does not entail consent to the use of the DNA information the sample contains.

[20] What we would have is, in effect, a variant or analogue of Bertrand Russell's theory of proper names, where names like 'Aristotle' are to be understood as implicitly *descriptive* (understanding a proper name is a matter of knowing a list of descriptions which serve to 'pick out' the referent). Philosophers have spent a century or so debating whether or not proper names are akin to descriptions. Our

possible, then *all* DNA information is potentially linkable, none of it can be irreversibly anonymised, and none of it should be used without consent from the relevant data subjects. Requiring such consent would put an end to virtually all genetic studies using lawfully held samples and data. It would also put an end to all legitimate use of information pertaining to other patients by clinical geneticists, unless consent could be obtained from those patients.[21]

Furthermore, since *DPA 98* views virtually *any* use of 'personal' data as impermissible without consent, it appears that *anonymising* will itself be a prohibited action if done without consent. The *Legal Guidance* to *DPA 98* provided by the Office of the Data Commissioner states that: 'In anonymising personal data the data controller will be processing such data and, in respect of such processing, will still need to comply with the provisions of the Act.'[22] If the data in question are sensitive 'personal' data (such as medical data) then the anonymising may be done *only* if the subject has given explicit, specific consent to that processing. Once the subject has consented to (irreversible) anonymisation, the data in question will no longer fall under the ambit of *DPA 98*. Given the breadth of definition of 'processing,' it seems that anybody who examines sets of tissue samples, or who organises or alters a genomic sequence, would have to be seen as processing sensitive 'personal' data in doing so. It may seem odd that such impersonal research should be prevented, hindered or restricted given that it is not invasive, not intrusive, not prejudicial, and does not affect, let alone harm, any source subject (or anyone else), and given that the researcher will often have no *actual* way of knowing who the source subject is. All of these problems are consequences of trying to protect informational privacy by regulating types of informational content, rather than types of action that use information.

point here is not meant to put an end to the 'game of the name' but merely to note that genomic profiling would allow a *de facto* way of identifying individual subjects from their 'profile' (most readily where a cluster of traits so identified is an unusual one).

[21] We discuss the use of genetic information, and arguments that there ought to be special 'genetic privacy' legislation in the next chapter.

[22] *Data Protection Act* 1998: *Legal Guidance*, p. 13; see also note 15.

We are very conscious that this criticism of *DPA 98* is unprofessional, the work of philosophers and not of lawyers. We think that it is nevertheless worth setting out these criticisms both because their practical implications, especially for biomedicine, are so extensive, and because we have not been able to find or work out any convincing justification for the Data Protection approach. At the beginning of this chapter we noted numerous disagreements and uncertainties about supposed rights to informational privacy. We could not find any more robust arguments for the approach by considering the *origins* of Data Protection legislation. The UK *DPA 98* was intended to implement the European Directive (95/46/EC) on data protection. The Directive *asserted* a particular conception of rights to informational privacy, and required that:

> In accordance with this Directive, Member States shall protect the fundamental rights and freedoms of natural persons, and *in particular their right to privacy with respect to the processing of personal data* (emphasis added).[23]

Yet the (supposed) informational privacy right is neither adequately specified in the Directive nor easily justified. It cannot even be closely linked to the broadly specified right to privacy (as opposed to a right to specifically informational privacy) asserted in Article 8 of the *European Convention on Human Rights*.[24]

Both the European Directive (95/46/EC) and its implementation in *DPA 98* tacitly *assume* that the conduit/container model of information and information transfer is coherent and workable.

---

[23] Article I (1), Directive 95/46/EC of the European Parliament and of the Council of 24 October 1995 on the protection of individuals with regard to the processing of personal data and on the free movement of such data.

[24] The preamble of Directive 95/46/EC refers to the *European Convention of Human Rights* (*ECHR*), http://www.pfc.org.uk/legal/echrtext.htm. However, Article 8 of *ECHR* sets out a very different general (rather than specifically informational) privacy right: '(1) Everyone has the right to respect for his private and family life, his home and his correspondence, and (2) There shall be no interference by a public authority with the exercise of this right except such as is in accordance with the law and is necessary in a democratic society in the interests of national security, public safety or the economic well-being of the country, for the prevention of disorder or crime, for the protection of health or morals, or for the protection of the rights and freedoms of others.'

Both construe supposed informational privacy rights as *rights over content*. Both impose informational obligations to 'process' (supposed) types of information in accordance with certain requirements, and both ignore the variety of epistemic and communicative acts that 'use' or 'process' 'personal' information, and the inferential links between information of various sorts. We do not think that data protection provides a satisfactory approach to informational privacy.

Our view, however, is emphatically *not* that there are no first-order informational obligations, and consequently no rights to informational privacy. Nor do we underestimate the importance of second-order informational obligations that secure the performance of first-order informational obligations, where necessary by means of legislation. We have pointed repeatedly to examples of epistemic and communicative actions that are impermissible. We have argued that such acts may be wrong if they violate any of a range of ethical and epistemic norms: they may be unintelligible, irrelevant, coercive, harmful, distressing, misleading, dishonest, and so on. Our view is rather that if we are to understand and justify these informational obligations, and any second-order obligations and measures used to reinforce them, thereby defining and protecting (a specific conception of) rights to informational privacy, we need to focus on action, on epistemic and ethical norms that specify informational and communicative obligations, and on the second-order informational obligations that secure their performance.

RETHINKING INFORMATIONAL PRIVACY

It is important, at this point, to bear in mind the *reasons* for introducing Data Protection legislation. Both the European Directive and *DPA 98* responded to changes in the way that we acquire, store and use knowledge. The acquisition, processing and use of information have become fantastically fast and cheap (relative to, say, thirty years ago), and this evidently has significant practical implications for the acquisition and use of information, including (if we can define it clearly) *'personal'* information. The new technologies also make a massive increase in the *recording* of data about individuals easy and cheap. The costs and benefits of new information technology may, however, not be equally shared between those who possess and process data, and those whom the data are about. A credit agency may not go bust if, say, 5 per cent of its data are false. But a 5 per cent error rate in millions of health or financial records may lead to a lot of individuals being harmed, and the costs of error may be very high indeed for individuals *about* whom the errors are made. *DPA 98* aimed to secure and enforce a higher standard of informational responsibility than that which mere prudence, or mere economic competitiveness, was likely to secure, partly in order to distribute the costs and benefits of constructing databases and of using new information technology more fairly.[25] So there were good reasons for enacting new protection for informational privacy. However, it could, we believe, have been better done by regulating specific types of communicative transactions than by trying to apply uniform standards to all uses of specific types of informational content.

If we could rethink informational privacy along the same lines as those on which we have rethought informed consent, a good number of the problems created by Data Protection legislation, particularly in biomedical practice, might be avoidable. On the surface there seem to be two options for rethinking informational privacy. One option would parallel the approach of Data Protection legislation, while trying to avoid its pitfalls. It might, for example, take a less extreme view of the requirements of anonymisation. However, the approach would still need to provide a convincing account of 'personal' information in order to define informational privacy rights and second-order informational obligations. This approach seems to us unlikely to succeed. It is based on the assumption that we can specify the type of informational content to be protected by informational privacy rights. Yet we have seen that it is hard to establish a well-specified – let alone definitive or well-justified – account of

---

[25] *DPA* 98 also specifies rights of 'access' for 'data subjects'. Data subjects should be able to check or monitor what information is held about them. It is arguable that this putative right has its place in a broad shift towards 'openness' and 'transparency' in a wide range of institutional contexts. We say more about transparency and accountability in Chapter 7.

such content, and impossible to guarantee that others do not come to know aspects of that content. But what alternatives could there be to Data Protection?

CONFIDENTIALITY: REGULATING COMMUNICATIVE ACTION RATHER THAN INFORMATION CONTENT

An alternative approach, in line with our strategy for rethinking informed consent, is to shift our focus to agency, and in particular to the communicative actions and transactions by which knowledge is obtained and communicated, and to the norms and obligations most relevant to communicative transactions. An agency-based approach provides a better framework for developing an account of informational obligations, which defines a configuration of informational rights, that include but are not limited to informational *privacy* rights. In effect, this approach extends the line of thought that that we developed in Chapter 4 and in the first part of this chapter in considering epistemic and ethical norms that are relevant to successful and acceptable communicative transactions. An agency-based approach can also offer a basis for an account of second-order informational obligations that support and assure respect for first-order informational obligations by identifying second-order epistemic and communicative obligations.

Obligations of *confidentiality* provide a good example of a second-order communicative obligation. Obligations of confidentiality presuppose a background of first-order epistemic and communicative transactions and of standards that they must meet. For example, they presuppose that communicative transactions must be intelligible and relevant to their intended audiences; accurate and honest; and they assume that the commitments entered into by means of communicative transactions must be observed. Against this background, professional and legal requirements for confidentiality provide second-order backing for first-order obligations to use information (both 'personal' and other) only as agreed. Confidentiality, we believe, may provide a more coherent and robust basis for thinking about second-order informational obligations than can be offered by approaches that rely upon putative informational privacy rights over specified types of informational content and their correlative obligations.

Obligations of confidentiality may hold between many different types of agent, in many different social contexts. Typically they are said to hold where there is a well-defined – but not necessarily *legally* defined – relation between two or more parties. Confidential relations may hold between friends; family members; business partners; doctors and patients; psychiatrists and patients; priests and confessors; lawyers and clients; bankers and account holders; employers and employees; employees and personnel officers, and so on. In a confidential relation, the confider discloses, or permits the confidant to act in such a way that she acquires or may acquire, certain kinds of knowledge that may not be a matter of public knowledge. In return the confidant assumes obligations not to use that knowledge to harm the confider, and not to communicate that knowledge to third parties without the consent of the confider.

The law of confidentiality has traditionally governed confidential disclosure in professional and commercial contexts. Recent court judgments extend its scope beyond formally constituted or legally recognised relationships to relationships of other sorts.[26] Obligations of confidence can make clear demands even where there is no explicit professional or contractual relationship. We can see this by considering the role of confidentiality in family life and friendships. We are also familiar with the idea that confidentiality is not simply a matter of process, and that it has clear ethical objectives. The basic aim of the law of confidentiality was set out by Lord Denning, in discussing whether legal action could be brought for breach of confidence in cases where no explicit contract exists between confider and confidant. He took the view that the legal notion of confidentiality 'depends upon the broad principle of equity that he who receives information in confidence *shall not take unfair advantage of it. He*

---

[26] Gavin Phillipson, 'Transforming Breach of Confidence? Towards a Common Law Right of Privacy under the Human Rights Act', *Modern Law Review* 66, 5 (2003) 726–58.

must not make use of it to the prejudice of him who gave it without obtaining consent' (emphasis added).[27]

Relations of confidentiality entail obligations: a confidant may not *tell* others certain things that he has come to know, and in particular may not use that information to the disadvantage of the confider, unless the confider consents. If this obligation is met, then confiders will have reason to trust confidants not to publicise or communicate information that was imparted in confidence without their consent. Like other trust relationships, confidential relationships may be supported by systems of accountability which add legal and regulatory force to obligations of confidentiality – however, it is important that any system of accountability be suitably designed for this purpose, and some are not. We shall turn to questions about the institutional reinforcement of second-order informational obligations, such as obligations of confidentiality, in Chapter 7.

Confidential relations and confidential communication, whether protected by law or not, can be of mutual value to confider and confidant, as well as to third parties. For example, patients might be reluctant to seek medical treatment, and clients reluctant to seek legal advice, if there was no confidential relation between client and professional. It is often important for the purposes of medical treatment or legal services that certain propositions are made known to, or come to be known by, another for a specific purpose whilst remaining unavailable for general broadcast. Consider, for example, relations of commercial confidentiality. Businesses would be at risk unless employees could be told certain facts in confidence, which it would be damaging for competitors to know. Confidential relations (whether strengthened by explicit, signed agreements or based on personal interaction) allow propositions to be communicated to those who need to know them, for specific purposes, without permitting them to be passed on to others. Confidentiality and the laws that cover it

---

[27] Cited in Mark Thompson, 'Breach of Confidence and Privacy', in *Confidentiality and the Law*, ed. Linda Clarke (London: Lloyds of London, 1990), pp. 65–79 (p. 67).

arose in well-defined relationships, but are now being interpreted more broadly by the courts as applicable in contexts where there is no formal relationship, but where, nevertheless, a reasonable presumption is made that certain information is not for wider consumption and will not be *made available to others* or *used for other purposes* without the agreement of the confider.[28]

The central point that we stress here is that confidentiality differs from data protection in that it seeks to regulate types of *action* – specifically, *types of speech act* – rather than the 'processing' of *types of information*. In this respect it is on a par with some of the epistemic and ethical standards for speech acts that are specified by epistemic and ethical norms and are in constant, ubiquitous use. Obligations of confidentiality differ from those norms in that they are not relevant to all communication, nor even to all communication of truth-claims. Confidentiality is relevant where information is received in confidence from others and requires that it not be imparted to third parties without the confider's consent. Rather than defining and protecting intrinsically 'personal' content, confidentiality is a way of protecting content *of many types* that the parties to a communicative transaction seek to protect, have agreed to protect or are required to protect. Confidentiality can be invoked for specific aspects of professional, commercial or other relationships, and can be waived

---

[28] There is renewed interest in exploring how the law of confidentiality might be extended to protect individual informational privacy. For example, Mr. Justice Scott notes in his introduction to *Confidentiality and the Law* (ed. Linda Clarke, p. xxiii) that it is his belief that 'the law of confidentiality can, in conjunction with the law of trespass and the law of nuisance, go a long way to remedy the alleged absence of a right to privacy under English law'. In the same volume Mark Thompson argues with regard to the English legal position on invasion of privacy that 'if any remedy is to be found [to invasion of privacy] it is the application of the law of confidence' (p. 66). In a similar vein Gavin Phillipson and Helen Fenwick argue that the legal 'doctrine of confidence is able to offer far more protection [of privacy] than is generally recognised' and explore how the legal notion of confidence can do work in protecting the Article 8 'right to respect for private life'. 'Breach of confidence as a Privacy Remedy in the Human Rights Act Era', *Modern Law Review*, 63, 5 (2000), 660–93 (p. 662).

by seeking consent from the confider. Confidentiality is also stand-ardly given second-order professional and legal backing.

By disclosing certain matters on a confidential basis, confiders gain *some* control over its further communication and its public dissemination. However, that control does not – and, we have argued, cannot – amount to a right to prevent others from coming to know that information. The inferential fertility of information means that there will often be many ways by which something can become known, rather than a single, pre-defined route. Matters imparted in confidence can and do become public knowledge with-out any breach of confidence having occurred. Obligations of con-fidentiality merely ensure that specific, 'direct' routes by which such matters might become known are 'closed off'; they do not offer an illusory guarantee that it is possible to block all routes. This is a corollary of the fact that confidentiality regulates communicative action, rather than the content of communicative or other informa-tional acts.

The law of confidentiality provides some protection against fur-ther communication of information imparted on a confidential basis, so can (*inter alia*) be used to assure a degree of privacy for some sorts of material. However, the privacy of information disclosed on a confidential basis does not and cannot amount to a general form of 'informational privacy' over 'personal' data such as data protection approaches aspire to provide. Equally, confidentiality is not confined to 'personal' data: much information that is disclosed on a confiden-tial basis would not generally be seen as private or 'personal': for example, the details of a tender for a contract, the management accounts (as opposed to the full company accounts) of a business. And when information disclosed on a confidential basis, such as intimate, familial or professional relations, is seen as 'personal' or private this is not because it has a distinctive sort of propositional content, but because of the acts by which, and the restrictions under which, it is imparted. Confidentiality provides a general way of protecting aspects of privacy, without any need to specify in general terms which types of information do and do not count as private or personal.

CONCLUSION

Any debate about informational privacy rights must acknowledge that persons have differing, sometimes competing, interests in *knowing* or *coming to know* certain facts about individuals. However, debates about informational privacy are often hindered by a reliance on the conduit/container model of information and communication. This model seeks to shape the approach to issues of privacy by assuming that there are discrete *types* of information, such as personal information, medical information, and so on. The model may tacitly encourage us to try to define distinctive obligations on those who seek to acquire, possess or 'process' information of these types. Yet, as we have already seen in the case of informed consent to invasive treatment, the conduit/container metaphor hides and obscures many important aspects of communication and other types of action by which knowledge is acquired and extended. In this chapter we have tried to expose some of the problems and difficulties that arise if we frame questions about good epistemic and communicative practice in terms of unclearly specified rights to informational privacy. We have offered alternative accounts both of first-order informational obligations to refrain from acquiring information (where such action would breach of a range of epistemic and ethical norms), and of second-order obligations whose purpose is to ensure that certain first-order informational obligations are met. We have argued that Data Protection legislation amplifies the effects of relying on the conduit/container metaphor, by assuming that it is possible to *regulate and control communicative transactions by reference to the type of information they contain* and to *specify* exacting obligations on all uses of specific types of information.

We also have pointed to some of the difficulties that data protection legislation creates for medical research, and especially for research that re-uses legitimately acquired, lawfully held medical data (so-called 'secondary use'). Such re-use is held to breach informational privacy rights, unless informed consent is given to specific further uses and the right is waived. Given the breadth of the *DPA 98* conception of processing, clinicians and researchers seem to be required to seek specific consent *even where the purpose of an investigation – which may be as minimal as reviewing a series of past patients or as large as a population cohort study – is not to find out anything about, or to do anything to, the individuals to whom the data refer.* It is hardly consoling that *DPA 98* permits such investigation provided all source subjects consent to it, and exceptionally if permission can be obtained from *PIAG.* Obtaining further consent from all source subjects is impractical, and selective reconsenting is likely to damage research findings by skewing their statistical basis. Moreover, even where it is in principle possible to re-contact and to seek renewed consent for all further work, doing so may not be feasible given the gaps between the informational complexity of the consent required and the real capacities – and limitations – of human individuals that we noted in Chapter 1.

Just as we argued in the last chapter that we need to rethink informed consent, and its second-order enforcement in regulating invasive treatment in clinical and research practice, so we have argued in this chapter that we should rethink informational privacy and its second-order enforcement. In both cases the basis of our approach has focused on epistemic and communicative action, rather than upon information content and information transfer. By focusing on communicative action and transactions, on speech acts rather than detached speech content, we were able to draw on a robust framework for thinking about epistemic and ethical norms for informational and in particular for communicative action. Norms of epistemic responsibility, ethical norms, and second-order legal and institutional requirements that reinforce norms of both sorts, constitute obligations, and thereby define and clarify certain rights. Action in accordance with such norms can protect the privacy interests that Data Protection legislation is meant to protect *without* invoking the flawed assumption that some *types* of information have intrinsic ethical significance while others do not.

CHAPTER 6

Genetic information and genetic exceptionalism

We have now set out our case for rethinking the role of informed consent in biomedical ethics. We have argued that informed consent is not simply a way of operationalising individual autonomy, and that its full importance can be seen only when it is integrated into a wider account of obligations (many of them with corresponding rights) that takes full account of the informational obligations that are particularly important in communicative transactions. Informed consent matters in biomedicine because patients and research subjects can use it to waive others' obligations (and their own rights), if and when they have reason to do so. In particular, they can use informed consent to waive others' obligations not to violate their bodily integrity, not to infringe other liberty rights, and not to intrude into private affairs.

We have argued that the point and purpose of informed consent is obscured unless it is set in the context of an agency-based model of informing and communicating. This model supports a steady focus on a wide range of obligations, including, in particular, the everyday informational obligations that bear on epistemic and communicative action and transactions. By considering a wide range of the informational obligations that are generally important in biomedical practice, we can gain a better and more focused understanding of the importance of informed consent, and so of the standards that it must meet.

A focus on informational obligations is particularly important where biomedical practice deals with apparently distinctive types of information.[1] In Chapter 5 we considered the role of these more

---

[1] We say *appears* to deal with distinctive types of information because, as we argued in Chapter 5, the very idea that information can be neatly partitioned into

specific informational obligations in supporting an account of informational privacy, and suggested that the topic might be better approached by rethinking and extending conceptions of confidentiality than by current approaches to data protection. In this chapter we will look at another aspect of medical and research practice in which informational claims are said to be of particular, indeed distinctive, importance.

Since their inception, discussions of human genetics, including genetic research, clinical genetics and uses of genetic technologies, have been dominated by a range of informational metaphors and claims. Some writers have concluded that genetic information is exceptional, and that there are reasons for thinking that the informational obligations that bear on it must also be exceptional. In this chapter we examine these claims, and consider how the account of informed consent that we have developed bears on genetic research, on clinical genetics and on the use of genetic technologies.

QUESTIONS ABOUT GENETIC INFORMATION

The past half-century has seen massive developments in scientific and medical knowledge, and in the technologies that allow such knowledge to be organised and applied. This is especially true of genetics and genetic technologies. Developments in scientific knowledge and technology make it possible to acquire and organise genetic knowledge of many kinds, in many contexts. Often the acquisition of genetic knowledge raises few, if any, ethical questions: a student who learns something general about the molecular structure of DNA acquires genetic knowledge; a person who reads Mendel's notebooks acquires genetic knowledge; a researcher who identifies a particular molecular mechanism by which gene activity is regulated acquires genetic knowledge. Such knowledge, we may think, is neither personal nor sensitive.

types – personal, medical, genetic etc. – is itself problematic, and not as harmless an assumption as it might seem.

But where genetic knowledge is about, or can be linked to, particular, identifiable individuals, acquiring and using it are thought to raise serious ethical and regulatory issues. For example, certain procedures performed upon an individual subject's DNA, or upon certain DNA products, may show something about that individual's origins; family relationships; future health; paternity; presence at a crime scene; gender; traits (such as eye colour); or the health (or otherwise) of future offspring, and so on. Various interventions – and in particular genetic tests – can clearly reveal significant information about identifiable individuals. *Genetic* knowledge, or information, about identifiable individuals is therefore often seen as *personal* information, indeed peculiarly sensitive personal information.

Unsurprisingly, then, many of the ethical and regulatory issues raised by uses of genetic knowledge are the same as those raised by the acquisition, use and communication of other 'personal' information. For example, those who acquire knowledge from genetic tests in a clinical context will typically be bound by relations of confidentiality to *refrain* from communicating the results of such tests to other parties, unless the individual who was tested *consents* to a communicative act that would otherwise breach confidentiality.

But some people have argued, and many more seem to think, that genetic knowledge derived from tests of an identifiable individual's DNA – often simply referred to as *genetic information* – is intrinsically distinct from other kinds of knowledge about individuals. This view is often called 'genetic exceptionalism' (and sometimes 'genetics exceptionalism').[2] Genetic exceptionalism is typically cast in terms of distinctive rights and obligations that hold for uses of genetic information.

In Chapter 3 we argued that normative debates about knowledge and communication are often distorted by relying on a range of

---

[2] G. J. Annas, L. H. Glantz and P. A. Roche, 'Drafting the Genetic Privacy Act: Science, Policy, and Practical Considerations', *Journal of Law and Medical Ethics* 23 (1995), 360–6. See also L. O. Gostin, 'Genetic privacy', *Journal of Law and Medical Ethics* 23 (1995), 320–30.

metaphors and assumptions that represent information as flowing or being transferred between individuals. In this chapter we will show why this way of thinking has particularly unfortunate implications for thinking about *genetic* information. Debates about the proper acquisition, use and communication of genetic knowledge are, we believe, particularly prone to distortion because the term 'information' has been co-opted by molecular biologists to denote something *other* than knowledge. Confusion is very likely if we conflate the conceptions of information assumed in our everyday discourse with those assumed in molecular biology. The conduit/container metaphors, however, pave the way for just such conflation.

Our aim here – as in the last chapter – is to illustrate our general contention that contemporary debates about information and communication are distorted and rendered inadequate by reliance on the conduit/container metaphor, and to suggest some of the advantages that can be gained by relying explicitly on an action based account of communication.

GENETIC PRIVACY AND GENETIC EXCEPTIONALISM

Consider a paradigmatic example of genetic exceptionalism. In the early 1990s, as part of the ELSI – ethical, legal and social issues – program for the Human Genome Project, George J. Annas and his colleagues produced a *Draft Genetic Privacy Act*.[3] The *Draft Act* was a proposal for US federal legislation that would address ethical issues raised by setting up DNA databanks. What is instructive for our

---

[3] We follow other authors in referring to Annas, Glantz and Roche's Act as the *Draft Genetic Privacy Act*. This is to indicate that the Act did not become part of US legislation (hence 'draft'). The 'Genetic Privacy Act and Commentary' was, originally, the final report of a project funded by the ELSI part of the Human Genome Project: 'Guidelines for Protecting Privacy of Information Stored in Genetic Data Banks' (Office of Energy Research, US Department of Energy, No. DE-FG02-93ER61626). The (draft) Act and Commentary are available online at: http://www.ornl.gov/sci/techresources/Human_Genome/resource/privacy/privacy1.html.

purposes is that it provides a clear, early and much-discussed formulation of genetic exceptionalism:[4]

The Act is based on the premise that genetic information is different from
other types of personal information in ways that require special protection.

How is genetic information different from other types of personal
information? Genetic information, the authors suggest, is 'highly
personal', in that it pertains to matters of bodily and mental health.
More strongly, the Act claims that 'Genetic information is *uniquely*
private and personal information',[5] and that such information is
'*uniquely* tied to reproductive decisions which are among the most
private and intimate decisions that an individual can make'[6]
(emphases added). Genetic information is *predictive* in that it may
pertain, albeit probabilistically, to *future* states of health. The introduction to the *Draft Act* suggests that 'the highly personal nature of

---

[4] *Draft Genetic Privacy Act*, 'Introduction', p. i. Although the *Draft Genetic Privacy
Act* did not become part of US legislation, the issues it addressed and the approach it
took influenced subsequent attempts to legislate to protect 'genetic privacy'. For a
database of subsequent US federal legislation and attempted legislation on the topic
see US National Institutes of Health, *Privacy and Discrimination Federal Legislation
Archive*, http://www.genome.gov/11510239.
For information about state legislation and attempted legislation see The National
Conference of State Legislatures, *State Genetic Privacy Laws*, and the comment that
by 2005 'the majority of state legislatures have taken steps to safeguard genetic
information beyond the protections provided for other types of health information.
This approach to genetics policy is known as genetic exceptionalism, which calls
for special legal protections for genetic information as a result of its predictive,
personal and familial nature and other unique characteristics', http://www.
ncsl.org/programs/health/genetics/prt.htm.
European legislators have also been active, if less frenetically so. This is unsurpris-
ing: most European states have national health insurance, and the opportunity for
insurers to use genetic information in ways that are feared are more limited.
Nevertheless there has been a great deal of public concern about genetics and
insurance in Europe. See the overview article by Godard, Raeburn *et al.*, 'Genetic
Information and Testing in Insurance and Employment: Technical, Social and
Ethical Issues', *European Journal of Human Genetics* 11 (December 2003), 123–142,
available at http://www.nature.com/ejhg/journal/v11/n2s/abs/5201117a.html.
[5] *Draft Genetic Privacy Act*, Part I, Section 2 (3).   [6] Part I, Section 2 (6).

the information contained in DNA can be illustrated by thinking of DNA as containing an individual's "future diary'".[7] Genetic information is also *familial*. Genetic test results may bear information about the current or future health of family members. Such tests may also be relevant to establishing biological familial relations: for example, by establishing paternity. Genetic tests may reveal information that is relevant to the reproductive decisions that other family members might make. Genetic information is thus (so the argument goes) unlike other kinds of private or health information.[8] The *Draft Act* also notes that DNA samples provide a stable, long-term source of information. There may be a very large *amount* of personal information that can, in principle, be acquired from a DNA sample. Moreover (in contrast to other kinds of medical information), neither the subject, nor those storing the samples, nor others may know exactly what information might be gleaned from the samples either in the shorter or in the longer run. Finally, it is pointed out that genetic information (and misinformation) has been – and could in the future once more be – used to *discriminate* against those who are 'genetically unfit'.

This exceptionalist line of thought is thought to offer the basis for a very broad individual 'genetic privacy right': a claim right of each individual against others engaging in actions of many different types that gain access to, or use, his or her genetic information. The informed consent of the individual from whom the DNA sample was taken – the individual genetic data subject – would be necessary to waive this right. Given the scope of the *Draft Act*, informed consent would be required for a very wide range of actions, including the acquisition, possession, analysis, use, transfer and disclosure of personal genetic information.[9] The *scope* of the obligations that might be based on genetic exceptionalism (of this kind) is very broad

---

[7] *Ibid.*

[8] The fact that genetic information is familial creates problems for informed consent procedures and for regulatory instruments (such as contemporary data protection legislation) that rely upon *individual* consent to determine what ought, or ought not, to be done with personal information.

[9] *Draft Genetic Privacy Act*, Part A, Sections 101, 102.

indeed. Complying with them would put serious obstacles in the way of research or other uses of genetic information and technologies unless the genetic information was irreversibly anonymised, or prior specific and explicit consent to each proposed use was obtained from the source subjects.

Are there good arguments for such extensive and distinctive privacy rights over genetic information? In the previous chapter we examined assumptions that shape more general debates about informational privacy. We raised worries about the very idea of framing a debate about epistemic and communicative action in terms of a putative set of informational privacy rights without paying attention to the informational obligations that shape any conception of informational privacy, or to the ways in which such obligations might be justified. Much of the debate about genetic privacy is framed in the same, problematic way: indeed, the aim of the *Draft Act* is to specify the basis and scope of a putative *genetic privacy right*. The genetic exceptionalist argues that there are obligations on those who use or seek to use information *of a particular kind*, because that kind of information is exceptional, and so the range of rights over that information is also exceptional.

But this is problematic. The class of *genetic information*, the class of *personal genetic information* and even the class of *personal genetic information derived from a DNA test* are all of them heterogeneous. *Some* information derived from gene tests may be of great significance for the source individual, but other information derived in the same way may be of little or no significance to him. For example, an analysis of a subject's DNA to test or calibrate genetic testing technology is a use of personal genetic information, but it aims to find out something about the technology rather than the person.

Worse still, genetic information, like other types of information, is *inferentially fertile*. Performing a genetic test is not like opening up a box that contains a unique, hitherto secret object. Genetic tests require a great deal of (theory-laden) interpretation. *What* genetic information is 'obtained' from a genetic test depends upon a vast amount of knowledge possessed and deployed by, for example, those who interpret the test results. Genetic information, like all information, may *pertain* to many different objects, and thus be of interest and use for many different purposes. A genetic test *on a particular identifiable individual* may be used to reveal, or provide, information that is *not about any particular identifiable individual* (e.g., in studies of the mechanisms of gene regulation). Indeed, the *aim* of many acts that use genetic information may be to find out things about biological mechanisms, about patterns of heredity in the aetiology of a disease, and so on. Moreover, this sort of inferential fertility is not an abstruse, technical affair. It is a commonplace part of everyday life. All of us come to know information that could correctly be called *genetic* information: for example, observing a pair of identical twins, or noticing someone's gender, provides a sound basis for inferences about the genetic material of individuals.

So, even if we restrict the definition of genetic information – as the *Draft Act* does – to *genetic information acquired in a particular way from a particular source* (tests upon DNA), 'genetic information' picks out a heterogeneous, overlapping, open-ended class of information that can be used in a wide variety of ways; and some of these uses do not appear to be ethically impermissible. Is this just a concern about *defining* genetic information? Could we dismiss the lack of a clear-cut distinction between genetic and non-genetic information as a 'merely abstract' point? We think that the point is indeed abstract – not a failing! – but that it is a telling one: it undercuts the putative justification – indeed the coherence – of a general genetic privacy right *over genetic information as such*.

Talk of a privacy right over genetic information may *sound* feasible, but looks far less feasible when one (a) tries to specify precisely *which* obligations are entailed by such a right (upon whom? in what contexts?), and (b) tries to justify this general right, across the entire, heterogeneous set of actions that use genetic information (many of them in no way invasive, harmful, deceitful, breaches of confidence or ethically questionable in other ways). The genetic exceptionalist aims to establish that there are distinctive obligations that hold for *all* acquisition, use and communication of (certain kinds of) genetic information. But *why* should we accept that there are

distinctive obligations with respect to such epistemic and communicative transactions? We accept, of course, that some acts – including
some uses of genetic information – are morally impermissible. Some
acts that acquire, use or communicate genetic information may
indeed be invasive, harmful, deceitful, coercive or distressing.
Communicating information about a person's genetic make-up, or
information derived from knowledge of DNA sequences, might, in
some cases, cause distress or breach confidence. Such action is
impermissible for these and other well-known reasons.

However, it is not clear how we add to the well-known reasons for
thinking these sorts of action wrong by trying to derive the relevant
obligations from claims about the exceptional character of genetic
information. Suppose, for a moment, that we *can* distinguish genetic
from non-genetic information. What then, given that medical
records may contain both genetic and non-genetic information,
should we make of the fact that non-genetic information can provide
an adequate inferential basis for genetic conclusions, and vice versa?
How is the *genetic* information to be kept apart from *non-genetic*
information, and how could it be used separately? Is information
about, or derived from, family history genetic information? Is
information about gender genetic information? If a clinician consults
a medical record to check some non-genetic aspect of a patient's
medical history, does she thereby use genetic information (given
that, on the conduit/container model the record *contains* both kinds
of information)?

Worse still, it is unclear what grounds there are for supposing that
there are distinctive obligations with regard to *genetic* information.
Take the claim that genetic information is *about*, or allows us to infer
something *about*, future health, about future generations, and so on.
An obvious rejoinder is: this claim is true of lots of other information –
for example, information about family fortunes. It cannot be the
mere fact that genetic information is about future traits, future health
or future generations, or that it supports inferences about them, that
provides the basis for special obligations not to acquire, use or
communicate such information without the consent of the source
subject.

Would it be easier to establish such obligations if we focused on the fact that genetic information can be *used* in ways that are harmful, prejudicial, and so on? This is clearly not enough to establish specific rights to genetic privacy or corresponding obligations, since many other sorts of information can be used in similar ways. Alternatively, might rights to genetic privacy and the corresponding obligations be based on the fact that acquiring genetic information can require an invasive process? Doesn't this provide us with grounds for treating genetic information in a distinctive way? This seems implausible because invasive interventions are neither necessary nor sufficient for acquiring genetic information. Genetic privacy rights are not needed for prohibiting invasive interventions (removing tissue or blood) done without consent, because these are subject to more general prohibitions. And, on the other hand, many ways of acquiring genetic information, such as obtaining lawfully held genetic data for secondary analysis, are not invasive.

Perhaps arguments for genetic privacy rights could be based on the striking fact that DNA contains a huge *amount* of information? There is no other molecule on earth, we might point out, that contains quite so much information, which might be of interest to so wide a variety of parties. But the fact that there is *lots of* genetic information contained in DNA does not tell us anything at all about the *content* or *significance* of that information. Every human being has a rich history, including lots of facts that most of us would prefer not to broadcast, or have widely known. Mature adults have longer histories than younger ones, but the fact that there is more 'private information' about older people does not imply that there are more, or special, privacy rights for older people. The fact that there is a large *amount* of 'private information' about each of us doesn't seem to make any difference at all to the justification of privacy rights. What matters is that certain *actions* – e.g., intrusive actions, or actions that breach confidentiality – are morally prohibited. *Some* knowledge acquired from genetic tests *may* be acquired or *used* by certain agents in ways that breach established norms, including certain rights and legitimate expectations. Other uses of the same information might be entirely permissible. It is intrusive action rather than distinctive informational content that may call for special measures.

Suppose, for the sake of argument, we accept that DNA 'contains' a huge amount of information. This still tells us nothing about the kinds of actions that will, could be, or are likely to be performed on the basis of that information. By analogy, a holiday resort beach may contain a large number of stones. Throwing stones in order to hurt children is morally impermissible. But this does not mean that there should be special laws pertaining to (and only to) very large beaches where there are lots of stones. It may be true that large beaches afford more opportunities for stone-throwing (because there are more stones to throw) but it would be odd to prohibit access to the beach, or innocent uses of the beach – such as sunbathing – because the size of the beach and the number of stones increase the *possibility* of performing a large number of impermissible actions. Such examples show quite clearly that it is the *action* of throwing stones that is impermissible, and it would be insane to frame a putative right in terms of the number of stones that could be *used* to perform impermissible actions.

An exceptionalist might respond by insisting that there is still something importantly distinctive about genetic information, by pointing out that genetic information may be acquired *without the source subject's knowledge*. However, once again, this is true of non-genetic information. Going back to our beach, a well-trained medical specialist may be able to identify various diseases by looking at people's skin. She may come to know something about a 'source' subject that the subject does not know himself (e.g., that he has a mole which may be a melanoma). The fact that the subject does not *know* that the other party has acquired this information may, in some cases, pose a *risk* to the subject (if the other party is unscrupulous and aims to use the knowledge so acquired in a prejudicial way). But here the actions that are impermissible are, once again, those that are invasive, or intrusive, or harmful or that involve a breach of confidence. There is nothing intrinsically impermissible about a doctor's learning something – even something of vital significance – about others without their knowledge.

Another line of argument to which exceptionalists might point is that the acquisition of genetic information provides an 'open-ended' source of knowledge, in that nobody today knows exactly *what* information might in the future be gleaned or inferred from, say, stored non-anonymised genomic sequences. However, the same is true of knowledge gleaned from a wide variety of *correlational* facts. Future science may reveal that eating meat *and* drinking red wine regularly *at the same meal* increases the likelihood of developing certain cancers, whilst consuming them separately does not. This is health information that pertains to individuals who eat meat and drink wine together, and to those who eat meat and drink wine separately. But we do not hold that knowledge about people's diets is private because such knowledge might, in the future, provide a basis for inferences about health. (Of course, in some cases there might be other reasons for thinking that information about someone's diet is private.)

The exceptionalist might reply that we *already* know that DNA is likely to provide a source of health information, but do not know *which* non-genetic facts might be correlated with health. However, genetic information is a heterogeneous category, and the significance of any item of genetic information becomes apparent only in the context of inferences and claims about health which typically also depend on knowledge of *non-genetic* facts. Possessing genetic information is not like possessing a crystal ball, and future facts are not 'contained' within DNA. Information about future health is inferred from information about a person's DNA on the basis of knowledge, interpretation and conjecture, including large ranges of non-genetic knowledge. The exceptionalist, in effect, singles out *one element* in a complex array of epistemic, communicative, inferential, and practical, actions and transactions. But this singling out is not justified. If we focus on the *actions* by which knowledge is acquired, used, and communicated there is little need to identify any putative class of significant *contents* of knowledge and communication: for, in principle, knowledge about *anything* might be used in some impermissible way in some context, and inferences typically draw on *lots of* knowledge of many different kinds.

At this point the exceptionalist may concede that the category of genetic information is not clearly defined, and that it may not be, in principle, different from other kinds of information, and may even agree that it is impossible to 'ring-fence' genetic information in a way that provides a focus for distinctively *genetic* obligations. However, the exceptionalist may then argue that distinctive obligations come into play precisely because people have certain *attitudes* – including misunderstandings and misapprehensions – about genetic informa-tion.[10] There are two kinds of argument here. The first line of argument (which looks decidedly unappealing when made explicit) is this: there are special obligations that apply when acquiring, using or communicating genetic information because those of whom the genetic information is true may *feel* a certain way: for example, they may feel that some putative right of theirs has been breached; or that they have been or are likely to be harmed; or that they will be likely to be subject to unfair or prejudicial treatment.[11]

There may sometimes be prudential reasons for taking account of the feelings that people have about genetic information, but they offer no basis for a general argument for the intrinsic ethical sig-nificance of genetic information, or to establish rights to genetic privacy. Any general claim that genetic information is ethically distinctive should be based on showing that its use bears on the claims, interests, costs and benefits, rights and obligations of the various parties involved or affected in distinctive ways. The fact that some individuals have distinctive feelings about genetic information, or that the media claim that they have (or should have) such feelings,

---

[10] Pamela Sankar discusses how popular beliefs about genetic determinism contribute to the genetic exceptionalist's arguments, suggesting that 'Genetic determinism provides the foundation of arguments supporting genetic exceptionalism': 'Genetic Privacy', *Annual Review of Medicine* 54 (2003), 393–407 (p. 404).

[11] Mark A. Rothstein notes that, in the US, legislators, and privacy advocates, have used public fears about genetic privacy as a way of securing privacy legislation that would, otherwise, be unlikely to become statutory. Rothstein gives a clear expo-sition of why this kind of 'legislative pragmatism' is extremely problematic, given the lack of a case for genetic exceptionalism, and given the practical unfeasibility of implementing such exceptionalist policies: 'Genetic Exceptionalism and Legislative Pragmatism', *Hastings Center Report* 35 (2005), 2–8.

may call for a range of responses. It might be important to improve public understanding, or to engage the public in discussion of genetic issues, or to listen more closely to the reasons behind these feelings. It is uncontroversially important to respect those who hold such views. But there is not likely to be any *general* case for accepting views that cannot be well supported, let alone for accepting views that are based on misunderstanding, ignorance, bias or prejudice.[12]

A second line of argument from received views to a demand for special restrictions on the use of genetic information claims that we ought to restrict access to genetic information because people are likely to misunderstand or abuse it. On such views, people *ought not* to acquire, use or communicate genetic information because *they – or the others with whom they communicate* – are likely to misunderstand it or abuse it. However, if this line of argument were taken seriously, it would provide just as good a basis for a wide range of comparable 'exceptionalisms', such as *probability exceptionalism*. Normal, intelligent human beings are notoriously poor at understanding information about probabilities and using it properly. Moreover, many people have been harmed by poor understanding of probability (e.g., parents have been convicted of killing their children by inadequate but 'authoritative' evidence given by expert witnesses). However, it would be odd, even perverse, to argue that *those who are competent* and epistemically responsible should be prohibited from acquiring, using or communicating information of some type whenever *some others* are incapable of doing so. What is needed is not a blanket prohibition on acquiring, using or communicating genetic (or any other sort of) information, but appropriate institutional

---

[12] There is considerable debate about these issues which might loosely fall under the rubric: public understanding of science (but note that one of the issues is whether it is public *understanding* that is the goal, or increased trust, or improved avenues for public *engagement* with the work of scientists *prior* to the development and application of scientific and technological innovation). Colin Blakemore, 'Cultivating a Thousand Flowers', *Journal of the Foundation for Science and Technology* 18 (2005), 10–11; and the report by the think-tank Demos: *See-through Science: Why Public Engagement Needs to Move Upstream* by Rebecca Willis and James Wilsdon (2004), available at http://www.demos.co.uk/catalogue/paddlingupstream.

mechanisms for ensuring that those who do so are epistemically competent and responsible, particularly when they use the information in ways that may have serious effects.[13]

Two further points count against basing a defence of genetic exceptionalism on claims about received views and attitudes. The first is that genetic exceptionalism, if framed in terms of rights to control a class of information, may be incoherent – so impossible to implement – for the very reasons outlined above. The second point is that the claim that people have a very poor understanding of genetics sits uneasily with the assumption that *informed consent* is necessary for the ethically sound use of genetic information. These two claims raise the problem noted in Chapter 1. How can people give full, explicit and specific consent to acts that are technical and complex, of which they do not have a good understanding? How can people give adequate consent to acts that use genetic information if (as is acknowledged) they have *false* beliefs about genetic information or understand it poorly? The exceptionalist seems to hold both (a) that most people's lack of understanding of facts about genetics imposes *special* obligations upon those who acquire, use or communicate genetic information, and (b) that the selfsame people have an intact ability to comprehend the complexities of genetic research or uses of genetic technologies, and so to give or refuse informed consent to proposed interventions. Such views are, we believe, untenable.

We conclude that the considerations appealed to in the debates surrounding the *Draft Genetic Privacy Act*, and in related debates on genetic privacy, fail to establish that genetic information is distinctive or provides a basis for distinctive obligations in acquiring and communicating *genetic* information. It is, of course, possible that we have only considered one strand of argument, and that a stronger case for genetic exceptionalism may come to view. For example, there may be arguments that establish distinctive obligations that

---

[13] For example, see Hilary Burton, *Addressing Genetics Delivering Health: A Strategy for Advancing the Dissemination and Application of Genetics Knowledge Throughout our Health Professionals* (Cambridge: Public Health Genetics Unit, 2003), available at http://www.phgu.org.uk/addressing_genetics.shtml.

bear on *particular* ways of obtaining or using genetic information. However, such arguments would not establish a *general* case for genetic exceptionalism, because they do not support any *general* claim that distinctive obligations come into play *because* genetic information is distinctive.

Our discussion of the *Draft Genetic Privacy Act* and similar legislative proposals and policy discussions raises problems that will arise for any version of genetic exceptionalism that 'is based on the premise that genetic information is different from other types of personal information in ways that require special protection'.[14] Any version of genetic exceptionalism will fail because of the heterogeneity of genetic information; the heterogeneity of uses of genetic information; the inferential fecundity of genetic information; the lack of a clear-cut genetic/non-genetic distinction; the *parity* with non-genetic information; and the practical problem of isolating or ring-fencing genetic information in medical records. In consequence *normative* claims that appeal to genetic exceptionalism will be hard to sustain. In thinking about the ethics of using and communicating information, including genetic information, it is both more feasible and more fruitful to focus on the ordinary range of informational obligations. In particular, we need to focus on the various norms that prohibit epistemic and communicative acts that are invasive, intrusive, harmful, deceitful, coercive, or that breach confidentiality. But when we frame issues in this way, it is hard to find any obligations that hold only for actions by which agents acquire, use or communicate specifically *genetic* information.

IS GENETIC INFORMATION CONTAINED WITHIN DNA?

We have argued that reliance on the conduit/container model of information transfer provides an unhelpful, misleading and problematic basis for discussing normative issues about knowledge and communication. These problems are particularly acute in debates about *genetic* information. In general the conduit/container model

---

[14] *Draft Genetic Privacy Act*, 'Introduction', p. i.

downplays the importance of agency, flattens or obscures the rich set of epistemic and ethical norms that make epistemic and communicative action possible and thus encourages a 'drift from agency'. For reasons that have nothing to do with genetic exceptionalism, these tendencies are particularly marked in discussions of genetic information.

In Chapter 2 we noted in passing that the mathematical theory of communication uses 'information' as a technical term. It views information as a measure of order, or of reduction of uncertainty, and measures information so conceived in *bits*. Information in this sense is not *about* anything; it does not refer; it is not true or false. Molecular biology adopted this *quantitative* conception of information from the early 1950s onwards.[15] Before this time, biologists had discussed how (as yet unidentified) genetic 'material' must 'specify' the particular proteins and protein constituents which are the building blocks of biological entities. Rather than talking of 'information', molecular biologists until the 1950s talked of 'specificity' and of the transmission of 'specificity' from one material element to another. Put in terms of the vocabulary of fifty years ago, the specificity of DNA determines amino acid production. Once DNA was found to be systematically structured out of four simple molecular constituents, their arrangement ('form'; 'specificity', or, later, 'in-formation') could be seen as determining which amino acid (if any) would be produced.[16]

When we use the *quantitative* conception of information to say that human DNA 'contains' the same amount of information as the New York phone directory we do not mean that DNA contains the same informational *content* as the phone directory. We mean only that it would take the same number of 'yes/no' questions to settle conclusively the specific arrangement of the nucleotides as it would to determine the order of letters in the phone book (leaving aside

---

[15] Lily E. Kay, *Who Wrote the Book of Life: A History of the Genetic Code* (Stanford, CA: Stanford University Press, 2000).

[16] See Brian Hayes 'The Invention of the Genetic Code', *American Scientist* 86 (1998), 8–14.

redundancy, compression algorithms and so on). The mathematical theory of communication views information quantitatively and entirely ignores its semantic features.

Genetic exceptionalism, and debates about privacy rights over genetic information, are not concerned with information in this quantitative sense. Their concern is with genetic information that is *about* things, such as health traits or paternity. It is, of course, common to speak of DNA as *containing* information *about* other things: about proteins, about phenotypic traits, and so on. If genes are understood as a blueprint *for* a living organism it is then easy to see them as bearing or containing information *about* the traits that the organism has, or will come to have. By itself this is not unusual: we may say that footprints contain information about the size of the feet of the person who made them; or that rain clouds contain information about future weather. The key point here is that *any* object can be viewed as 'containing' or 'carrying' information about some other situation or state of affairs provided that some conscious agent knows of a causal or logical relationship between that object's being a certain way and the state of affairs in question. For example, if Robinson Crusoe knows that foot-shaped imprints in sand are made by human feet, this will allow him to draw inferences about events and situations *other* than the imprints immediately before him.[17] So, when we talk of DNA 'containing' information *about* phenotypic traits, what we actually mean is that *if* someone knew of the correlation between, say, a particular allele and a Mendelian trait, knowledge of an instance of the former would provide a basis for drawing conclusions about instances of the latter.

On this view, information is first and foremost the knowledge that people possess. But the conduit/container model makes it all too easy to airbrush the conscious agent out of the picture, and to assume

---

[17] As Fred Dretske puts it, 'A state of affairs contains information about X to just that extent to which a suitably placed observer could learn something about X by consulting it'. Fred Dretske, *Knowledge and the Flow of Information* (Cambridge MA: MIT Press, 1981), p. 45.

that information is a kind of stuff that is 'out there', somehow contained *in* the footprint, *in* the clouds, or *in* the DNA. This 'reification' of information (and of its 'location') is especially tempting and pronounced in discussions of DNA, both because biologists have adopted the mathematical notion of information to talk about degrees of order in DNA sequences, and because biologists and others have used linguistic and communicative metaphors to talk about the structure of DNA and about many intracellular causal transactions involving DNA. Reliance on these metaphors is evident in such claims as: 'DNA is *translated* into RNA'; 'Every functional gene is *read by* the cellular machinery to produce the product of that gene';[18] or 'Cells must *decipher the information* for the corresponding trait to be revealed. The *process of deciphering a gene's information* involves several steps, which are collectively called gene *expression*' (emphases added).[19] These metaphors represent molecules as *communicating* with one another and molecular systems as capable of *translation errors*. Indeed, the 'central dogma' of molecular biology is cast in terms of information flow: 'genetic information' flows from DNA to RNA to proteins.[20]

These metaphors draw upon the *functional* similarities between a person copying a text accurately and DNA transcription. That is, the 'outputs' systematically depend upon which determinate arrangement out of a number of possibilities is 'written' in the 'text'. Molecular entities are treated *as if* they were conscious subjects communicating with one another. The *sequence* of nucleotides in DNA is treated *as if* it were a text of some kind (a *blueprint*; a *code*). The tropes appropriate to characterising propositional communication are then deployed to characterise certain causal relations that

---

[18] Anthony J. F. Griffiths *et al.*, *An Introduction to Genetic Analysis* (New York: W. H. Freeman, 2000), p. 6.

[19] Paul Berg and Maxine Singer, *Dealing with Genes: The Language of Heredity* (Mill Valley, CA: University Science Books, 1992), p. 36.

[20] Francis Crick, 'On Protein Synthesis', *Symposium of the Society of Experimental Biology* 12 (1958), 138–63 and 'Central Dogma of Molecular Biology', *Nature* 227 (1970), 561–3.

obtain amongst these entities.[21] RNA is cast as a *messenger* within the molecule. These metaphors and tropes are mutually supporting, and their widespread use shapes the way that we think about genetic information, and, importantly, about the *significance* of genetic information.[22]

CONCLUSION

Let us take stock. Consent, we have argued, can be used to waive important norms, rules and standards, and so has considerable ethical importance. But since its use always presupposes whichever norms are to be waived, it cannot be basic to ethics, or to bioethics. Thinking about consent can become distorted and unrealistic if certain deeply entrenched ways of thinking about information and communication are taken too literally. This can be avoided by building on an agency-based model of informing and communicating, taking full account of standards for successful and acceptable epistemic and communicative transactions, and of their importance for informed consent transactions and for meeting informational obligations.

In this chapter, as in Chapter 5, we have developed this approach to cover the case of specifically informational obligations. We have aimed to expose the influence of the conduit/container model and to outline the advantages of the agency model for considering activities

---

[21] Some biologists, and a number of philosophers, argue that our talk of DNA containing information is *not* merely metaphorical. They argue that DNA really does contain information *about* other things and that talk of DNA as a 'code' or 'language' that can be interpreted, translated or deciphered is not metaphorical either (e.g., John Maynard Smith, 'The Concept of Information in Biology', *Philosophy of Science* 67 (2000), 177–94). Others are more cautious. Sahotra Sarkar, for example, argues that 'there is no clear, technical notion of "information" in molecular biology. It is little more than a metaphor that masquerades as a theoretical concept': 'Biological Information: A Sceptical Look at Some Central Dogmas of Molecular Biology', in S. Sarkar (ed.), *The Philosophy and History of Molecular Biology: New Perspectives* (Dordrecht: Kluwer, 1996), pp. 187–232.

[22] For further discussion see Neil C. Manson 'What is Genetic Information and Why is it Significant? A Contextual, Contrastive Approach', *Journal of Applied Philosophy* 23 (2006), 1–16.

that are intrinsically informational. In Chapter 5 we showed how an approach to informational privacy gained some clarity if we abandoned the illusory aim of defining certain types of information as intrinsically personal or private, hence protected by privacy rights, and concentrated instead on articulating informational obligations that are relevant to thinking about information and communication. In our discussion of informational privacy we showed how problematic it is to frame normative discussions about who ought to know what about whom, and who ought to communicate what to whom, in terms of supposed privacy rights over distinctive classes of information (personal information, sensitive information).

In this chapter we extended this approach by arguing that attempts to show that genetic information is intrinsically special or exceptional fail, and that normative debates about the use of genetic information should focus upon the ways in which obligations bear on acts of informing and communicating. The debate about genetic information may in fact be even more prone to distortion by reliance on the container/conduit model of information than the general debate about informational privacy. For it is especially easy to conceive of genetic information in ways that divorce it from the social and normative context of epistemic and communicative transactions, indeed from the context of agency. The widespread practice of talking of genetic information as something *contained within* DNA[23] suggests that particular care needs to be exercised when raising and framing normative questions about genetic information.

The conduit/container metaphor blurs the distinction between at least three very different senses of 'genetic information': genetic

---

[23] A study by the UK Human Genetics Commission of public attitudes to human genetic information posed the question: 'When I say "human genetic information" what, if anything, springs to mind?' The most common response was something to do with DNA fingerprinting (18 per cent) closely followed by – as summarised in the report – 'Make-up of human genes/characteristics/genetic info of the body' (15 per cent): *Report to the Human Genetics Commission on Public Attitudes to the Uses of Human Genetic Information*, p. 18.
Available at http://www.hgc.gov.uk/UploadDocs/DocPub/Document/public_attitudes.pdf.

information viewed as an intrinsic non-semantic feature of DNA; genetic information viewed as a semantic, but causal and relational feature of DNA; and genetic information viewed as propositional knowledge. On the conduit/container model, these different senses of information become intertwined, and even confused. We may overlook the differences between the thought that DNA contains a huge amount of information (non-semantic); that DNA contains information about proteins, or about traits (causal-relational); and that a genetic test may *reveal* or give *access* to the genetic information that is contained in the DNA (propositional). The conduit/container metaphor supports the thought that there is *continuity* between these radically different senses of 'information'.[24] This apparent continuity is problematic. It may seem to support the untenable conclusion that there is a homogeneous class of *genetic* information contained within DNA that can be accessed or acquired by human beings via certain kinds of technological interventions. This approach seeks to classify information or knowledge by its *source*. But, as we have stressed above, countless propositions come to be known via a range of sources: some may be important and others trivial; some may be general, others quite specific; some may be about individuals, others not; some of ethical significance, most not.

The conduit/container metaphor readily underpins a certain kind of 'slippage' in thought and talk about the *significance* of genetic information. Genetic information, viewed as something contained in DNA, may seem to be of unparalleled *causal* significance. On the conduit metaphor, however, this information can be *acquired* by certain parties. But it simply does not follow that acquiring genetic

---

[24] This is because the metaphors support certain inferences: if genetic information about traits is *contained* within DNA, then when one comes to *know* about traits, by learning something about DNA sequence variation it may seem that one has *acquired* the very thing that was *contained* in the DNA all along. Imagine a culture that does not deploy such metaphors and, instead, thinks of knowledge as something *constructed*. In this culture there is no access to something contained in DNA; rather, agents *construct* their genetic information by acting in certain ways. The point here is not to argue for, or endorse, an alternative metaphorical scheme, the example is given by way of illustrating how metaphors shape our thought.

information has any distinctive significance. The conduit/container metaphors may make it seem as if there is a special kind of potent stuff – genetic information – and any action that involves, uses or communicates such a potent stuff must surely be worthy of special consideration. Now, it *may* be that nobody has ever exhibited this kind of slippage in their thought. But, even if this is the case – and detailed empirical study would be required to establish that – we believe that it is still worth making explicit the (potentially) distorting effects of the conduit/container metaphor. First, it allows us to make explicit a danger for those engaged in normative debates about genetic information. Second, it may also help *explain* the appeal of genetic exceptionalism. The exceptionalist argues that special genetic regulation is required *because* genetic information is a special kind of 'stuff'.

More speculatively, the very fact that we conceive of DNA as 'containing' information *about* future traits surely reinforces popular views of genetic determinism (which, in turn, may distort debates about the regulation of genetic information). Conceiving of genes in this way radically downplays the importance of the environment (including the cellular, chemical, uterine, environmental and social environments). Once genetic information is viewed as something *about the future* that is *in the DNA*, the emergent traits may be seen as foretold or predicted by that information. Yet the reality of the matter is that DNA by itself *does nothing at all*, without an exquisitely finely tuned and extremely heterogeneous set of environmental conditions and events.[25]

Rather than thinking about the proper regulation of genetic information, we should focus on the various, heterogeneous actions that acquire, use and communicate genetic knowledge. We fully accept that many ways of using genetic information would be impermissible. Some acts of acquiring, using and communicating genetic information will be wrong because they are invasive,

---

[25] For further discussion of the tendency to assign DNA a potency that it does not possess see Susan Oyama, *The Ontogeny of Information*, 2nd edn (Durham, NC: Duke University Press, 2000); and P. E. Griffiths and R. D. Gray, 'Developmental Systems and Evolutionary Explanation', *Journal of Philosophy* 91(2004), 277–304.

intrusive, harmful, unjust, coercive, breach confidentiality, and so on. But what makes these actions wrong is that they breach a range of important obligations that are very generally accepted and have a wide range of application that has nothing to do with protecting putative rights of 'genetic privacy'.

CHAPTER 7

Trust, accountability and transparency

CONSENT, PATERNALISM AND TRUST

Informed consent cannot, we have argued, serve as an ethical panacea in biomedicine. It is inapplicable where public rather than private goods are to be provided. It fails where individual capacities to consent are not adequate for grasping the relevant information. Even where capacities are adequate, it fails where consent transactions are defective; and consent transactions can fail in many ways. These failures are exacerbated rather than remedied by attempts to set higher and supposedly better standards for consent, for example, by gesturing to excessive and impractical conceptions of 'fully explicit' or 'fully specific' consent. The difficulties cannot be remedied by invoking implausible or ungrounded conceptions of individual autonomy or of informational privacy.

These realities cast a sobering light on attempts to make informed consent the key to justifiable clinical and research interventions. Where consent transactions fail, any ostensible consent will be bogus; and bogus consent can offer only bogus justification. Even when more limited forms of consent can be sought and given, they will not *by themselves* provide a sufficient ethical justification. Since consent works by waiving other norms and standards in specific ways for specific purposes, it has to be understood against the background of a wider range of normative standards, including ethical standards. Informed consent is never more than a part of any justification for medical and research interventions.

These are challenging conclusions. If informed consent can play only a limited part in justifying clinical or research practice, we face serious problems. In Chapter 1 we pointed to an uncomfortable trilemma. If a great deal of current clinical and research practice does not and cannot meet adequate standards for genuine, legitimating consent, how should we proceed when we know those standards have not been – perhaps cannot be – met? Should we pretend that they have been met, and continue with business as usual? Should we curtail clinical and research practice in drastic ways because adequate standards have not been – even cannot be – met? Or should we rethink informed consent? We took the latter course. But taking it has only confirmed that informed consent can play no more than a limited part in justifying either invasive clinical or research interventions or (potentially) intrusive uses of 'personal' information for clinical and research purposes.

In this chapter we ask how clinical and research interventions are to be justified when informed consent cannot be secured. We realise that even those who take the limits of informed consent seriously, and accept that it cannot be obtained in many cases where treatment is apparently needed, or research apparently beneficial, may worry that any alternative will be risky and retrograde. Should we set aside the achievements of twenty-five years of bioethics? Should we revert to a culture of medical and scientific paternalism? Would that require us to trust doctors or researchers blindly? Many will recoil at such thoughts, and point to the dispiriting tally of experts, including clinicians and scientists, who have proved untrustworthy. They will emphasise the risks and disappointments of misplacing trust.[1] Both reinstating paternalism and relying on trust will seem to them to turn the clock back and to put individuals at risk in a variety of ways.[2]

---

[1] Major recent cases of medical untrustworthiness in the UK include events at Alder Hey, at the Bristol Royal Infirmary and the crimes of Dr Shipman. See *The Report of the Royal Liverpool Children's Inquiry*, http://www.rlcinquiry.org.uk/; *The Bristol Royal Infirmary Inquiry*, http://www.bristol-inquiry.org.uk/; *The Shipman Inquiry* http://www.shipman-inquiry.org.uk/reports.asp.

[2] For an account of some of the harms and dangers created by paternalism see: Allen Buchanan, 'Medical Paternalism', *Philosophy and Public Affairs* 7 (1978), 70–390; Gerald Dworkin, 'Paternalism', *The Monist* 56 (1972), 64–84; John Kleinig, *Paternalism* (Manchester: Manchester University Press, 1983).

It is no part of our argument to advocate any *unnecessary* return to paternalism. However, we accept that paternalism cannot be wholly avoided in clinical practice. Where competence to consent does not match up to the complexity of the information that would have to be grasped to give genuine consent that waives others' obligations, we cannot insist on consent. Patients who are unable to give such consent cannot be denied treatment, so others must decide what treatment they will receive. Since gaps between patient competence and the level of understanding required for consent to needed treatment are very common, paternalism is not always avoidable in medical practice. The need for paternalistic decisions may be reduced by making informed consent procedures clearer and easier, but the gap between patient capacities and those that would be needed for consent cannot always be eliminated. Moreover, even when competence matches up to complexity, patients may be inattentive or fail to grasp relevant information accurately, particularly if it is emotionally laden. So paternalism is ineliminable in medical practice.[3] On the other hand, where competence is adequate for consent, and consent transactions meet adequate standards, we see every reason not to revert to medical paternalism.

Paternalism could be more readily eliminated in medical research, since research *need not* be done on those who cannot consent. But this does not show that research *should not* be done on conditions that render patients incompetent or partially incompetent to consent, some of them common and distressing conditions. So there are questions to be raised and considered. Might some non-invasive (or minimally invasive) research, done without consent but with

---

[3] It is arguable that informed consent practices themselves are *essentially* paternalistic at some level given that they are based on taking a view of others' epistemic or informational interests. Informed consent practices typically involve the disclosure of the information that certain expert authorities believe that the patient *ought* to know, whether or not she actually does want to know it. They are based on decisions about the patient's *epistemic* interests. Taking into account what the 'reasonable patient' would want to be told, it is no less paternalistic than deciding what the 'reasonable patient' would want to have done. See Carl E. Schneider, *The Practice of Autonomy* (New York: Oxford University Press, 1998) for a discussion of the various reasons patients have for not wanting to know.

other safeguards, be permissible or even morally required? In particular, might retrospective non-invasive research, that uses information or tissues already obtained and retained with consent, be permissible without further consent? It is often *claimed* that such research would be unacceptable, and that further consent is required for *any* retrospective research. Yet, in practice, returning to patients to seek further consent for retrospective research may prove impossible: they may be dead, untraceable or have become incompetent to consent.

What, we may reasonably ask, justifies requiring further, more specific consent for non-invasive retrospective research that uses reversibly anonymised information or reversibly anonymised tissues that have been lawfully obtained and retained?[4] Two considerations show that answers to this question are not obvious. First, since all patients are treated on the basis of knowledge and experience that is based on information and tissues obtained from other patients, much of it not irreversibly anonymised, a supposed right to refuse to allow the use of one's own information for the benefit of other patients may be hard to justify. Second, retrospective study of (reversibly) anonymised tissues or information cannot harm or injure the sources of those tissues or information. In this case, informed consent is not needed to permit invasive actions, since none are proposed. Nor is it needed to waive rights to informational privacy of the sort that are adequately secured by reversible anonymisation. It is needed *only* if we assume a very strong conception of informational privacy that views the very *possibility* of intrusive action as violating privacy. This suggests that even if we reject a *general* return to paternalism, medical research without informed consent would be justifiable where the research is non-invasive and information and tissues are lawfully held and reversibly anonymised. In effect, retrospective studies, such as secondary data analyses and epidemiological studies, would not require consent: this research

---

[4] This was a central issue in debates surrounding the passage of the UK *Human Tissue Act 2004*. See Kathleen Liddell and Alison Hall, 'Beyond Bristol and Alder Hey: The Future Regulation of Human Tissue', *Medical Law Review* 15 (2005), 170–223.

does *nothing* further to the former patient or former research subject who was the source of information or tissue. Accepting these points would not, however, establish any *general* case for paternalism in biomedical research.

However, these considerations are not relevant to the case of patients who cannot consent to clinical interventions, or of research subjects who cannot consent to participate in prospective research. Here proceeding without informed consent would manifest a degree of trust in clinicians or researchers. Although rejecting paternalism – where it is avoidable – does not show whether or not trust should always be refused, a reliance upon trust is often seen as unacceptable. Trust is often seen as one more form of deference, and the rejection of trust as one more aspect of rejecting avoidable paternalism. A suspicion of trust is central to contemporary autonomy-based bioethics, and typically reflects fears that trust can be misplaced, and that the cost of trusting the untrustworthy can be high.

Since there is no guarantee that medical and research practice will always be trustworthy, it may seem prudent to refuse all trust, and to concentrate simply on ensuring that clinicians and researchers are (more) trustworthy. This is usually done by introducing more robust and reliable ways of holding clinicians and researchers, and the institutions within which they work, to account. Accountability is then seen as the successor to trust. Robust forms of accountability are widely seen as making trust obsolete. In this chapter we shall query many aspects of these standard views. We shall suggest that trust is not dispensable, and that it cannot be replaced by systems of accountability that support trustworthiness without requiring any form of trust. As we see matters, some forms of trust are not dispensable, need not be deferential, can be intelligently placed (or refused), and can be epistemically and ethically justified.

Decisions to place or refuse trust are typically individual decisions – just as giving or refusing informed consent is an individual decision. However, the epistemic and other norms that must be met for intelligent placing and refusal of trust are less demanding than those that must be met in giving and refusing informed consent. Requiring patients and research subjects to give or refuse informed consent is, we have seen, all too often a demand too far. Relations of trust may sometimes offer a more realistic basis for medical and research practice if – but only if – reasonable evidence to support the placing or refusal of trust is available. If medical and research practice can be anchored in trustworthy structures and practices, which offer others reasonable evidence of their trustworthiness, they may earn others' trust, while untrustworthy structures and practices may fail to do so. Where biomedical institutions and practices are trustworthy, and where patients and research subjects judge that they are trustworthy, there is no need to place trust blindly. On the contrary, trust can be intelligently placed and intelligently refused.

PLACING AND REFUSING TRUST INTELLIGENTLY

We are well aware that these suggestions will be greeted with great scepticism. It is a commonplace of contemporary debate to claim that trust is intrinsically immature, risky and unintelligent, and to recommend that we concentrate on ensuring that others are trustworthy. Trustworthiness, it is held, can be improved by establishing robust and transparent systems of accountability in all areas of life. If we can ensure trustworthiness, trust – supposedly – will no longer matter. In effect, accountability can supersede trust. We believe that this picture seems plausible only if we rely on a limited, indeed unintelligent, conception of trust, and overlook convincing reasons for thinking that placing and refusing trust are ineliminable in human life.

Trust matters, in biomedicine as elsewhere, because individuals have limited epistemic and practical capacities. Each of us has a wide range of needs, interests, goals, desires, wants, and so on, and none of us is self-sufficient. Our survival, development and well-being depend upon others from the moment we are born. Although adults are not wholly dependent upon others, as infants are, they always depend on others' knowledge, expertise and goodwill to lead a viable and minimally secure life, let alone anything like a life worth living. So we need to be able to judge when to rely on what others say and on their commitments. The stakes can be high: misplaced trust may lead to risk, harm and injury. So it matters to understand what trust is and what we need to place and refuse it intelligently. Three ranges of considerations are relevant.

Placing and refusing trust

When we trust we rely on others' words and deeds. This is not the same as *relying on* or *expecting* others to display certain regularities. We rely on the fact that people do not become invisible or dissolve without warning, and on countless other regularities in human life, in just the way that we rely on the daily rising of the sun. Trust, however, is not merely a matter of expecting or relying on certain events or outcomes. It is specifically a matter of relying on *what others say*; on *what they undertake to do*; on the truth of their claims; and the reliability of their commitments.

Trust is primarily given or refused to others' speech acts. It is directed primarily to what is said or to what is done in speaking, to truth-claims or to undertakings, and secondarily to those who make truth-claims or undertakings. Tom may tell Sue that you can fly to Amsterdam from Stansted, and she may – or may not – trust what he says. Sue may tell Tom that she will pick his children up from school, and he may – or may not – trust her undertaking. Sometimes – but not always – Sue and Tom may reach a general judgement that the other is a trustworthy – or untrustworthy – person.

Trust is well placed when it is given to trustworthy claims and commitments, and ill placed when it is given to untrustworthy claims and commitments. In placing trust in others' truth-claims, we aim to place it where their words accurately match the way the world is (or comes to be) and to refuse it where their words do not accurately match the way the world is (or comes to be). If Sue trusts Tom's word, she accepts that the world is as he says it is (and may act on that basis); if he is indeed trustworthy, what he claims will be the case. If Tom trusts Sue's undertaking, he accepts that she will act in accordance with her commitment; if her undertaking is indeed trustworthy she will live up to it by shaping the world (in small part) to match her words. We aim to place trust in those who fit their words to the world, and in those who shape the world (in small part) to their words, and we aim to refuse trust to those who do not fit their words to the world, or who do not, or are not likely to, live up to their word. Regardless of the 'direction of fit', we aim to place trust where words and the world fit, and to refuse it where they do not.[5]

Doing without trust can have high costs for those mistrusted. Most of us are trusted in many ways, by many people. Our family and friends trust us with their confidences and secrets; strangers who ask for directions trust us to give true, relevant information; colleagues trust us in numerous matters. Others' trust, like their respect, is of fundamental value to most of us. When others treat us *as if* we were untrustworthy, the results can be psychologically and socially devastating. Those who (correctly) view themselves as trustworthy and competent may feel undermined by social practices that query their trustworthiness, or that demonstrate mistrust by imposing excessive forms of assessment, review and monitoring. Trust may not be the only 'cement of society'[6] – but societies with little trust are likely to be societies of fear and divisiveness. Yet relying on trust may still seem undesirable because of the high cost of mistakenly trusting the untrustworthy.

So if all trust were blind we would face an intolerable dilemma: we would either have to accept the social costs of a society without trust, or those of a trusting but high-risk society. But fortunately not all trust is blind. Childish trust is indeed blind at first, a matter of attitude and affect rather than of judgement: children do not weigh up evidence in favour of trusting or decide to trust in the light of evidence. However, nearly all of us move on from blind trust as we learn that some people are more trustworthy than others, and that they can be trusted in some ways but not in others. As we grow

---

[5] The phrase 'direction of fit' is used to distinguish two ways in which mental states (e.g., beliefs, desires) can aim to 'fit' the world. Beliefs (and other cognitive states) succeed if we adjust them to tally with, or correspond to, the way the world is. Desires succeed if we adjust the world to fit the desires. See Elizabeth Anscombe, *Intention* (Oxford: Blackwell, 1957), p. 56.

[6] See Jon Elster, *The Cement of Society: A Study of Social Order* (Cambridge: Cambridge University Press, 1989).

up, we refine these skills and learn how to place and refuse trust more intelligently, how to provide others with the evidence that they need to place and refuse trust in us, and (alas) how to exploit the epistemic norms required for intelligent placing and refusal of trust in order to get others to place their trust poorly. We get better at placing trust so that it tracks trustworthiness, and at refusing trust so that mistrust tracks untrustworthiness, and we realise that intelligent trust is highly differentiated. We get better at placing and refusing trust.

Can we do without trust?

Still, trust is never without risks. Intelligent trust aims to track trustworthiness. Trust in truth-claims aims to track their *truth*; trust in others' commitments aims to track their *reliability*. But judging truth and reliability are both of them demanding, and can go wrong. We place and refuse trust *despite* lack of conclusive evidence or proof, and *despite* lack of complete control or guarantees of future performance. Indeed, where we have full evidence or proof, or complete control or guarantees, trust is redundant. Given that trust is placed and refused on the basis of incomplete evidence or incomplete guarantees, it can be misplaced. This can cost those who misplace it – and others – a great deal. Nevertheless, we cannot do without trust. Those who suggest that since trust can be misplaced we should do without it are, we believe, recommending the impossible. They typically suggest that we replace trust with what they take to be trust-free ways of protecting ourselves against the risk of placing trust in false claims or unreliable commitments. In place of trust, they look for stronger forms of accountability. In effect they concentrate on improving trustworthiness, and suggest that we can forget about trust. The currently favoured methods for improving trustworthiness advocate stricter and stronger systems of accountability that clarify powers, obligations and rights, imposed by formal contracts and codes, backed by monitoring and inspection of performance, by sanctions for failure (professional, financial or criminal) and by redress for those who are let down (complaints procedures; compensation schemes).[7] Systems of accountability are seen as ensuring that institutional and professional action meets acceptable standards. How deep this justification reaches will, of course, depend on the standards achieved by a particular system of accountability.

However, even the most impressive systems of accountability cannot eliminate the need for trust. Rather they invite us to transfer trust from the primary agents who provide some good or service (nursing care, a DNA test, a blood test) to those who devise or impose second-order systems for holding those primary providers to account. Good systems of accountability, we shall argue below, can improve trustworthiness, and may offer helpful evidence for placing and refusing trust intelligently. *But they do not and cannot supersede trust.* Those who rely on systems of accountability in effect place their trust in second-order systems for controlling and securing the reliable performance of primary tasks, and in those who devise and revise such systems of accountability. Pushing trust one stage, or several stages, back does not eliminate the need to place or refuse trust, and to do so intelligently.

Trust is therefore ineliminable in human affairs. It is always important to place and refuse trust intelligently, in ways that are responsive to evidence of truth or reliability, with the aim of tracking trustworthiness. This is the most, and the best, that we can do to reduce the risk of trusting misleading claims or unreliable commitments. Yet this reality is overlooked by those who dismiss all trust as blind, and as disconnected from evidence. They overlook the possibility – and the importance – of placing it intelligently. In our view, this is a disaster: the intelligent placing and refusal of trust is important in all areas of life, and while misplaced trust and misplaced refusal of trust can have costs, systematic refusal of trust is not even an option. Even an approximation to a systematic refusal of

---

[7] Informed consent procedures are sometimes incorporated into systems of accountability, but generally play only a minor role.

trust – e.g., adopting an attitude of undifferentiated cynicism – does not truly eliminate trust, and has enormous costs.[8]

Intelligent trust is differentiated

A lot of current discussion of the supposed 'crisis of trust' ignores the possibility of placing trust intelligently, in ways that are sensitive to available evidence. For example, it may depict trust in doctors, scientists or others as intrinsically unintelligent, as a mere matter of attitude or affect,[9] as gullible or deferential, and, at the limit, as blind. If trust were invariably unintelligent in these and similar ways, there would indeed be little reason to trust. Blind trust may be placed in untrustworthy claims and untrustworthy commitments, and may expose those who place it to risk, harm and injury. But there is little reason to assume that trust always has to be placed without evidence of trustworthiness, or that trusting is invariably foolish. Good reasons for rejecting blind trust are not good reasons for rejecting intelligent trust.

[8] Philosophers have, for many centuries, enjoyed toying with (and bewitching their students with) the idea of radical mistrust. Descartes' 'method of doubt' is a classic example of a thought experiment in systematic mistrust. Descartes tries to secure a trust-free epistemology, one that does not require trust in the authority or expertise of others, and that will even survive a general mistrust of our senses (e.g., see Rule III of 'Rules for the Direction of our Native Intelligence', in *Selected Philosophical Writings*, ed. and trans. J. Cottingham, R. Stoothoff and D. Murdoch, (Cambridge: Cambridge University Press, 1988). By pulling away the scaffolding of trust, however, Descartes is left high and dry with the claim that a thinking thing exists: the one claim that he thinks has its trustworthiness – or *certainty* – 'built in'. His subsequent arguments to reinstate a divine guarantee of the general reliability of our epistemic capacities have won little support.

[9] Trust is often seen by sociologists as a social attitude that reflects intermediate institutions and social rather than individual virtues. See Francis Fukuyama, *Trust: The Social Virtues and the Creation of Prosperity* (New York: Free Press, 1995), especially Ch. 2, 'The Idea of Trust'; Robert Putnam 'Bowling alone: America's declining social capital', *The Journal of Democracy* 6 (1995), 65–78; *Bowling Alone: The Collapse and Revival of American Community* (New York: Simon & Schuster, 2000). For congruent philosophical views that see trust primarily as an individual attitude, that incorporates good will, see Annette Baier, 'Trust and Anti-Trust', *Ethics* 96 (1986), 231–60; and 'Trust', *Tanner Lectures on Human Values*, vol. 13 (Salt Lake City: University of Utah Press, 1991), available at http://www.tannerlectures.utah.edu/abcd.html; and Karen Jones, 'Trust as an Affective Attitude', *Ethics* 107 (1996), 4–25. For an alternative view that stresses epistemic conditions for trust see Richard Holton, 'Deciding to Trust, Coming to Believe', *Australasian Journal of Philosophy* 72 (1994), 63–76.

Since intelligent trust aims to track trustworthiness, it must be responsive to specific evidence for the truth of *certain* claims or the reliability of *certain* commitments. We may trust – or alternatively mistrust – A's claim that *p*; we may trust – or alternatively mistrust – B's commitment to do *x*. Anyone who seeks to place and refuse trust intelligently must try to discriminate the various claims and commitments that agents make. I may trust a genetic diagnosis if it is based on reputable tests and upon a thorough consideration of clinical evidence and family history, but not if it is based on quirky views of heredity. I may trust a hospital clinic to keep my 11.00 a.m. appointment, but probably will not trust them to keep it to the minute. The discrimination with which we place and refuse trust is also important in confidential relationships. We may trust a banker not to reveal details of our financial affairs, but be unsure whether she will reveal personal information disclosed in a social setting (even bankers may be gossips).[10]

---

[10] Trust is not only directed at many objects, and focused in various ways, but may reflect varied reasons. For example, S, may trust T, to perform some task *x* and to refrain from doing *y* for any of the following reasons:

(a) S believes that T has strategic reasons to do *x* and refrain from doing *y*;
(b) S believes that T has prudential reasons to keep S's trust;
(c) S believes that T's occupation/role makes it likely that T is reliable about doing *x* and refraining from *y*;
(d) S believes that T values what S values;
(e) S believes that T is too stupid to seize the opportunity to do *y*;
(f) S believes that T's actions will be monitored and checked by a truly reliable third party, X;
(g) S believes that T has been trustworthy in the past;
(h) S believes that T is endorsed by X as trustworthy, and S has further reasons for trusting X;
(i) S believes that *x* is the morally correct thing to do and believes that T is a morally worthy person.

At a more abstract level, in each case, S believes that T is 'bound' to the doing of *x* and refraining from *y*. The abstract element these examples have in common may be thought of as a *fiduciary binding factor*. When we are deliberating about whether to trust someone, we need to determine whether there are any fiduciary binding factors that will 'bind' them to act in certain ways but not in others. The variety of such reasons makes it plain that systems of accountability are not the only way of providing reason to trust.

Since evidence for the truth of specific claims and the reliability of specific commitments is highly differentiated, it would be astonishing if we had reason to place a uniform level of trust in every claim or commitment a given individual makes. It would be even more astonishing if we had reason to place a uniform level of trust in everything said by all those holding some type of office or role (e.g., doctors, nurses, scientists), or in every commitment they make. Public opinion pollsters who ask undifferentiated questions such as 'Do you trust doctors (nurses, scientists) to tell the truth?' assume – and do not show – that trust is unintelligent and undifferentiated, hence unrelated to evidence.[11] Their questions take it that respondents will have a single level of trust in *all* the claims and commitments made by *types* of agents. Yet the only intelligent answers any respondent could give to these undifferentiated questions would have to take the form 'I trust some (but not other) claims and commitments made by some (but not other) doctors (nurses, scientists)'.

Questions that are framed on the assumption that trust must be blind, undifferentiated trust (and mistrust blind, undifferentiated mistrust) are likely to ignore the discrimination and judgement that intelligent placing and refusal of trust requires. It is hardly surprising that if questions are framed on the assumption that no evidence differentiates the various claims and commitments made by agents of a given type, respondents are driven to equally undifferentiated replies. They are in effect asked to choose between blind credulity and equally blind suspicion or cynicism. Neither invitation is particularly appealing. We cannot

---

[11] For example, a MORI poll in February 2000 on the public's 'confidence' in doctors (post-Shipman), asked: 'For each of these different types of people would you tell me if you generally trust them to tell the truth, or not?' Eighty-seven per cent of those asked (2,072 adults) answered that they would trust doctors to tell the truth, compared with 21 per cent for government ministers and a mere 15 per cent for journalists (are we to assume that people don't trust journalists to tell them football results or is it restaurant reviewers that we do not trust?). See MORI website 'Public Still Regards Doctors As The Most Trustworthy Group', http://www.mori.com/polls/2000/bma2000.shtml.

reach reliable views of levels of trust, or of changes in levels of trust, on the basis of aggregating responses to such unintelligent questions.[12]

If we cannot but place or refuse trust, we have every reason both to secure and encourage trustworthiness, and to find practical ways of distinguishing trustworthy from untrustworthy claims and commitments. This is a complicated task in contemporary societies, where we cannot rely wholly or mainly on the testimony and claims of others whose reputations for truth telling and reliability are familiar to us. We often have to rely on more indirect ways of securing trustworthiness and of obtaining evidence of trustworthiness. This is why accountability matters for us. Systems of accountability do not offer an alternative to trust, but they can improve trustworthiness, and can provide useful evidence for placing trust intelligently. Good systems of accountability should do both. They should incentivise and promote trustworthy claims and commitments, and they should make it easier for those who need to decide whether to place or refuse trust to distinguish true from false claims, and reliable from unreliable commitments. At their best, systems of accountability should make placing trust intelligently easier not only for experts and office holders, but for all who may have reason to place or refuse trust in the words and action of individuals and of institutions.

Systems of accountability are highly varied, but they have a common formal structure. They are used to define, assign and help enforce *second-order obligations* to account for the performance (or non-performance) of *primary* or *first-order tasks or obligations*. For example, employees, students and companies have both primary

---

[12] Opinion polls offer good evidence of attitudes – but no more. This is clear from the ways in which people rely on the very types of professional they claim to mistrust: their mistrust is a matter of attitude rather than displayed in action. Most of those who mistrust doctors seek their services – and many of those who mistrust journalists believe many of their claims.

tasks and obligations, and second-order obligations to account for the way they meet their primary obligations. Those who hold them to account also have second-order obligations to see that others discharge their primary obligations. An employee may be held to account by appraising how well she has done her job; a student may be held to account by examining how well he has mastered course material; a business may be held to account by auditing and publishing its accounts. Each of them also has second-order obligations to account for their performance of those primary tasks or obligations, and others have second-order obligations to hold them to account. In speaking of obligations to account for one's performance, or to hold others to account for their performance as *second-order* obligations, we mean simply that these obligations *refer to* the relevant primary obligations. The second-order obligations that make up a system of accountability remain wholly indeterminate until primary obligations are specified. Putting matters quite generally, accountability is achieved when obligation-bearers also have – and meet – second-order obligations to account for their performance of their primary obligations to others, who in turn have second-order obligations to hold them to account for that performance. Accountability is always second-order, and always presupposes that those who are to be held to account have adequately specified, internally coherent and feasible sets of primary obligations. (See the appendix to this chapter for a more explicit and detailed exposition of the formal structure of systems of accountability.)

In other respects systems of accountability vary greatly. They may be democratic or corporate, bureaucratic or professional, collegiate or military, managerial or regulatory, and of many other sorts; often accountability is multiple and hybrid. We shall not offer a taxonomy of systems of accountability. However, we note that accountability can have many purposes. Traditionally the most common purposes were to ensure *proper use of funds* and *proper process*. But systems of accountability are also often used for wider purposes such as *controlling* others, *censuring* or *sanctioning* poor performance, *rewarding* good performance, providing *redress* for those short-changed by poor performance and *ranking* the performance of different agents or institutions (the latter may be needed to determine the allocation of scarce goods such as employment, promotion or funding). However, behind this variety there is a common structure and a common aim. Systems of accountability establish second-order obligations (to render an account of performance; to hold to account for that performance) with the aim of securing trustworthy performance. They may or may not have the secondary aim of supporting the intelligent placing and refusal of trust.

ACCOUNTABILITY, TRUSTWORTHINESS AND TRUST IN BIOMEDICINE

In the UK, as elsewhere, demands for accountability have mushroomed. Systems of accountability are more numerous, detailed, intrusive, expensive and sophisticated than they were twenty or thirty years ago.[13] Nowhere is this more evident than in the growth of accountability requirements for medicine and biomedical research. If accountability supports rather than replaces trustworthiness and trust, we might expect these changes to have increased levels of trustworthiness, of trust or of both. But this has not happened. Trustworthiness is constantly questioned by pointing to cases of actual, presumed or possible medical or scientific dereliction.[14] And trust is widely thought to have

---

[13] Michael Moran, *The British Regulatory State: High Modernism and Hyper-innovation* (Oxford: Oxford University Press, 2003).

[14] There is a great deal of media coverage of untrustworthy action by individual clinicians (from Shipman down to local hospital errors), and widespread suspicion of the motivation and activity of researchers and those who fund and employ them. Public debates about the proper remedies initially advocated greater *public understanding of science*, subsequently greater *public engagement with science*, and most recently greater *public engagement with science policy and science funding* (so-called *'upstream engagement'*). For a summary of the stages of this debate in the UK and references to the relevant reports see references in note 12, p. 143 and http://www.foundation.org.uk/pdf18/fst18_8.pdf.

declined.[15] Although the decline in reported trust in GPs and nurses is slight, decline in reported trust in 'hospital doctors' and scientists, and in other professions, is larger. And there is considerable reported public mistrust of genetics, and of the use, or potential future use, of genetic information and genetic technologies.[16] The coincidence of supposedly rising standards for accountability with supposed declines in trustworthiness and in trust might have various causes. For example, it might reflect reliance on inadequate conceptions of accountability, or inadequate ways of providing evidence to those whose trust is sought.

Different approaches to accountability may be more or less useful for different purposes. Some may be particularly well designed to control the performance of those held to account; some to incentivise maximal, or reliable, performance of primary tasks; some for penalising inadequate performance or deterring risk-taking. Those who hold others to account can have a wide range of purposes: they may be concerned with the bottom line, with the quality of work done, with avoiding failure, or with ranking performance.

We shall illustrate some of these differences by contrasting two specific approaches to accountability with contrasting strengths and weakness. The two approaches are respectively *managerial* and *professional*. Each plays a large part in discussions of accountability in medicine and in biomedical research. Each takes a distinctive approach to issues that arise in placing trust under conditions of

---

[15] The evidence is not uniform. Much of it is taken from public opinion polls, which (as noted in the second section, 'Placing and Refusing Trust Intelligently') mainly seek answers to undifferentiated questions, which, in turn, invite undifferentiated responses, and so may offer evidence only that blind trust has declined. These polls suggest that in the UK trust in technologies for genetic modification is low; trust in clinical genetics rather greater; and trust in forensic uses of genetic technologies and information often quite high.

[16] See Parliamentary Office of Science and Technology, *The 'Great GM Food Debate': A Survey of Media Coverage in the First Half of* 1999 (May 2000), 138; see also MORI and The Human Genetics Commission, *Public Attitudes to Human Genetic Information* (2001), http://www.hgc.gov.uk/business_publications_morigeneticattitudes.pdf; and the US Genetics and Public Policy Center Report, *Reproductive Genetic Testing: What America Thinks* (2004).

informational asymmetry and power. We concentrate on these particular forms of accountability and neglect others because they are much used and have been at the centre of controversy.

The critique of medical paternalism that underlies the bioethics of the last twenty-five years, like the continuing critique of science and scientists (and in particular of genetics and genetic technologies) that has emerged in the last fifteen years, highlights the asymmetric relations between experts and others. Doctors know more than their patients. They are also more powerful than individual patients, who need their doctor more than doctors need any individual patient. This asymmetry may have been slightly reduced by the rise of the 'expert patient', by the availability of greater information for patients on the internet and by the rise of patient support groups. However, we take it as read that asymmetric knowledge and power persist and will persist in medical practice. Equally, biomedical scientists know more about their areas of research than their research subjects. Indeed, the knowledge gap between researchers and research subjects may be greater than that between doctors and patients, and particularly great in highly complex investigations and innovations such as those based on genetics or genetic technologies. However, the asymmetry of power may sometimes be less: researchers sometimes need the participation of volunteers more than any volunteer needs to participate in research. In both areas, however, there is a large gap between the knowledge of experts and that of typical patients and research subjects. The reality of this gap makes the task of constructing serious systems of accountability for experts a demanding one.

Traditional approaches relied on forms of professional accountability: professional bodies aimed to ensure that their members were sufficiently competent and sufficiently upright to provide trustworthy service. Competence was secured – and still is secured – by requiring qualifications for professional practice. Upright performance was secured by informal and cultural means, backed by (sometimes inadequate) sanctions for unacceptable performance. Professional approaches to accountability have one distinctive merit, and one distinctive defect. The distinctive merit is that professionals who hold other professionals to account understand what it takes to meet the relevant primary obligations. They can make complex and accurate judgements about professional competence and about standards of performance. The defect is that professionals may be too close to fellow professionals to hold them to account rigorously, and may do too little to ensure that standards are met. They may make *insider*, rather than *independent*, judgements of levels of performance. Professional accountability, in short, is *informed* but not *independent*. As is well known, professional accountability has been widely criticised for masking professional cosiness, professional capture and, at worst, professional corruption.[17]

In many developed societies, and in particular in the UK, professional self-regulation has now been subordinated to external regulation and management of professionals, and professional accountability has been replaced by increasingly demanding forms of managerial accountability. This deep social transformation addresses the core accusation that professional accountability permits experts to police experts, and so relies on insider rather than independent judgement. Managerial accountability is intended to remedy these defects by ensuring that institutions and the professionals whom they employ – including doctors and scientists – are accountable to a range of external and non-expert bodies – including government departments and agencies, regulators, inspectors, examiners or funders. This has become the standard practice of an 'audit society'.[18]

This view of changing systems of accountability is accurate enough, but may provide less to celebrate than its advocates claim. The forms of managerial accountability that have been widely introduced also have unwelcome effects. The portmanteau term 'managerial accountability' encapsulates the difficulty: management and accountability are quite different matters, and their combination is problematic. In general, management is *downwards* and *prospective*,

---

[17] For evidence see Michael Moran, *The British Regulatory State*.

[18] Michael Power, *The Audit Explosion* (London: Demos, 1994), and *The Audit Society: Rituals of Verification* (Oxford: Oxford University Press, 1997).

but accountability is *upwards* and *retrospective*. In business, managers manage the workforce and the work prospectively, but are retrospectively accountable to a board and to shareholders, whom they do not manage. In universities, heads of department manage a range of academic activities within the units they head, but are retrospectively accountable to a university council and to funding bodies, whom they do not manage. In schools, head teachers manage the staff and work of a school, but are retrospectively accountable to governors and education authorities, whom they do not manage. In the UK, NHS hospital trusts – those who manage the delivery of clinical services – are retrospectively accountable to the trust board and through it to a range of external bodies, whom they do not manage.

However, the currently fashionable managerial systems of accountability conflate management and accountability. They use the methods of management to discharge the task of holding to account. The very means that are used prospectively to secure performance of tasks are re-used retrospectively to hold to account those who carried – or failed to carry – out those tasks. For example, professionals and institutions may be managed by setting them objectives and targets, and then held to account by judging perform-ance against these targets, rewarding good performance and sanc-tioning poor performance. A managerial approach to accountability makes good sense where those who manage others (prospectively) later hold them to account (retrospectively), using the same meas-ures of performance for both tasks. It makes much less sense if those who hold to account *but do not manage* try to set detailed managerial targets in order to provide themselves with convenient and uniform measures by which to hold others to account. Yet this bizarre form of managerial accountability at a distance is now quite common.

Managerial approaches to accountability are now used far beyond the confines of a given professional setting or institution and its management. The reasons given for doing so are simple. Managerial approaches to accountability are thought to prevent insiders from judging their colleagues' performance in undemanding ways. It confronts problems of professional cosiness and capture head on, by ensuring that professional work is not merely accountable to, but in many respects managed or controlled by, external bodies who may be at considerable distance from the work. This form of *management-at-a-distance* secures independent judgement of performance of primary obligations, but at high cost. For it undermines – or perhaps overrides – the managerial responsibility of those who actually are supposed to manage, and may end up holding them to account for 'succeeding' in meeting standards set without adequate attention to *professionally informed judgement* of quality of performance. This conflation of management with accountability can create requirements to 'perform' to standards that are counterproductive and which undermine high-quality professional work.

Managerial forms of accountability might nevertheless work for complex professional tasks if it were possible to agree on salient measures of adequate performance that could provide a basis both for managing and for holding to account. However, professional tasks do not always have a well-defined set of simple and easily measurable outcomes that provide a basis both for managing and for holding to account. That is why it was traditionally assumed that informed (expert, professional) judgement was essential for holding those with complex primary obligations to account. Yet once management and accountability are merged, targets will often be simplified so that they can be used to control professional action and to reduce the influence of professional judgement. For example, because managerial approaches to accountability aim to marginalise professional judgement, they typically focus on relatively simple surrogate *indicators* of performance, which can be easily defined and measured, rather than on informed, professional evaluation of the performance of primary obligations. Surgeons may be judged by success rates (regardless of patient mix); hospitals by waiting times for non-urgent surgery (regardless of circumstances); schools by the number of A to C exam marks at GCSE (regardless of subject mix).[19]

---

[19] Reliance on over-simple performance indicators, and over-complex regimes of accountability that use them, is widely criticised, even by those who enforce them, who now commonly pay lip-service to 'lighter touch regulation'. The criticisms are well articulated in the work of the *Better Regulation Commission,* formerly the *Better Regulation Task Force,* which advises the UK government on action intended to

Reliance on simplified *performance indicators* supposedly has a number of merits: it is said to be cheap and objective; it is said to provide a clear ranking of the performance of different individuals and institutions. Supposedly it can be complemented by requirements for transparency (to which we turn below), and so offers the inexpert – both affected individuals and the public at large – a means to judge performance. However, these supposed merits will be illusory unless performance indicators *actually* provide reliable measures of quality of performance. Unfortunately this is often in doubt, for two basic reasons. First, there are sometimes no reliable and simple indicators of quality of performance for complex tasks. Good performance of complex primary obligations may not be readily measurable by simple indicators. Second, even when a performance indicator offers a reasonably useful measure of some aspect of performance, its use may create perverse incentives to concentrate on that aspect of performance at the expense of others, and to pursue high 'scores' on the salient indicators (the so-called 'key performance indicators') rather than good performance. The costs of marginalising informed judgement can be high.

But can judgement be both informed and independent? If we insist on extreme conceptions of these two requirements, they will be incompatible. For example, if we deem anybody who has trained as a pathologist, a psychiatrist or a pharmacist as *ipso facto* incapable of independent judgement of performance in these fields, we will have boxed ourselves into a position in which we see insider judgement as the price of informed judgement. Equally, if we deem all outsiders as *ipso facto* incompetent to make an informed judgement of performance, we box ourselves into a position in which we have to accept ignorant judgement as the price of independent judgement.

But generally we are not so stupid. It is typically not impossible to find outsiders with the necessary competence or expertise, and to

make regulation and its enforcement accord with 'the five Principles of Good Regulation', which it identifies as *Proportionality, Accountability, Consistency, Transparency and Targeting*. See http://www.brc.gov.uk/. Unfortunately, lively debate is not the same thing as lively progress towards better regulation.

provide institutional support for their independence. A considerable degree of independence is achieved by school examiners who do not teach the pupils they examine; by university examiners who work for other universities; by health and safety inspectors who are not employed by the companies they inspect; by auditors who are barred from selling further services to those whom they audit. Medical and scientific practice can achieve similar, or better, standards. Methods for securing the independence of those who hold to account in some areas of professional life may need improving: but improvement is neither impossible nor obscure. A large range of measures, including those set out in successive reports of the *Committee on Conduct in Public Life* (originally the Nolan Committee), are relevant.[20]

If we drop the artificial pretence that expertise and independence are intrinsically incompatible, we can aim for forms of accountability that combine informed and independent judgement. Professional cosiness, laxness and impropriety can be limited by robust institutional measures to secure independence.[21] Such measures may include rigorous certification of competence to practice, proper appointment processes and measures to bear down on lax professional practice or casual approaches to failure. In each activity, accountability for good practice can combine *informed* with *independent* judgement.

So if we want serious and intelligent accountability we can *neither* turn our backs on professionalism and expertise *nor* rely on cosy, unmonitored professionalism, in which conflicts of interest persist unchallenged and professional solidarities swamp the needs of those whom professionals are meant to serve. But there is no forced choice. It is possible to support and maintain robust and expert ways of monitoring standards, investigating failure, disciplining the slipshod

---

[20] See http://www.public-standards.gov.uk/.

[21] The 2002 Enron scandal illustrates the dangers of ignoring these standards. Although not all issues have been resolved in the courts, it appears in 2005 that Arthur Andersen, Enron's auditors, may not have been adequately independent of the corporation whose accounts they audited, and may have provided a 'soft' audit. The US *Sarbanes-Oxley Act 2002* subsequently tightened US standards for company accounting and auditing.

and removing the incompetent. To achieve these standards some professions and organisations may need to change, and all will need to demonstrate that they have effective procedures in place for securing independent judgement. There may be good reasons to include 'lay' voices in processes by which poor performance is judged, to limit periods of accreditation by requiring continuous professional development, to require and make public declarations of interest and to require those with conflicts of interest to stand down.

This sort of attention to securing the real institutional conditions for informed and independent judgement can do more for trust-worthy performance than any reliance either on purely professional or on wholly managerial accountability can achieve in isolation. However, trustworthy performance will not be enough for those who seek to place or refuse trust intelligently, unless they are able find evidence for trustworthiness.

ACCOUNTABILITY WITH TRANSPARENCY

Systems of accountability may secure or support trustworthiness, yet still fail to provide others with the evidence they need to place and refuse trust intelligently. Merely *knowing* that professionals and institutions are generally held to account may not provide any individual, or the public at large, with an adequate basis for placing and refusing trust in particular claims or commitments.[22] Many people cannot or do not read auditors', inspectors' or examiners' reports, or institutional reports and company accounts. Sometimes such reports are not made public; sometimes they are public but hard to find; and sometimes they can be found but are hard to follow. From the public's point of view, the reports that emerge from some systems of accountability may seem arcane. Some members of the public may be sceptical of the very idea of accountability – however

---

[22] However, sometimes knowing that there is a system of accountability may be enough for 'fiduciary binding'. For example, if I know that you are held account-able (not to me, but to some other party) I may take that as evidence that you can be relied upon, at least for the activities for which you are held accountable.

expert, however independent. They may respond to organised evidence with an added worry that 'they're all in it together'; the very fact that information is presented in a detailed, meticulous way, may trigger a thought that 'they are trying to cover things up with all these figures'. Even if the same material is presented in simplified form, such as rankings and league tables, a suspicious person may simply conclude that this is only 'presentation' or 'spin'.

The most common proposal for making evidence more available to members of the public is that institutions and professionals should be *transparent* or *open* about their activities. *Transparency* or *openness* is supposed to improve trustworthiness by exposing misleading claims or failing performance and by creating incentives for institutions and office-holders to be trustworthy, thereby discouraging attempts to play upon others' gullibility in order to gain an unearned reputation for trustworthiness.[23] An expectation of disclosure creates clear incentives for proper behaviour. But *by itself* transparency does not provide the evidence that is needed to support the intelligent placing and refusal of trust. Since transparency is only a matter of disclosure or dissemination, it may limit secrecy, yet fail to ensure successful communicative transactions with others, including, in particular, communication with others for whom a decision to place or refuse trust may be important. Transparency requirements can be satisfied by limited and partial disclosure of material, which is neither accessible to, nor assessable by, supposed audiences.[24]

Throughout this book we have drawn attention to the costs of taking a one-sided view of communication. We suggested that the conduit/container metaphors that underlie many discussions of communication downplay agency and its normative context, by casting communication merely as the 'transfer', 'conveyance' or 'disclosure'

---

[23] The international NGO *Transparency International*, founded in 1993, now with chapters in eighty-five countries, views transparency as a way of combating untrustworthiness, and in particular corruption. See http://www.transparency.org/.

[24] For a more systematic account see Onora O'Neill, 'Transparency and the Ethics of Communication', in *Transparency: The Key to Better Governance?* eds. David Heald and Christopher Hood, *Proceedings of the British Academy* 135 (Oxford: Oxford University Press, 2006), pp. 75–90.

of determinate 'items' of 'stuff' ('ideas'; 'content'; 'messages' etc.). We have pointed out various damaging effects of thinking about information and communication in these ways, in particular the ways in which they shape thinking about informed consent, 'personal information', 'informational privacy' and 'genetic privacy'.

However, the conduit/container model can also distort accounts of uses of information that is not personal or private. Similar deficiencies arise when *non-personal* information – such as information about the trustworthiness of institutions and professionals – is *disclosed* or *disseminated* to meet requirements for transparency. On the conduit/container model of information transfer, non-personal information is seen as material for dissemination, and dissemination is equated with placing material in the public domain – which can often be done by the click of a mouse. Yet, material that is disseminated in this way may not reach any relevant audience: it may achieve even less than disclosure, which is at least directed towards some specific audience. Even if disseminated material reaches some audience, it may not be tailored to their capacities, with the result that they may not understand it or grasp its relevance to judging others' truth-claims and commitments. Those to whom material is disseminated may be unable to use the information they acquire as part of a reasoned basis for placing or refusing trust.[25] Transparency sets too *low* a standard for communicating the evidence that others need if they are to place and refuse trust well. Transparent dissemination need not be audience-sensitive; it need not meet epistemic or ethical standards; it need not lead to successful communicative transactions; it need not be open to others' queries, checks or challenges. In consequence it need not, and often does not, support the intelligent placing and refusal of trust. The mere fact that arcane requirements for disclosure and dissemination have been imposed on those performing complex tasks – even if widely known – offers a

---

[25] Some disclosed evidence – e.g., rankings and league tables – may reach very large audiences and may seem simple enough. After all, it is not hard to see who comes 'top' or 'bottom'. Yet interpreting this sort of information and setting it in context may be surprisingly difficult.

slender basis for deciding where to place or to refuse trust. Only those who can make a second-order judgement that performance has been subjected to a form of independent scrutiny in which they have some trust will be able to transfer some of that trust to those who have been scrutinised and held to account.

We have suggested that an agency model of communication provides a better basis for thinking about informational obligations and rights, including second-order informational obligations such as duties of confidentiality. That model also has advantages for those who seek to place and refuse trust intelligently. Where agents and institutions enter into communicative transactions with others, they open themselves to epistemic and ethical assessment. Interlocutors can investigate truth-claims, or challenge commitments. A process of checking and challenging may allow them to detect forms of epistemic and ethical failure. They may bring to light others' ignorance or dishonesty, or the unreliability of their commitments. When this can be done, the basis for placing or refusing trust becomes clearer.

We have argued that trust is ineliminable in human affairs, yet that it cannot be intelligently placed unless evidence that is relevant to placing and refusing trust is made available. Systems of accountability are important for collecting or recording relevant evidence available, but they do not ensure that the evidence is made available to those who may most need to place or refuse trust. Unless those who hold others to account are informed, unless they judge matters independently and unless they communicate intelligibly to relevant, specific audiences, accountability may do little to support trust, or to resolve a 'crisis' of trust. Speech acts that need not engage with audiences – such as *disclosing, distributing, disseminating*, or even *publishing* – do not provide enough for those who seek to place or refuse trust. Such speech acts may not secure comprehension, uptake or assimilation. Augmenting accountability with the fashionable ideal of transparency avoids secrecy and repudiates the cosy world of insider accounting and self-certification: it is important for trustworthiness. But, transparency does not offer an adequate basis for placing or refusing trust intelligently. It supports a world of one-sided and defective communication that may dissolve rather than help build trust. By contrast, genuine communication supports a world in which judgements about accountability can be made, and in which trust can be intelligently placed and refused.

APPENDIX: THE STRUCTURE OF ACCOUNTABILITY

The starting point for any system of accountability is an accurate view of the relevant primary tasks or obligations. Accountability always begins with *first-order* normative claims about action that ought to be done, of the form:

1. *X ought to be done.*

However, normative claims or obligations are vestigial without identifiable agents who ought to do what ought to be done. So a more perspicuous rendering of the basic normative structures on which all systems of accountability build has the form:

2. *X ought to be done by A.*

In some, but not in all, cases the performance of primary tasks or obligations is claimable by a right-holder, and in those cases the structure of the underlying, primary normative relations can be more completely expressed as:

3. *X ought to be done by A, and B has a right to X being done by A.*

Accountability adds a range of *second-order* normative claims or obligations to the primary normative requirements that specify first-order obligations (and rights). The structure of any form of account-ability can be rendered most simply as:

4. *X ought to be done by A, B has a right to X being done by A, and A is accountable (alternatively: answerable) to C for doing X.*[26]

---

[26] As a special case of 4., obligation-bearers are sometimes accountable for their performance to those who hold the counterpart rights:
  4*. *X ought to be done by A, B has a right to X being done by A, and A is accountable to B for doing X.* However, since right-holders may be unavailable, incompetent, intimidated or partisan, such forms of 'private justice' risk revenge and vendettas. This approach to accountability fell from favour a long time ago, although it still

This can be made more explicit by distinguishing those aspects of accountability that consist of obligations to *render an account* of performance of primary obligations and those that consist of obligations to *hold to account* for performance of those primary obligations. Accountability is a complex normative relation between at least two (and often more) parties. Where A is accountable to C, A has a second-order obligation to *render* an account of performance of A's first-order obligations to C, and C has a second-order obligation to hold A to account for (non-) performance of those first-order obligations.

Setting this out schematically we have:

4*. *X ought to be done by A; B has a right to X being done by A; A has a further obligation to render an account of success or failure in doing X to C; C has an obligation to hold A to account for success or failure in doing X.*

Obligation-bearers are seen as *accountable* (alternatively: *answerable*) for their (non-) performance when they have second-order obligations to render an account of their (non-) performance to others, who have corresponding second-order obligations to hold them to account for their (non-) performance of those primary obligations. Generalising these points, since in any complex activity or institution there are *many* required act types, *many* obligation-bearers, *many* right-holders and *many* agents and/or institutions to whom obligation-bearers may be accountable, the structure of *a system of accountability* has the form:

5. $X_1 \ldots X_n$ *ought to be done by the relevant As; the relevant Bs have rights to $X_1 \ldots X_n$ being done by the relevant As; the relevant As are accountable to the relevant Cs for doing $X_1 \ldots X_n$; and the relevant Cs ought to hold the relevant As to account for doing $X_1 \ldots X_n$.*

sometimes surfaces, for example, in suggestions that victims should play a part in determining sentences. Usually accountability is 'socialised' by appointing third parties – the courts, professionals, inspectors, regulators – to carry second-order obligations to hold to account.

Some conclusions and proposals

Informed consent is the most discussed, indeed the most hackneyed, theme in bioethics. Yet many widely accepted accounts of informed consent are riddled with problems. They offer justifications that are less than convincing, and set standards that are less than feasible. In this book we have proposed a new way of thinking about informed consent. We believe that our approach offers a more convincing account of informed consent, of reasons why it matters and of standards it should meet.

We looked first at widely accepted accounts of informed consent requirements, and found that they typically propose exaggerated and impractical standards. Unsurprisingly these standards are routinely flouted and ignored in biomedical practice. While some 'failures' arise because clinicians and researchers do not live up to standards that they could have met, many arise because the standards advocated propose – or presuppose – inaccurate, excessive or even impossible views of informing and consenting. We identified three possible responses to these mismatches between aspirations and realities.

The first response would be to look for lower, more practicable, standards that could be satisfied either by current practices, or by making feasible changes in those practices. The second would be to reaffirm current standards and continue with current clinical and research practices, in the full knowledge that practice and standards diverge, and that there is no prospect of patching matters up by introducing a few favoured 'improvements'. We thought that lowering standards and systematic hypocrisy were both unattractive options, and so chose to rethink informed consent in a more radical and systematic way.

INFORMED CONSENT AND EPISTEMIC NORMS

Our strategy for rethinking informed consent has been straightforward, although some of the details proved complex and intricate. We started from the thought that informed consent cannot be achieved, so cannot be required, unless it sets feasible standards for those who are to seek, give or refuse consent.

This point may seem trivial and obvious, but is widely ignored. Most discussions of informed consent in bioethics – and beyond – focus rather narrowly on the *disclosure of information* by those who seek consent, and on *decision-making* by those whose consent is sought. This narrow focus ignores or underplays what is actually needed for effective communication and commitments between the parties. Yet tendencies to think about informed consent in terms of 'disclosure for decision-making' are underpinned and supported by a range of deeply entrenched metaphors that shape the way that we tend to think and talk about information and communication. The conduit and container metaphors cast information as a kind of 'stuff' that can be acquired and stored, and can be transferred and conveyed between agents. We argued that these metaphors were not in themselves mistaken, but that they highlight and accentuate some aspects of knowledge and communication by hiding or downplaying others. Disclosure by itself may not reach its intended audience, so may fail to communicate what is proposed, or which commitments are offered; decision-making by itself may fail to communicate whether consent is given or refused or which commitments are assumed in consenting. Our strategy for rethinking informed consent and its relevance to a range of related normative issues in biomedicine began by making the distorting effects of these metaphors explicit, and by showing how they contribute to a partial and inadequate view of communication, and so of informed consent.

A more convincing account of informed consent, we argued, would focus on the communicative transactions by which it is sought, given and refused. Each element of a successful informed consent transaction must meet adequate standards. Informed consent cannot be achieved by communicative transactions that ignore norms of intelligibility and relevance that are essential for effective communication. Even where norms of intelligibility and relevance are respected, and where effective communication is secured, informed consent transactions will still fail unless they respect a wide range of epistemic and ethical norms, including norms of accuracy and honesty. Speech acts that confuse or baffle, that mislead or manipulate, that peddle false or dishonest claims are likely to leave others unable to judge what is claimed and what is offered, what is understood and what is agreed to, and are unlikely to secure informed consent. We concluded that adequate informed consent must be grounded in communication that satisfies a wide range of epistemic and ethical norms. The shift from a thin 'informational' conception of informed consent to a fuller communicative account has numerous implications and corollaries, some of them of great practical importance.

INFORMED CONSENT AND INDIVIDUAL AUTONOMY

Across the last forty years informed consent requirements in bio-medical practice have grown enormously. The scope of these requirements has been extended from medical research to clinical practice, and standards have been prescribed with increasing specificity and (supposed) rigour. The reason most commonly given for the expansion, entrenchment and elaboration of informed consent requirements is that they are needed to secure respect for individual autonomy.

We entirely accept that seeking and giving informed consent displays a *minimal* form of individual autonomy. Those who consent to some action choose that it be done, and might have refused. But the fact that a consented to action is chosen shows very little about reasons for requiring consent for all medical and research interventions. That some act is chosen is, after all, neither necessary nor sufficient to justify doing it. Choice and consent cannot be *necessary* for all medical interventions: some health provision creates public goods, which cannot be varied to suit individual choice. Much treatment is and must be given to patients who cannot take part in epistemically adequate consent transactions. Equally, choice and consent cannot be *sufficient* for medical intervention: many possible interventions are not on offer, so cannot be chosen. Choice may seem at first blush to offer a more plausible standard for permissible research interventions: but here too some 'choices' – such as participation in clinical trials – are poorly understood by many who 'choose' them, and other 'choices' – e.g., variations in research protocols that individuals might prefer – are not on offer. Evidently choice is neither necessary nor sufficient for acceptable medical or research practice, so cannot be required for all biomedical interventions. Yet if choice, manifested by informed consent or refusal, is required only in some cases, we need to understand what distinguishes those cases. Appeals to the claim that informed consent matters because it secures respect for (some version of) individual autonomy seemingly reiterate the claim that informed consent is important, rather than anchoring it. And if weak conceptions of autonomy raise these problems, stronger and more exacting conceptions are likely to raise even greater problems.

A common response to these realities is to hold on to the view that consent is required in order to respect (some version of) individual autonomy, but to accept that (this version of) individual autonomy is only one among a number of important ethical requirements in biomedical practice. On such views, individual autonomy has to be 'balanced' against other important principles, such as beneficence, non-maleficence, justice and others. While this move takes some of the heat off the conceptions of individual autonomy invoked to justify informed consent requirements, it does little to explain why and when informed consent should be required. If autonomy is only one among a range of important standards, perhaps informed consent is not always important? If so, when should it be required and when can it be dispensed with or even overridden? A convincing justification of informed consent should, we believe, answer these questions, and cannot do so merely by appealing to the importance of respecting (some conception of) individual autonomy.

INFORMED CONSENT AS WAIVER

In clinical and research practice, and beyond, informed consent is seen not merely as desirable and important, but as a standard way of avoiding breaches of significant obligations. Consent is ethically important in medical practice where interventions would *otherwise* breach underlying obligations, such as obligations not to assault, coerce, imprison falsely, poison, and so on. Consent provides a way of waiving such obligations and the corresponding rights, in order to avoid their breach; whilst acting without consent simply breaches those obligations and rights. However, little is gained – and a good deal is lost – by subsuming these very strong reasons for seeking informed consent under a blanket heading such as 'respect for individual autonomy'.

A focus on the communicative transactions by which consent is sought, given and refused provides a much clearer view of the reasons why consent is important and of the relation between consent and other significant ethical standards. Informed consent transactions are used to waive other requirements in specific ways and for specific purposes. So informed consent has a role to play only where certain underlying requirements, such as ethical, legal and professional obligations and legitimate expectations of various sorts, are accepted. We did not – sensibly, we think – try to offer any complete or extensive list of the underlying norms, obligations and expectations that can be waived by informed consent. But we pointed out that in medical and research practice they were likely to include very significant ethical, legal, professional and other obligations not to invade others' bodily integrity, not to constrain their liberty of action, not to deceive them and not to violate their privacy, or any rights that correspond to these obligations.

These obligations and expectations are *presupposed* by informed consent practices. When they are waived by giving consent, they are not discarded or marginalised: they are merely waived in limited ways, for a limited time, for a limited purpose. In consenting to an appendectomy I do not consent to other irrelevant incisions, or to incisions by persons other than the relevant surgeon. In consenting to take part in a clinical trial I do not consent to swallow other novel medicines, let alone medicines that are irrelevant to my condition. Informed consent matters because it offers a standard and controllable way of setting aside obligations and prohibitions for limited and specific purposes. There are nearly always good, indeed overwhelming, reasons to maintain and uphold prohibitions on action that may injure, poison or violate bodily integrity, and to uphold requirements not to restrict others' liberty or invade their privacy. But in specific circumstances, patients and others may have good reasons to waive these prohibitions and requirements in limited ways and for limited purposes. That is the point and purpose of informed consent transactions. Informed consent is used where an agent has reason to permit derogation from a significant obligation or expectation that would otherwise be breached; it is prominent in biomedical practice because many medical and research interventions would otherwise breach underlying obligations and expectations. We cannot have medical or research interventions unless we permit limited action that would otherwise constitute a breach of bodily integrity, personal liberty or privacy: informed consent is a way of granting permission for such action. It is not, and certainly not primarily, a way of exercising individual autonomy, however conceived.

We took a parallel approach to the use of informed consent to waive informational obligations. We argued that many informational obligations, including obligations to respect privacy and confidentiality, were not best thought of as obligations that apply to specific types of semantic content, such as 'personal' or 'medical' information. Attempts to subject certain types of information to distinctive requirements and regimes are based on a misconception. Although the conduit and container metaphors make it seem as if information is a quasi-spatial stuff that comes in different types, we argued that this seemingly obvious and innocuous assumption is in fact both suspect and problematic. Types of information cannot be neatly defined and ring-fenced, and it is futile to try to construct obligations that bear directly on types of informational content. Since information is inferentially fertile, there are often many ways in which it can be reached. Rather than construing informational obligations – ranging from obligations to respect privacy, to obligations to maintain confidentiality, to act accountably and to support the placing and refusal of trust – as bearing directly on types of informational or propositional content, we argued that they are better construed as obligations that bear on the speech acts and other epistemic actions by which information is acquired, used and conveyed. Informational obligations apply to communicative transactions, and are distorted if they are seen as bearing solely or primarily upon their informational or propositional content.

PRACTICES AND POLICIES FOR INFORMED CONSENT

Framing discussions of informed consent in this way casts light on a number of debates in bioethics, and has significant practical implications. We point to some changes in approach and in practice that might be feasible and important.

Standards for consenting

Approaching informed consent in the way we propose allows for a differentiated view of standards for consent requirements. Instead of thinking of successful informed consent transactions as all-or-nothing affairs that respect, or alternatively fail to respect, individual autonomy, we focused on the epistemic and other norms that must be met by adequate consent transactions, and upon the reasons for waiving specific underlying obligations in specific cases. This alternative approach offered a realistic basis for distinguishing cases in which informed consent must be more robust and detailed from cases where it may – and often should – be less robust and less detailed.

An uncontroversial example illustrates the point well. Failure to discuss a common complication of a medical procedure and to seek consent for performing the procedure may be not only acceptable, but required in a medical emergency, because taking time to discuss the matter and seek consent would, in effect, set aside even more significant professional and ethical obligations to limit rather than prolong pain and risk. Failure to discuss a similar complication at a routine consultation could be a different matter, since time taken for discussion would not then set aside obligations to limit rather than prolong pain and risk. On the other hand, failure to mention a rare and minor side effect of a prescribed drug may not constitute failure: it is implausible to think that everything can be mentioned, or that patients can attend to every scrap of information that could in theory be made available for their consideration and consent.

We therefore argued against gestural and unrealistic demands that consent be *specific* or *explicit* (still worse, *fully explicit* and *fully specific*) and more generally against demands for uniform standards prescribing the amount or specificity of information to be incorporated in informed consent transactions. We could find no reason for thinking that an ever-more elaborate and prescriptive approach to the ways in which informed consent is sought, given or recorded is ethically required, advisable or even acceptable.

In place of such approaches we developed an approach to informed consent that focuses on the obligations and expectations to be waived, and on the reasons for waiving them in specific cases. We believe that this approach offers advantages. Where medical interventions would not breach significant obligations or expectations – as with much routine medical care – there is no case for elaborate or formalised consent requirements. What is done will either be entirely permissible, creating no need for any waiver of any obligation, or so minimally invasive or intrusive that unrecorded implied consent – perhaps inferred from a patient's seeking an appointment with a doctor or rolling up a sleeve for an injection – is entirely adequate.

There may be a better case for using standardised consent forms in seeking consent to routine treatments that would otherwise breach significant obligations. However, such forms will need to vary with the treatment offered, and it is pointless, and perhaps risky, to seek for a single canonical protocol for all informed consent transactions. Neither standardised nor elaborated consent forms and protocols for treatment or for research will generally guarantee that better or more genuine consent is obtained. On the contrary, their use, and above all their routine use, may encourage an over-casual attitude to the epistemic standards that must be met for adequate informed consent transactions. Such practices may lead to an excessive focus on formalities in place of efforts to ensure the seeking of genuine informed consent.

On standard ways of thinking about informed consent, with an emphasis on disclosure of information in order to secure respect for individual choice, it may seem problematic to argue that medical interventions might be permissible without explicit, proactive, specific informed consent disclosures. It might seem, then, that we are treating informed consent as a trivial matter, or perhaps advocating a 'return to paternalism' in medicine. However, in calling standardised and elaborated consent procedures and forms into question we do not treat informed consent as a trivial matter. Rather the contrary. We think that it is important for those undertaking invasive treatment to attend to the obligations and expectations that would be breached if they proceeded without consent, to the reasons that there may be for a particular intervention, and to the epistemic standards that must be met for adequate informed consent transactions. We concluded that seeking consent by offering a standardised set of boxes to be ticked, forms to be signed and witnessed and lists of countersignatures to be obtained is not ethically required, and can be ethically risky.

The risks that arise from a misplaced emphasis on uniform or over-elaborate consent forms and procedures will not be obvious if we assume that the informed consent is no more than a matter of 'disclosure for decision-making' that enables individual choice, thereby respecting (some conception of) individual autonomy. An excessive emphasis on individual choice does not ensure sufficient attention to the full range of ethical, legal and professional obligations that are important in biomedical practice. It falsely suggests that action of any sort (other than action that provides public goods) could be a matter of choice. It falsely suggests that providing more information will always support better-informed choice. Yet disclosing ever more information in a standardised way risks breaching fundamental epistemic norms, and will not ensure – indeed may obstruct – adherence to underlying ethical norms.

The thought that there need be no uniform procedure for seeking consent in biomedical practice will not surprise – and may encourage! – many clinicians and researchers, patients and research subjects. Consent seeking in biomedical practice is known to be variable and selective, and nobody realistically expects it to be otherwise – although they do expect that there will be no breach of significant underlying obligations and expectations. *In practice*, consent seeking has *always* been selective, and the amount of information provided has *inevitably* been limited. *In practice*, professionals are usually realistic about the limits of effective communication, even if they pay lip service to fashionable demands for ever more complete disclosure of information. *In practice*, patients and research subjects are generally – and sensibly – not keen on receiving more and more technical information than they can put to use, and are adept at making second-order judgements of the reliability and trustworthiness of those who offer medical treatment or invite research participation.

The only parties who may be genuinely opposed to a retreat from the excessive formalisation of informed consent procedures and protocols may be those who value it as a source of evidence that protects them against liability for clinical or scientific malpractice. Yet if boxes ticked and forms signed provide inadequate evidence of epistemically sound informed consent transactions, they do not provide satisfactory evidence that underlying obligations have been waived. Signatures, let alone ticks in boxes, may have *legal* weight, but they lack *ethical* weight, and often do not provide evidentiary weight that genuinely informed consent has been given. It is a further question – which we did not explore – whether routine and formalised indicators of consent should be taken as protection against liability. Should disclosures count as disclaimers if they are epistemically defective informed consent transactions? We must leave this question for another occasion.

Consent and non-competence

Thinking of informed consent as waiving underlying norms also illuminates the unending discussions of informed consent and patient non-competence. When individual autonomy is seen as the sole justification for informed consent practices, there seems to be nothing left when individual capacities fail or falter, either because patients are generally incompetent to consent or because they cannot genuinely consent to specific proposals. But if we see informed consent requirements as the way in which patients and research subjects waive, or refuse to waive, underlying obligations, we can see in outline what matters for non-competent patients.

Non-competent patients are by definition unable to determine for themselves which specific obligations, rights or expectations to waive in specific circumstances. However, there can be just as solid reasons for waiving specific norms, obligations and expectations in their case as in others. Hence those who have to determine whether non-competent patients shall receive medical treatment can and ought to think in entirely parallel terms about waiving obligations, rights and expectations. In appealing to the 'best interests' of the patient they can draw on the very considerations that are relevant when competent patients determine what they will consent to. The threatening disparity between the case of competent and of non-competent patients is reduced, and with it the temptation to think that the central issue in medical ethics is to find ingenious ways for the partially competent to register consent to complex proposals. Rather the central issue is that obligations to those who are non-competent or partially competent should not be waived for reasons that would not be sufficient for a competent patient to waive an obligation in the same way in similar cases. Misuse of paternalism is of course a serious issue, and measures to prevent such misuse are needed: but refusal or denial of treatment for the sake of marginal or missing autonomy is an even more serious one.

Parallel considerations arise in considering whether individuals who cannot consent may legitimately take part in research. Here too, the task is not to find a new way of obtaining consent that is easier for those whose ability to consent is impaired. Rather the task is to ensure that underlying obligations to those with cognitive or other impairments are not waived, unless for reasons that would also be adequate in the case of the fully competent. Cases will differ, and there may be no case for including those who are not competent to consent in research where there are alternatives, or where risks are serious. However, in other cases there may be few alternatives. If the condition for which a drug is being tested renders sufferers incompetent to consent, it may – given proper safeguards – be judged in their interest to be included in a clinical trial despite incapacity to consent.

Consent and information

A third advantage of the approach that we have developed here is that it allows for a more plausible account of obligations not to misuse information that pertains to others. Current conceptions of data protection seek to protect 'personal' data by prohibiting any use other than those specifically authorised by the informed consent of the data subject. This approach to privacy is built on an assumption that all data can be classified exclusively as personal or non-personal: unless this distinction could be drawn, privacy obligations could not be adequately defined on this basis. In a parallel way, advocates of 'genetic exceptionalism' claim that data can be classified exclusively as genetic or non-genetic, and seek to provide special protection for genetic data, and to prohibit any use other than those specifically authorised by the informed consent of the source subject. Again this approach to privacy is built on an assumption that all data can be classified exclusively as genetic or non-genetic: unless this distinction could be drawn, genetic privacy obligations could not be adequately defined on this basis.

We have argued that the background assumptions that underlie these accounts of privacy obligations and privacy rights are incoherent. Although it may not be apparent if we rely on the conduit and container metaphors, all information, including personal and genetic information, is inferentially fertile. Others may come to know something about a person's medical condition or genetic make-up by many different routes, and not all ways of acquiring such knowledge violate obligations to respect privacy. Consequently it is absurd to view the mere *possibility* that others come to know 'personal' or 'genetic' information as a breach of privacy. An adequate account of informational privacy cannot construe it as a right that nobody come to know certain facts, with matching obligations on others not to come to know those facts, since facts may often be inferred from matters entirely in the public domain, or by others with legitimate access to the relevant data. For example, an experienced doctor may infer that somebody seen in a public place suffers from a clinical condition or has a certain genetic characteristic from information that is publicly displayed; twins may infer something about one another's genetic make-up from information to which each has legitimate access. Inferential fertility means that there *cannot* be rights that others' not know certain matters, just as surely as cognitive limitations mean that there cannot be rights to know certain matters. Informational obligations are obligations to undertake – or to refrain from – communicative transactions of certain sorts; informational rights are rights that correspond to obligations to undertake – or refrain from – communicative transactions of certain sorts. They are not and cannot be obligations to ensure that others know or do not know certain matters, any more than informational rights could be rights to know or not to know certain matters.

A 'right to privacy' can therefore at most be a right that others not come to know certain matters by unacceptable epistemic or communicative transactions such as prying in diaries, breaching confidentiality or hacking into medical records. Obligations not to intrude into others' privacy can at most be obligations not to perform intrusive epistemic or communicative acts. It follows, we believe, that the sorts of anonymisation used in biomedical practice should aim to make information *effectively* anonymous to those who do not need to know the identity of a data subject (or of a source subject in cases where the information is embodied in tissue samples). There is no good ethical reason to insist on irreversible anonymisation (delinking; deidentification) of medical and research data, thereby destroying the data linkages that are essential for medical databases, and making many sorts of research impossible. Effective yet potentially reversible anonymisation can secure respect for privacy without undermining the possibility of constructing medical data-bases, of doing public health research or of undertaking secondary data analyses. Potentially reversible anonymisation is also enough to ensure that consulting clinical notes pertaining to past patients and publishing case notes without specific consent does not violate individual privacy. Some of the more exorbitant consent-based forms of privacy protection associated with data protection legislation permit such practices only where it is possible to get prior or retrospective consent to the specific work or use envisaged, or where specific permission is obtained (e.g., from PIAG). We believe that these measures are unnecessary, and that their entrenchment in current legislation and regulation is an aberration rather than a reflection of good ethical standards.

We concluded that respect for privacy is an informational obligation that matters in biomedical practice, but not because medical, personal or genetic data are intrinsically private. Obligations to respect privacy, and many other obligations, matter because there certain things that should not be done with information, or with information acquired in specific ways. Inaccurate information should not be misrepresented as true; information that is imparted in confidence should not be transmitted without consent; information that is intended for a particular audience should be put in ways that are intelligible to that audience, and so on. Taken together these obligations define quite robust informational obligations, including obligations to respect privacy, but are not based on untenable assumptions about the intrinsic privacy of certain sorts of information content. For the same reasons, retrospective research that uses the medical records of non-competent patients without specific consent need not breach any obligations, or violate their privacy. If there are no convincing reasons for prohibiting merely potential violations of privacy in the case of competent patients, as we have argued, there will no convincing case for prohibiting merely potential violations of privacy for non-competent ones. Seeking to prevent actual violations of privacy by legislating to prevent possible violations of privacy is a precaution too far.

Consent and accountability

Obligations to respect privacy are only one of a range of informational obligations that matter for biomedical practice. Some other informational obligations are essential if clinicians and researchers, and the institutions within which they work, are held to account. Professional certification and clinical audit provide well-known and long-established examples of practices in which informational obligations play a central and well-known part. However, many other informational obligations matter in biomedical practice, particularly for ensuring that there is proper professional and institutional accountability.

Accountability is achieved by second-order obligations to others. Those providing medical care typically have second-order obligations to provide information about their performance to others, who, in turn, are subject to second-order obligations to monitor that information, and to use it to hold professionals and institutions to account for their performance. In discharging these (and other) second-order informational obligations both professionals and institutions often have to take account of large amounts of information, including information about the primary tasks for which others are responsible and the standards to which those tasks are carried out.

On the conduit and container model of information and communication, accountability is often said to require the 'transparent' disclosure of information that makes it available to others. Our focus on communicative action and the epistemic standards it must meet stresses obligations to communicate rather than to disclose. Systems of accountability can come in many forms and serve a variety of purposes. As we see it, systems of accountability are well structured when they protect the legitimate interests and expectations of various parties and provide evidence for the intelligent placing and refusal of trust. None of these informational obligations can be discharged without effective communication between the relevant parties, which meets the necessary epistemic norms.

AFTER RETHINKING: THE POSSIBILITY OF CHANGE

Although the details are complex, we believe that the everyday views that practitioners, patients and research subjects take of informed consent, and of the reasons why it matters, are closer to the picture that we have offered than they are to the more fashionable views that we have criticised. We see informed consent as a way in which individuals can waive others' underlying obligations and expectations in specific ways, when they have reason to do so. Informed consent works on the assumption that those individuals and institutions have many underlying obligations, including informational obligations, to others. We cannot understand informed consent, the standards that it must meet, or the limits to its use, without taking that background picture seriously. Nor can we understand it without taking seriously the epistemic norms that must be met by effective communicative transactions. By contrast, the conduit and container model of information and communication, conjoined with the assumption that respect for individual choice or autonomy provides a justification for informed consent practices which can distort and mislead, supports numerous untoward implications and consequences. We believe that our strategy for rethinking informed consent both avoids these distortions and their untoward implications and consequences, and provides a useful and coherent way of thinking about the importance and use of informed consent in biomedical practice.

We realise that implementing the changes for which we have argued would require a massive change of direction in biomedical practice, and in the legislative and regulatory framework in which it is conducted. Some changes and improvements could be instituted piecemeal by medical and scientific institutions and professionals. Others would require action by various parts of government. A few might need better primary legislation, and in particular more coherent legislation for the protection of individual privacy. Philosophical work, we know, can take us only part of the way.

However, it can at least take us part of the way, and there are many things that could be done. In the first place, we could stop trying so hard to travel in the wrong direction. Rather than shouldering the Sisyphean task of subjecting all aspects of biomedical practice to ever more exacting forms of informed consent, or persisting with fruitless endeavours to base all of medical and research ethics on an appeal to individual autonomy, anybody – and any body – whose work bears on biomedical practice *could* seek change. The NHS – and similar healthcare institutions in other countries – *could* stop trying to implement ever more rigorous and numerous informed consent requirements, and *could* remove requirements that are either dysfunctional or unjustifiable (or both). Research Councils and other research funders *could* stop funding work on 'improving' consent procedures to make them fit for unachievable purposes, and *could* stop demanding the use of such procedures where they cannot or need not be used. Manuals for Research Ethics Committees *could* be rewritten to ensure that the point and limits of informed consent and the standards it must meet are clearly set out, and to deter inflationary elaborations of these requirements. Regulators *could* insist that it is communication to relevant audiences rather than disclosure and dissemination that matters. They *could* judge medical and research performance by the quality of the communication achieved, and not by compliance with informed consent protocols whose use cannot be justified. In the UK, medical and scientific institutions *could* open an urgent and unaccommodating dialogue with the Information Commissioner, in the hope of securing agreement on an interpretation of the *Data Protection Act 1998* for biomedical practice that supports justifiable rather than illusory conceptions of privacy (and similar points apply for other jurisdictions with similar data protection legislation). Patient support groups *could* insist on forms of accountability that support rather than undermine the intelligent placing and refusal of trust by patients, and *could* challenge regulatory demands that impose dysfunctional forms of accountability. Both individuals and institutions *could* do more to strengthen and support the parts of government that argue for – but so rarely achieve – 'lighter touch' regulation.

We realise, all too well, that change across a wide spectrum of institutions and practices will need the support and the collaboration of many players. We hope that the arguments we have proposed will be helpful to those who seek change. We hope they will be encouraging to those who have come to suspect that informed consent is not fundamental to good biomedical practice, and that attempts to make it so are neither necessary nor achievable. We hope that the juggernaut of informed consent requirements that has been constructed across the last fifty years will be reformed and reduced within a far shorter period.

Bibliography

Annas, G. J., Glantz, L. H. and Roche, P. A., 1995, 'Drafting the Genetic Privacy Act: Science, Policy, and Practical Considerations', *Journal of Law and Medical Ethics* 23, 360–6.

Annas, G. and Grodin, M., 1992, *The Nazi Doctors and the Nuremberg Code*, Oxford: Oxford University Press.

Anscombe, Elizabeth, 1957, *Intention*, Oxford: Blackwell.

Austin, J. L., 1962, *How to Do Things With Words*, Oxford: Clarendon Press.
  1962, *Collected Philosophical Papers*, Oxford: Clarendon Press.

Baier, Annette, 1986, 'Trust and Anti-Trust', *Ethics*, 96, 231–60.
  1991, 'Trust', *Tanner Lectures on Human Values*, vol. 13, Salt Lake City: University of Utah Press.

Beauchamp, Tom L., and Childress, James F., 1994, *Principles of Biomedical Ethics*, 4th edn, New York: Oxford University Press.

Bennett, Colin J., 1992, *Regulating Privacy: Data Protection and Public Policy in Europe and the United States*, Ithaca, NY: Cornell University Press.

Berg, Paul, and Singer, Maxine, 1992, *Dealing with Genes: The Language of Heredity*, Mill Valley, CA: University Science Books.

Beyleveld, Deryck, and Brownsword, Roger, 2001, *Human Dignity in Bioethics and Biolaw*, Oxford: Oxford University Press.

Blakemore, Colin, 2005, 'Cultivating a thousand flowers', *Journal of the Foundation for Science and Technology*, 18, 10–11.

Brody, B., 1998, *The Ethics of Biomedical Research: an International Perspective*, New York: Oxford University Press.

Brownsword, Roger, 2004, 'The Cult of Consent: Fixation and Fallacy', *King's College Law Journal*, 15, 223–51.

Buchanan, Allen, 1978, 'Medical Paternalism', *Philosophy and Public Affairs*, 7, 70–390.

Burleigh, Michael, 1994, *Death and Deliverance: 'Euthanasia' in Germany, c.1900–1945*, Cambridge: Cambridge University Press.

1997, *Ethics and Extermination: Reflections on Nazi Genocide*, Cambridge: Cambridge University Press.

Burton, Hilary, 2003, *Addressing Genetics Delivering Health: A Strategy for Advancing the Dissemination and Application of Genetics Knowledge Throughout our Health Professionals*, Cambridge: Public Health Genetics Unit.

Callahan, Daniel, 1996, 'Can the Moral Commons Survive Autonomy?', *Hastings Center Report*, 26, 41–2.

Carey, James, 1990, *Communication as Culture*, New York: Routledge.

Carlson, Robert V., Boyd, Kenneth M., and Webb, David J., 2004, 'The Revision of the Declaration of Helsinki: Past, Present and Future', *British Journal of Clinical Pharmacology*, 57, 695–713.

Christman, John, 1988, 'Constructing the Inner Citadel: Recent Work on the Concept of Autonomy', *Ethics*, 99, 109–24.

ed., 1989, *The Inner Citadel: Essays on Individual Autonomy*, New York: Oxford University Press.

Coady, C. A. J., 1992, *Testimony: A Philosophical Study*, Oxford: Clarendon Press.

Cox, K., 2002, 'Informed Consent and Decision-making: Patients' Experiences of the Process of Recruitment to Phases I and II Anti-cancer Drug Trial', *Patient Education and Counselling*, 46 (1), 31–8.

Crick, Francis, 1958, 'On Protein Synthesis', *Symposium of the Society of Experimental Biology*, 12, 138–63.

1970, 'Central Dogma of Molecular Biology', *Nature*, 227, 561–3.

Dalla-Vorgia, P., Lascaratos, J., Skiadia, P., and Garanis-Papadotos, T., 2001, 'Is Consent in Medicine a Concept Only of Modern Times?', *Journal of Medical Ethics*, 27 (1), 59–61.

Dawson, Angus, 2004, 'What Should We Do About It? Implications of the Empirical Evidence in Relation to Comprehension and Acceptability of Randomisation?', in Holm, S. and Jonas, M., eds., *Engaging the World: The Use of Empirical Research in Bioethics and the Regulation of Biotechnology*, Netherlands: IOS Press, pp. 41–52.

Day, Ronald E., 2000, 'The "Conduit Metaphor" and The Nature and Politics of Information Studies', *Journal of the American Society for Information Science*, 9, 805–11.

Descartes, Rene, 1988, *Rules for the Direction of our Native Intelligence*, in *Selected Philosophical Writings*, ed. and trans. Cottingham, J., Stoothoff, R., and Murdoch, D., Cambridge: Cambridge University Press.

Dretske, Fred, 1981, *Knowledge and the Flow of Information*, Cambridge, MA: MIT Press.

Dworkin, Gerald, 1972, 'Paternalism', *The Monist*, 56, 64–84.

Eckstein, Sue, ed., 2003, *Manual for Research Ethics Committees*, 6th edn, Cambridge: Cambridge University Press.

Elster, Jon, 1989, *The Cement of Society: A Study of Social Order*, Cambridge: Cambridge University Press.

Faden, Ruth R., and Beauchamp, Tom L., 1986, *A History and Theory of Informed Consent*, New York: Oxford University Press.

Fiske, John, 1990, *Introduction to Communication Studies*, 2nd edn, London: Routledge.

Fletcher, George P., 1996, *Basic Concepts of Legal Thought*, Oxford: Oxford University Press.

Fukuyama, Francis, 1995, *Trust: The Social Virtues and the Creation of Prosperity*, New York: Free Press.

Geach, Peter, 1965, 'Assertion', *Philosophical Review*, 74, 4, 449–65.

Godard, Raeburn *et al.*, 2003, 'Genetic Information and Testing in Insurance and Employment: Technical, Social and Ethical Issues', *European Journal of Human Genetics* 11, 123–142.

Gostin, L. O., 1995, 'Genetic privacy', *Journal of Law and Medical Ethics*, 23, 320–30.

Griffiths, Anthony J. F., *et al.*, 2000, *An Introduction to Genetic Analysis*, New York: W. H. Freeman.

Griffiths, P. E., and Gray, R. D., 2004, 'Developmental Systems and Evolutionary Explanation', *Journal of Philosophy*, 91, 277–304.

Hardwig, John, 1985, 'Epistemic Dependence', *Journal of Philosophy*, 82, 335–49.
    1991, 'The Role of Trust in Knowledge', *Journal of Philosophy*, 88, 693–708.

Hayes, Brian, 1998, 'The Invention of the Genetic Code', *American Scientist*, 86, 8–14.

Hill, Thomas E., Jnr, 1992, 'The Kantian Conception of Autonomy', in Hill, Thomas E., Jnr, *Dignity and Practical Reason*, Ithaca, NY: Cornell University Press, pp. 76–96.

Holton, Richard, 1994, 'Deciding to Trust, Coming to Believe', *Australasian Journal of Philosophy*, 72, 63–76.

Jones, James H., 1993, *Bad Blood: The Tuskegee Experiment*, New York: Free Press.

Jones, Karen, 1996, 'Trust as an Affective Attitude', *Ethics*, 107, 4–25.

Kant, Immanuel, 1996, *Critique of Practical Reason*, in Kant, Immanuel, *Practical Philosophy*, tr. Gregor, Mary, Cambridge: Cambridge University Press.

Kass, Leonard R., 2002, *Life, Liberty and the Defence of Dignity: The Challenge for Bioethics*, New York: Encounter Books.

Kay, Lily E., 2000, *Who Wrote the Book of Life: A History of the Genetic Code*, Stanford, CA: Stanford University Press.

Kegley, J. A., 2002, 'Genetics Decision-making: a Template for Problems With Informed Consent', *Medical Law* 21(3), 459–71.

Kleinig, John, 1983, *Paternalism*, Manchester: Manchester University Press.

Lakoff, George, and Johnson, Mark, 1980, *Metaphors We Live By*, Chicago: University of Chicago Press.

Laurie, Graeme T., 2002, *Genetic Privacy: A Challenge to Medico-Legal Norms*, Cambridge: Cambridge University Press.

Liddell, Kathleen, and Hall, Alison, 2005, 'Beyond Bristol and Alder Hey: The Future Regulation of Human Tissue', *Medical Law Review* 15, 170–223.

Manson, Neil C., 2006, 'What is Genetic Information and Why is it Significant? A Contextual, Contrastive Approach', *Journal of Applied Philosophy* 23, 1–16.

Maynard Smith, John, 2000, 'The Concept of Information in Biology', *Philosophy of Science*, 67, 177–94.

Mill, John Stuart, 1962, *On Liberty*, London: Fontana.

1989, *On Liberty, and Other Writings*, ed. Collini, Stefan, Cambridge: Cambridge University Press.

Moran, Michael, 2003, *The British Regulatory State: High Modernism and Hyper-innovation*, Oxford: Oxford University Press.

Moreno, Jonathan D., 2000, *Undue Risk: Secret State Experiments on Humans*, London: Routledge.

O'Neill, Onora, 2000, 'Kant and the Social Contract Tradition', in Duchesneau, François, Lafrance, Guy, and Piché, Claude, eds., *Kant Actuel: Hommage à Pierre Laberge*, Montreal: Bellarmin, pp. 185–200.

2000, *The Bounds of Justice*, Cambridge: Cambridge University Press.

2002, *Autonomy and Trust in Bioethics*, Cambridge: Cambridge University Press.

2003, 'Autonomy: The Emperor's New Clothes, The Inaugural Address', *Proceedings of the Aristotelian Society*, supp. vol. 77, 1–21.

2004, 'Self-Legislation, Autonomy and the Form of Law', in *Recht, Geschichte, Religion: Die Bedeutung Kants für die Gegenwart*, eds. Nagl-Docekal, Herta, and Langthaler, Rudolf, *Sonderband der Deutschen Zeitschrift für Philosophie*, Berlin: Akademie Verlag, pp. 13–26.

2004, 'Informed Consent and Public Health', *Philosophical Transactions: Biological Sciences*, vol. 359, no. 1447, 1133–6.

2005, 'The Dark Side of Human Rights', *International Affairs*, 81, 427–39.

2006, 'Transparency and the Ethics of Communication', in *Transparency: The Key to Better Governance?*, eds. Heald, David, and Hood, Christopher, *Proceedings of the British Academy* 135, Oxford: Oxford University Press, pp. 75–90.

Oyama, Susan, 2000, *The Ontogeny of Information*, 2nd edn, Durham, NC: Duke University Press.

Parent, W. A., 1983, 'Privacy, Morality and the Law', *Philosophy and Public Affairs*, 12, 269–88.

Phillipson, Gavin, 2003, 'Transforming Breach of Confidence? Towards a Common Law Right of Privacy under the Human Rights Act', *Modern Law Review* 66, 726–58.

Phillipson, Gavin and Fenwick, Helen, 2000, 'Breach of confidence as a Privacy Remedy in the Human Rights Act Era', *Modern Law Review*, 63, 660–93.

Power, Michael, 1994, *The Audit Explosion*, London: Demos.

1997, *The Audit Society: Rituals of Verification*, Oxford: Oxford University Press.

2004, *The Risk Management of Everything: Rethinking the Politics of Uncertainty*, London: Demos.

Putnam, Robert, 1995, 'Bowling Alone: America's Declining Social Capital', *The Journal of Democracy*, 6, 65–78.

2000, *Bowling Alone: The Collapse and Revival of American Community*, New York: Simon & Schuster.

Raymont, Vanessa, *et al.*, 2004, 'Prevalence of Mental Incapacity in Medical Inpatients and Associated Risk Factors: Cross Sectional Study', *The Lancet*, 364, 1421–7.

Reddy, Michael, 1979, 'The Conduit Metaphor: A Case of Frame Conflict in our Language about Language', in Ortony, A., ed., *Metaphor and Thought*, Cambridge: Cambridge University Press, pp. 284–324.

Rhodes, Rosamond, Batting, Margaret P., and Silvers, Anita, eds., 2002, *Medicine and Social Justice: Essays on the Distribution of Health Care*, New York: Oxford University Press.

Rothstein, Mark A., 2005, 'Genetic Exceptionalism and Legislative Pragmatism', *Hastings Center Report*, 35, 4, 2–8.

Sankar, Pamela, 2003, 'Genetic Determinism Provides the Foundation of Arguments Supporting Genetic Exceptionalism', *Annual Review of Medicine* 54, 393–407.

Sarkar, Sahotra, 1996, 'Biological Information: A Sceptical Look at Some Central Dogmas of Molecular Biology', in Sarkar, Sahotra, ed., *The Philosophy and History of Molecular Biology: New Perspectives*, Dordrecht: Kluwer, pp. 187–232.

Schneider, Carl E., 1998, *The Practice of Autonomy*, New York: Oxford University Press.

Searle, John, 1969, *Speech Acts: An Essay in Philosophy of Language*, Cambridge: Cambridge University Press.

Sugarman, Jeremy, *et al.*, 1999, 'Empirical Research on Informed Consent: An Annotated Bibliography', *Hastings Center Report*, Special Supplement, January–February, 1–42.

Thompson, Mark, 1990, 'Breach of Confidence and Privacy', in Clarke, Linda, ed., *Confidentiality and the Law*, London: Lloyds of London, pp. 65–79.

Wacks, Raymond, 1993, *Personal Information: Privacy and the Law*, Oxford: Clarendon Press.

Warlow, Charles, 2005, 'Over-regulation of Clinical Research: a Threat to Public Health', *Clinical medicine*, 5, 1, 33–8.

Warren, Samuel D., and Brandeis, Louis D., 1890, 'The Right to Privacy', *Harvard Law Review*, 4, 193–220.

Weinreb, Lloyd L., 2000, 'The Right to Privacy', in Frankel Paul, Ellen, Miller, Fred D., Jnr., and Paul, Jeffrey, eds., *The Right to Privacy*, Cambridge: Cambridge University Press.

Welbourne, Michael, 2001, *Knowledge*, Chesham: Acumen.

Westin, Alan, 1967, *Privacy and Freedom*, New York: Atheneum.

Weston, J., Hannah, M., and Downes, J., 1997, 'Evaluating the benefits of a patient information video during the informed consent process', *Patient Education and Counselling*, 30 (3), 239–45.

Wilkinson, T. M., 2001, 'Research, Informed Consent, and the Limits of Disclosure', *Bioethics*, 15, 4, 341–63.

Williams, Bernard, 1985, *Ethics and the Limits of Philosophy*, London: Fontana.

Willis, Rebecca, and Wilsdon, James, 2004, *See-through Science: Why Public Engagement Needs to Move Upstream*, London: Demos.

Wolpe, P., 1998, 'The Triumph of Autonomy in American Bioethics', in Devries, R., and Subedi, J., eds., *Bioethics and Society: Constructing the Ethical Enterprise*, Englewood Cliffs, NJ: Prentice Hall, pp. 38–59.

Institutional sources and documents

Council of Europe
European Convention on Human Rights and Fundamental Freedoms
(1950)
http://www.pfc.org.uk/legal/echrtext.htm

Council of Europe
European Convention for the Protection of Human Rights and Dignity of the Human Being with regard to the Application of Biology and Medicine: Convention on Human Rights and Biomedicine (1996)
http://conventions.coe.int/treaty/en/Reports/Html/164.htm

European Parliament
Directive 95/46/EC *On the protection of individuals with regard to the processing of personal data and on the free movement of such data* (1995)
http://europa.eu.int/comm/justice_home/doc_centre/privacy/law/index_en.htm

MORI, for the British Medical Association,
'Public Still Regards Doctors As The Most Trustworthy Group' (2000)
http://www.mori.com/polls/2000/bma2000.shtml

MORI and UK Human Genetics Commission
Public Attitudes to Human Genetic Information
http://www.hgc.gov.uk/UploadDocs/DocPub/Document/morigeneticattitudes.pdf

The Bristol Royal Infirmary Inquiry
Report (2001)
http://www.bristol-inquiry.org.uk

The Royal Liverpool Children's Inquiry
Report (The Redfern Report) (2001)
http://www.rlcinquiry.org.uk/contents.htm

The Shipman Inquiry
Reports (2002–5)
http://www.the-shipman-inquiry.org.uk/reports.asp

Transparency International
http://www.transparency.org/

UK Better Regulation Commission
http://www.brc.gov.uk/

UK Committee on Standards in Public Life
http://www.public-standards.gov.uk/

UK Data Protection Act 1998
http://www.hmso.gov.uk/acts/acts1998/19980029.htm

UK Data Protection Act 1998: *Legal Guidance*
www.ico.gov.uk/documentUploads/
Data%20Protection%20Act%201998%20Legal%20Guidance.pdf

UK Department of Health
Section 60 of the Health and Social Care Act 2001: Consultation on Proposals to Revise Regulations
http://www.dh.gov.uk/assetRoot/04/07/14/32/04071432.pdf

UK Department of Health
Confidentiality: NHS Code of Practice (2003)
http://www.dh.gov.uk/assetRoot/04/06/92/54/04069254.pdf

UK Health and Social Care Act 2001
http://www.opsi.gov.uk/ACTS/acts2001/20010015.htm

UK Human Genetics Commission
Report to the Human Genetics Commission on Public Attitudes to the Uses of Human Genetic Information (2000)
http://www.hgc.gov.uk/UploadDocs/DocPub/Document/public_attitudes.pdf

UK Human Tissues Act 2004
http://www.opsi.gov.uk/acts/acts2004/20040030.htm

UK Parliamentary Office of Science and Technology
The 'Great GM Food Debate': A Survey of Media Coverage in the First Half of 1999 (2000)
www.parliament.uk/post/report138.pdf

UK Patient Information Advisory Group (PIAG)
Your Health Records: Safeguarding Confidential Information
http://www.advisorybodies.doh.gov.uk/piag/HealthRecords.pdf

UK Public Health Genetics Unit
Addressing Genetics Delivering Health: A Strategy for Advancing the Dissemination and Application of Genetics Knowledge Throughout our Health Professions (2003)
http://www.phgu.org.uk/pages/work/education/addressing.htm

US Counsel for War Crimes
'The Nuremberg Code' (1949)
Trials of War Criminals before the Nuremberg Military Tribunals under Control Council Law no. 10, vol. 2, pp. 181–2.
http://www.ushmm.org/research/doctors/Nuremberg_Code.htm

US Department of Energy
Draft Genetic Privacy Act and Commentary (1995)
http://www.ornl.gov/sci/techresources/Human_Genome/resource/privacy/privacy1.htm

US Department of Health, Education, and Welfare
The Belmont Report: Ethical Principles and Guidelines for the

Protection of Human Subjects of Research (1979)
http://ohsr.od.nih.gov/guidelines/belmont.html

US Genetics and Public Policy Center
Reproductive Genetic Testing: What America Thinks (2004)
http://www.dnapolicy.org/tools-content/pdfs/6/66756.pdf

US National Conference of State Legislatures
State Genetic Privacy Laws (2005)
http://www.ncsl.org/programs/health/genetics/prt.htm

US National Institutes of Health
Privacy and Discrimination Federal Legislation Archive
http://www.genome.gov/11510239

World Medical Association
Declaration of Helsinki
Declaration of Ethical Principles for Medical Research Involving Human Subjects (2004)
http://www.wma.net/e/policy/b3.htm

All URLs tested and working 29 March 2006.

Index

accountability 167–82, 197
  first- and second-order obligations involved
    in 167–8
  managerial 172–4
  professional 171
  promoting trust 167
  purposes served by systems of 168
  structure of 181–2
  variety of systems of 167–9, 170
Alder Hey Hospital 14
anonymisation
  of DNA samples 118–19
  of personal data 116–19, 157–8, 195–6
autonomy 16–22, 69–72
  individual 18, 20, 185–6
  Kantian 17
  limitations of an appeal to 69–72
  principled 17
  rational 21

commitments
  cognitive and practical 50–7
  communication and 90–4
  consent and 90–4
communication
  agency model of 65, 66, 180
  communicative commitments 90–4
  conduit and container model of 34–5, 65
  mathematical theory of 37, 146–7
  two models of 64, 68–9, 130–1
  via action. *See* communicative actions
communicative actions 54–7
communicative norms 41–2, 57–64,
  84–90
communicative obligations 123–7
conduit and container metaphors 34–5,
  194–5, 197
  and genetic information 147–9, 150–2
  and information privacy 105–11
  and informed consent 68–9
  and transparency 178–81

confidentiality 123–7
  contrast with data protection 126–7
  legal discussion of 124–6
consent. *See also* informed consent
  and non-competence 71, 192–4
  as waiver 72–7, 189
  bogus 92, 95, 154
  explicit and implicit 8, 10–11, 80
  generic and specific 8, 11–12, 80, 190
  hypothetical 6
  impossibility of fully explicit 12
  in data protection legislation 112, 116, 128
  opacity of 12–15
  proxy 6
  reasons for waiving prohibitions 75–6
  to cannibalism or torture 70
consent requirements
  varying standards for 81–2

Data Protection Act 1998 22, 111–21, 128
  and personal information 113–15
  broad definition of information processing 114
declaration of Helsinki. *See* Helsinki, declaration of
direction of fit 52, 161
Draft Genetic Privacy Act 133–7

epistemic norms 63 *See also* informational
  obligations
  and informed consent 184–5
epistemic responsibility 60–1
European Directive (95/46/EC) on data
  protection 120
explicit consent. *See* consent, explicit and implicit

generic consent. *See* consent, generic and specific
genetic exceptionalism 132
genetic information
  attitudes to 142–3
  conduit and container metaphors for 147–9,
    150–2
  contained in DNA 145–9

genetic information (cont.)
  in molecular biology 146–7
  nature of 145–9
  privacy rights over 133–45
  risk of abusing 143–4
  variety of uses of 140–2
genetic knowledge 131–2
genetic privacy. *See* privacy, genetic
Genetic Privacy Act. *See Draft Genetic Privacy Act*
genetic privacy legislation 23

Helsinki, declaration of 7–9, 80, 82
Human Tissues Act 2004 23
hypothetical consent. *See* consent, hypothetical

implicit consent. *See* consent, explicit and implicit
implied consent. *See* consent, explicit and implicit
individual autonomy. *See* autonomy, individual
inferential fertility 46
  and genetic information 136–7
  and information privacy 105
information and informing
  as a type of action 34–5
  classifying information by content 28–9
  informing, nature of 41–8
  informing, rationality of 43–5
  non-semantic conception of information 37
information privacy 97–101, 194–6
  and personal information 103
  as right over information content 105–11
  basis of 100–1
  rethinking of 121–3
informational obligations 101–5, 196
  distorted view of 110–11
  first-order 29–30, 105–11
  second-order 31, 111–21
informational privacy. *See* information privacy
informational rights. *See* informational obligations
informed consent
  and communicative norms 90–4
  and standardised consent forms 190–1
  as communicative transaction 69, 84–90, 94–6
  as disclosure for decision making 69
  as waiver. *See* consent, as waiver
  assumptions underlying informed consent
    procedures 27–33
  conduit and container metaphors and 68–9

distortions of 34
extended scope of 4–6
justification in terms of individual autonomy
  16–22
no uniform standard for 83
practical proposals 189–97
regulatory reinforcement of 22–4
rethinking justification of 72–7
rethinking scope of 77–84
standards for 6–16, 189–92
transactional model of 69
two models of 68–9

Nuremberg Code 2–4, 79

paternalism 72, 155–8, 171
  not always avoidable in clinical practice 156
performance indicators 175
personal information
  nature of 104
  used for impersonal ends 108–9
placebos 9
privacy
  differing conceptions of 97–8
  genetic 23, 133–45
  right to 98 *See also* information privacy;
    informational obligations
privacy interests 98
proxy consent. *See* consent, proxy
public goods 19

referential opacity 12, 45
research ethics 7–9, 199
respect for autonomy 16–22

specific consent. *See* consent, generic and specific

transparency 177–81
  reasons for transparency requirements 178
  role of conduit and container metaphors 178–81
trust 158–77
  and 'direction of fit' 161
  differentiation of 164–7
  ineliminability of 162–4
  placing and refusing 159–62

waiver. *See* consent, as waiver